TOWARD A SOCIOLOGICAL
IMAGINATION

Bridging Specialized Fields

Edited by
Bernard Phillips
Harold Kincaid
Thomas J. Scheff

University Press of America,® Inc.
Lanham · New York · Oxford

Copyright © 2002 by
University Press of America,® Inc.
4720 Boston Way
Lanham, Maryland 20706
UPA Acquisitions Department (301) 459-3366

12 Hid's Copse Rd.
Cumnor Hill, Oxford OX2 9JJ

ISBN 0-7618-2342-5 (paperback : alk. ppr.)

Contents

Preface

Although many sociologists have criticized the division of our discipline into fields which largely fail to communicate with one another, we have yet to see a movement throughout the discipline to build bridges connecting those fields and thus fulfill the ideals of the scientific method. For example, Mills' idea of "the sociological imagination" remains no more than a vague ideal. The result of this situation is a failure to achieve rapid cumulative development of our knowledge as well as limited credibility even to ourselves. Given sociology's breadth, we might well be showing the way for the other social sciences to build similar bridges, yet we fail to do this as well. We revere classical sociologists like Marx, Durkheim, Weber and Simmel in large measure because of their breadth, yet--granting our modern accomplishments--we have not been able to emulate that breadth. And for those of us who are much concerned with sociology's potential for enlightening society on its massive and perhaps increasing social problems, there is much justified disappointment, cynicism and pessimism. This is reflected in the influence of some postmodernist ideas which question the utility of the very idea of "the scientific method."

We believe that such current questioning of the utility of the traditional approach to the scientific method is a most useful development, since it opens up questions that we sociologists should be addressing. For example, why have we proceeded so far from the scientific ideal of rapid cumulative development? Are there fundamental problems with our approach to the scientific method?

What is wrong with our orientation to sociological theory? Why have we in fact come to be so divided? Granting that such questions have been raised many times in the past, we believe that they can prove to be most important at this time, provided that some alternative way of doing sociology which attempts to answer those questions adequately can be presented. We need both an effort to answer such questions in the abstract as well as illustrations of how those answers can be applied to substantive sociological research in a variety of fields. Our approach is much like that suggested by Thomas Kuhn's analysis of scientific revolutions. In order for a scientific paradigm to change, a new paradigm which promises to resolve contradictions within the old one must be put forward. To the extent that such a promise comes to be fulfilled, the new scientific paradigm will, over time, replace the old one. Yet if we follow Kuhn's argument, then changing our sociological paradigm is no easy matter.

The problem that we are confronting is nothing less than reconstructing the scientific method so that it can handle the incredible complexity of human behavior. We believe that sociologists along with other social scientists have failed to address that complexity, opting instead for oversimplified and highly specialized approaches. They hope that somehow, somewhere, specialized knowledge will come together. Like the fable of nine blind men meeting an elephant for the first time, disparate pieces of knowledge--the elephant is like a snake (the tail), like a tree trunk (the leg), like a wall (the side), like a hose (the trunk)--do not form a coherent picture when each piece of knowledge is itself deficient. This is the situation for human behavior, since the very partial knowledge developed by each specialist omits background knowledge that is required for understanding. Most current practices do not only yield lack of cumulative development, integration of knowledge and credibility for sociology and the social sciences. They also fail to help society. Social problems appear to be increasingly threatening and urgent all the while we social scientists continue to go around in circles.

Given this situation, we remain divided theoretically, methodologically and substantively, burying our vision of "the promise of sociology" as we continue with our specialized work. Dissatisfaction with the editorial policies of the American Sociological Review was clearly manifested at the 1999 Chicago ASA meetings. We believe that behind that dissatisfaction lay a deep concern with the failure of the discipline to make the cumulative progress we all have hoped for but have largely given up on. Pessimism and cynicism about sociology's prospects appear to be the order of the day.

This volume collects revisions of papers given by "the sociological imagination group" at evening sessions of its research conference simultaneous with the meetings of the American Sociological Association in August, 2000. It also includes several other papers. The group was formed during the preceding year, largely based on concern over the lack of rapid cumulative development and credibility of the discipline at a time in history when its voice should be heard. Through continuing communication via e-mail, the group grew to include 22 individuals: Albert Bergesen, David Britt, Thomas Conroy, Richard Edgar, Susan Haworth-Hoepper, Matthew Hoover, Chanoch Jacobsen, James Kimberly, Harold Kincaid, Richard Lachmann, Bronwen Lichtenstein, Guenther Lueschen, John Malarkey, David Maines, Keith Oatley, Joseph Perry, Bernard Phillips, Suzanne Retzinger, Martin Sawzin, Thomas Scheff, Jay Weinstein and Andrew Ziner.

We see our volume as responding to a deep chord of dissatisfaction among sociologists. Mills' *The Sociological Imagination* was voted the second most influential book among sociologists of the twentieth century (behind Weber's *Economy and Society*) by the membership of the International Sociological Association, as reported at their 1998 meetings in Montreal. Mills appears to represent not just a commitment to a broad theoretical approach but also to confronting the fundamental problems of modern society. In our volume we carry forward Mills' ideas, building on his general orientations so as to yield a systematic approach to reconstructing the scientific method. We believe that we have developed an approach that will yield rapid cumulative development within sociology and the other social sciences. Equally important, we see it as enabling us to get our act together as sociologists, giving us the integrated knowledge required as a platform for launching effective social technologies.

Our approach is strengthened by the just-published book by the first editor, *Beyond Sociology's Tower of Babel: Reconstructing the Scientific Method* (2001). That monograph provides a description of the methodological and theoretical approach we have adopted along with illustrations detailing its use. The present volume, by contrast, tests the utility of that approach for yielding insights in diverse areas of the discipline that go beyond those obtained via a traditional methodological approach. It was indeed difficult for us to come together within this volume. We feel that our accomplishment augurs well for the potential impact of the volume. If we authors have been able to join hands in this way, it should be possible for sociologists within the forty Sections of the American Sociological Association and the hundreds of even more specialized subfields of sociology to do the same. We have opened a door and given a number of illustrations of how one might walk through that door. We are offering a path directed toward fulfilling "the promise of sociology." We believe that few have given up completely on that possibility. And beyond a vague and programmatic approach, we are offering a systematic effort with illustrations bearing on a variety of different fields.

The breadth of our theoretical approach is illustrated by the nine concepts in Table 1-1 of Chapter 1: anomie, cultural values, social stratification, labeling, relative deprivation, conformity, worldview, alienation and addiction. That breadth is also illustrated by the range of Sections within which the authors are known: Methodology, Crime, Law & Deviance, Theory, Social Psychology, Sociological Practice, Mental Health, Comparative Historical, Sociology of Emotions, Science, Knowledge and Technology, Rational Choice, and the Sociology of Religion. What is crucial is not just that range but the possibility-- with the aid of our reconstructed scientific method--of linking material not only in those Sections and in the other Sections of the discipline, but also in fields and subfields throughout the social sciences.

The volume is organized into two parts. Part One, "The Framework," consists of two chapters: "Reconstructing the Scientific Method": and "Toward a Reflexive Sociology." The former is based largely on Mills' *The Sociological Imagination*. But it goes on from there to develop a systematic philosophical foundation based on Kincaid's work in the philosophy of social science. And it also details relevant modern work within sociology. The second chapter begins with Gouldner's work on reflexive sociology, proceeding to develop the idea of reflexivity as a key component of our approach to the scientific method. Gouldner, like Mills, never was able to develop his seminal idea in a systematic way. These two chapters mesh with the stance of the first editor in *Beyond Sociology's Tower of Babel*; they are a collaborative effort and not every aspect of two chapters fully represents the views of each editor.

The nine chapters of Part Two, "Building Bridges," go where few have gone before. We sociologists have been taught from early on to be individualists, new Columbuses who stake out innovative areas of the discipline, and certainly not to stand on the shoulders of giants. We give lip service to reviewing the literature, and we generally avoid using earlier concepts in any systematic way, treating them much like a novelist would treat clichés. However, our reconstructed scientific method requires a much different approach. It is one that builds on earlier work with the aid of abstract concepts, yet comes far down language's ladder of abstraction to data, and it uses this ability to shuttle up and down to define fundamental problems in society. The reflexive approach enables us to confront our very worldview and, in the process, open up to the interactive nature of the research process in ways that are rarely achieved with traditional research procedures. Most significant is the ability of each of the authors in Part Two to join in a new approach that also follows the ideals of the scientific method.

As for the specific chapters in Part Two, Jacobsen's use of concepts like "alienation" and "bureaucratic order" in Chapter 3 enables us to view secularization as linked to increasing deviance and anomie throughout modern society. In Chapter 4, Kimberly uses abstract concepts to tie together two distinct small-group theories, and also to relate those theories to large-scale social structures. In Chapter 5 Kincaid employs the web approach to suggest how to go far beyond the 1967 analysis of stratification and occupational mobility by Blau and Duncan. Lachmann's Chapter 6 gives us a taste of the complexities unearthed by modern historical analysis, using abstract sociological concepts to generalize beyond the beginnings of capitalism in England. Maines and Britt in Chapter 7 suggest the power of a methodological approach broad enough to include both narrative prejudice in Chapter 8 throws light on the ways in which our basic social and individual structures yield prejudice and aggression. In Chapter 9 Retzinger shows links between feelings of shame and patterns of social interaction, implying the failures of psychiatrists and social scientists to recognize those links. Scheff's analysis of unacknowledged shame and anger among working-class individuals in Chapter 10 suggests the potential impact of learning to become aware of such emotions on the reduction of violence. And Becker's view of Goffman's Asylums in Chapter 11 (appearing prior to the idea for this volume: published as "*La politique de la presentation Goffman et les institutions totales*, pp. 59-77 in Charles Amourous and Alain Blanc, editors, *Erving Goffman et les institutions totales*, Paris: L'Harmattan, 2001) shows Goffman's verbal approach to be technical or theoretical conceptually and not merely vernacular.

In comparison to other edited volumes, the methodological and theoretical bridges linking widely diverse fields which we have achieved is unique. Every substantive chapter is based on a secondary analysis of some previously published piece. Our approach to the scientific method is by no means limited to secondary analyses, but this format is useful in helping us to compare the utility of our methodology with a traditional approach to the scientific method. Can we in fact achieve new and important insights with our reconstructed scientific method? Would it indeed be difficult to achieve such insights with traditional methodology? The reader will be in a position to answer these questions. Our own conclusion is emphatically positive. Since we are dealing with a general approach to the scientific method, the implications of this conclusion are far-reaching. We see no field or subfield within the social sciences which escapes severe limitations in employing a traditional approach to the scientific method. And we see every field and subfield gaining from our reconstructed approach. We also expect that a volume as unified as ours is will be an effective tool for instruction, given its combination of a general framework with diverse and extended illustrations.

In some ways the volume parallels the studies of *The American Soldier* following World War II, which helped to usher into the discipline a new emphasis on quantitative procedures. Now, half a century later, sociologists generally have learned the limitations of those procedures along with their strengths. Our approach includes qualitative as well as quantitative procedures and is broad enough to encompass the full range of theoretical approaches within the social sciences. Our own excitement parallels that felt about sociology's possibilities during the late sixties. Our volume's broad methodological, theoretical and problem-solving approach opens up to sociologists in the Sections and subfields of the discipline and to other disciplines as well. We look forward to their following our lead by continuing to test the utility of this reconstructed scientific method. We have not worked it out in final detail, but we do claim to have made considerable progress. We see the volume as addressing a need within the discipline: to find a path that fulfills the promise of sociology. That need has become an urgent one at this time in history.

Contributors

Howard S. Becker <hbecker@alishaw.ucsb.edu> lives and works in San Francisco. He is the author of *Outsiders, Art Worlds, Writing for Social Scientists,* and *Tricks of the Trade,* and co-author of *Boys in White* and *Making the Grade.* He has taught at Northwestern University, the University of Washington, and the University of California at Santa Barbara.

David W. Britt <David_Britt_sr@hotmail.com> is a research professor in the Department of Obstetrics and Gynecology at Hahnemann/Drexel University. He is the author of *A Conceptual Introduction to Modeling: Quantitative and Qualitative Perspectives.* His recent articles are in the areas of medical sociology and mixed-method epistemology.

Chanoch Jacobsen <chanoch@ie.technion.ac.il> is emeritus professor of sociology in the Faculty of Industrial Engineering and Management at the Israel Institute of Technology. He is the author of *Social Dynamics: Theory and Research* and co-author of *Simulating Violators.* Recent articles center on deviant behavior and simulation models using the system dynamics approach to computer simulation.

James Carlton Kimberly <jbkimber@msn.com> is emeritus professor of sociology at the University of Nebraska, Lincoln. He is the author of *Group Processes and Structures: A Theoretical Integration.* Formerly chair of the Social Psychology Section of the ASA, his articles in many journals and books center on small groups, social psychology, theory, and inequality.

Harold Kincaid <kincaid@uab.edu> chairs the Department of Philosophy at the University of Alabama at Birmingham. He is co-editor of the Aldine series, "Sociological Imagination and Structural Change." He has authored *Philosophical Foundations of the Social Sciences* and *the Unity of Science: Essays on Reduction, Explanation, and the Special Sciences,*as well as numerous articles.

Richard Lachmann <RL605@CSC.ALBANY.EDU> is associate professor in the Department of Sociology at SUNY, Albany. He is the author of *Capitalists in Spite of Themselves: Elite Conflict and Economic Transitions in Early Modern Europe* and *From Manor to Market: Structural Change in England, 1536-1640.* Articles stress omparative and historical as well as cultural and political sociology.

David R. Maines <maines@oakland.edu> chairs the Department of Sociology and Anthropology at Oakland University, Rochester, Michigan. He has written *The Faultline of Consciousness: A View of Interactionism in Sociology.* He received the George Herbert Mead Award for lifetime contributions to scholarship from the Society for the Study of Symbolic Interaction.

Bernard Phillips <bernieflps@aol.com> has taught at the Universities of North Carolina and Illinois and Boston University. He cofounded the ASA section "Sociological Practice" and is co-editor of the Aldine series, "Sociological Imagination and Structural Change." His recent book is *Beyond Sociology's Tower of Babel.* He is currently writing "Confronting the Accelerating Crisis of Modern Society."

Suzanne M. Retzinger <sretzinger@mindspring.com> is a practicing mediator and psychotherapist with a doctorate in sociology from the University of California, Santa Barbara. She has authored *Violent Emotions: Shame and Rage in Marital Quarrels* and co-authored *Emotions and Violence* with Thomas J. Scheff. Her articles emphasize the sociology of emotions, interpersonal relations, and conflict.

Thomas J. Scheff <scheftj@mindspring.com> is emeritus professor of sociology at the University of California, Santa Barbara. Recent books are *Emotions, the Social Bond, and Human Reality, Bloody Revenge,* and *Microsociology.* His "part/whole" approach anticipated the web approach within this volume. He was President of the Pacific Sociological Association and has received international recognition.

PART ONE   THE FRAMEWORK

Part One outlines a reconstructed scientific method. Our focus is on the failure of traditional methods and theory in sociology to achieve rapid cumulative development and credibility for the discipline. Those aspirations have been central to most of us since the times of Marx, Durkheim, Simmel and Weber. Vidich's and Bensman's *Small Town in Mass Society* (1960) yields insight into our current efforts to fulfill those aspirations with their analysis of the failures of Springdalers to fulfill their own dreams. Their "falsification of memory" and "technique of particularization" enabled them to hide from those dreams. The Springdaler, "instead of entertaining the youthful dream of a 500-acre farm, entertains the plan to buy a home freezer by the fall." We sociologists bury our aspirations in different ways. We work hard to publish articles in highly specialized journals which will bring us, in the words of Vidich and Bensman, "some degree of satisfaction, recognition and achievement," even if we realize that few colleagues pay attention to those articles and almost no one is influenced by them. We delude ourselves into believing that in the future the pieces of the puzzle of society--represented by the forty Sections of the American Sociological Association--will somehow come together, yet deep down we suspect that this will never happen.

Our own vision for sociology points us back to the future, centering on those earlier ideals for sociology's possibilities. We believe that the specialized approach that has emerged within sociology--coupled with limited communication connecting our disparate fields--has taken us away from the directions embodied by Marx, Durkheim, Simmel and Weber. Yet it *is* possible to build on the broad and historical approach taken by those classical figures, provided that we re-examine just how we are interpreting the scientific method. As a result, we can alter that interpretation. This is in fact what we proceed to do in Part One. Chapter 1 presents a sketch of what we call our bureaucratic orientation to the scientific method by contrast with an interactive orientation. And Chapter 2 develops in more detail a key aspect of an interactive scientific method: reflexivity. Part One is designed to open a door to a different way of doing sociological and social science research. It is a door that we editors have only begun to enter. It is in Part Two that we shall focus on entering that doorway. Whatever the limitations of our efforts prove to be, we hope that readers will take up the task of addressing them.

Chapter 1

Reconstructing the Scientific Method

INTRODUCTION

In a study of the aging process recently reported in *Science*, over 6,000 genes of individuals in different age groups were viewed with the aid of "gene chips," DNA-coated microchips the size of a postage stamp. Some 60 genes were located which either speeded up or slowed down many manifestations of old age, ranging from gray hair and wrinkled skin to organ failure. Richard Lerner, president of Scripps Research Institute in La Jolla, California, a lead scientist on the new study, stated:

> We have spent 100 years of reductionism trying to understand bio-
> logical processes by looking at the pieces. Now we're going to try
> to understand complexity, how the pieces work together (*Sarasota
> Herald-Tribune*, March 31, 2000: 4A).

Lerner is making an argument against reductionism, or the kind of specialization in biological research which reduces complex phenomena into simplistic "pieces" and fails to see the forest for the trees. It is not the knowledge laboriously gathered by specialists which is the problem, but rather the failure of those specialists to look beyond their own narrow fields.

Lerner is engaged in a procedure, a method, for getting at complexity by using DNA-coated microchips, and he expects to achieve as a result a broader theoretical understanding of the aging process. He questions a narrow or piecemeal approach to the scientific method because it has failed to yield the kind of theoretical understanding which awaits a broader methodological approach. By so
doing he illustrates our own approach to sociology.

This volume is not an effort to come up with a comprehensive theory of everything or even a set of theories about a variety of substantive and applied problems within the discipline. Rather, it is a focus on an interpretation of the scientific method which we believe will face up to the complexity of human phenomena more adequately than our existing piecemeal practices. And as a result we believe that it will yield broader theoretical understanding of human behavior. But the theoretical conclusions in the volume are no more than illustrative of the potential of our approach to the scientific method. They are the icing on the cake rather than the cake itself. Those theoretical conclusions are not meant to replace the existing literature within the many specialized areas of the discipline. Rather, we would like the reader to assess whether or not *our approach to the scientific method* contributes important insights to the specialized areas where it is applied.

If Lerner indicts the failure of contemporary biological research to take into account the enormous complexity of biological phenomena, then arguably that indictment must apply far more convincingly to contemporary sociological research. If biological phenomena are complex, then sociological phenomena--with their social and personality structures based on language and culture, the necessity of taking history and momentary changes into account, and all of this in addition to the biological nature of the human being--constitute an order of complexity many fold greater. Yet reductionism to simplistic perspectives exists within our discipline as well as outside of it. We sociologists are much concerned about the activities of psychological reductionists or biological reductionists, but we too attempt to oversimplify human behavior. For example, Homans' "Bringing Men Back In" (1964) weighs in against our general exclusion of biological phenomena, and Wrong's "The Oversocialized Conception of Man in Modern Sociology" (1961) argues against a too-heavy focus on social structure to the exclusion of forces within the individual. Apparently, a simplistic orientation to phenomena pervades sociology as well as biology and psychology despite the enormous complexity of human behavior. We argue that the source of that orientation lies in a narrow interpretation of the scientific method which fails to open up to that complexity.

Presently we have some forty Sections of the American Sociological Association, and they point toward forty relatively distinct literatures. Those literatures generally are overwhelmingly reductionist in their failure to embody an approach to the scientific method which opens up to the importance of other literatures within sociology. The fairy-tale that most of us would like to believe is that somehow, somewhere, in some way, sociological knowledge from our many specialized fields is being pulled together. But the facts of the case tell a different story. Sociology's present situation in this regard appears to be much worse than in earlier times, when classical sociologists like Marx, Durkheim, Simmel and Weber reached out broadly and historically in their efforts to understand society and the individual. The fact that we still pay homage to their ideas somehow does not manage to stir us to pay much attention to that breadth and historical perspective. Many of us like to think that our current methodology is much advanced over that of the early sociologists, and in some ways it surely is. But with respect to a broad openness to phenomena--fundamental to our scientific ideals--it appears to be lacking. We recall literally thousands of situations we have observed over the years where individuals in Departments of Sociology or at professional meetings would politely recognize the presence of other sociologists in different fields but would fail to open up to the possibility of learning anything of importance from them.

A metaphor can help us to understand our situation more fully, one that comes from the Old Testament:

> Throughout the earth men spoke the same language, with the same vocabulary. Now as they moved eastward they found a plain in the land of Shinar where they settled. They said to one another, "Come, let us make bricks and bake them in the fire."--For stone they used bricks, and for mortar they used bitumen.--Come," they said, let us build ourselves a town and a tower with its top reaching heaven. Let us make a name for ourselves, so that we may not be scattered about the whole earth."
> Now Yahweh came down to see the town and the tower that the sons of man had built. "So they are all a single people with a single language!" said Yahweh. "This is but the start of their undertakings! There will be nothing too hard for them to do. Come, let us go down and confuse their language on the spot so that they can no longer understand one another." Yahweh scattered them thence over the whole face of the earth, and they stopped building the town. It was named Babel therefore, because there Yahweh confused the language of the whole earth. It was from there that Yahweh scattered them over the whole face of the earth (Genesis 11: 1-9).

Applying the metaphor of the tower of Babel, we sociologists appear to speak much the same language, but that is no more than appearance. In fact, the distinct literatures within our specialized fields--whatever are their contributions to knowledge--work to divide us. We follow Merton's emphasis on "theories of the middle range" rather than abstract concepts which could build bridges across our specialized areas of knowledge:

> every effort should be made to avoid dwelling upon illustrations
> drawn from the "more mature" sciences--such as physics and
> chemistry. . .because their very maturity permits these disciplines
> to deal fruitfully with abstractions of high order to a degree which,
> it is submitted, is not yet the case with sociology (1968: 139-140).

Merton's approach appears to be a classic illustration of what he himself called a "self-fulfilling prophecy." By defining sociology as imma-
ture and unable to employ "abstractions of high order," we create that
very situation of immaturity. By centering on a method that opposes
the abstract concepts needed to bridge disparate fields, we create a
tower of Babel among ourselves where we no longer understand or are
interested in what sociologists in other fields are learning.

As an example of our tower of Babel, consider the concept of social
stratification.   We deal with different kinds of social stratification
within our forty Sections of the American Sociological Association:
ageism within the Sociology of Aging, *racism* and *ethnocentrism*
within Racial and Ethnic Minorities, *prejudice* within the Sociology of
Asia and Asian America, *weightism* in Social Psychology, *discrimination* in Latino/a Sociology, *homophobia* in Sociology of Sexualities,
sexism within Sex and Gender, *classism* in Marxist Sociology, *hegemony* in the Sociology of Culture, *power* and *elitism* within Political Sociology, *credentialism* in Organizations, Occupations and Work, *bureaucracy* in Community and Urban Sociology, *hierarchy* within Economic Sociology, *authoritarianism* in Peace, War and Social Conflict,
labeling in Crime, Law and Deviance, *meritocracy* within the Sociology of Education, and *dominance* within the Sociology of the Family.
Those italicized concepts certainly do have different meanings to an
extent, but they have a shared meaning as well. An emphasis on that
shared meaning by using abstract concepts like social stratification
would help sociologists in each of those fields of the discipline to interact with and learn from one another. Instead, we follow Merton's advice to avoid such concepts since our discipline is not sufficiently "mature" as yet. Our own assessment of immaturity thus creates the very
conditions which that assessment predicts.

Some three decades ago Willer and Webster launched a profound
critique of Merton's approach to the scientific method, basing their
argument largely on the philosophy of science (1970; see also Peirce,
1955; Hempel, 1965; Willer, 1967). They maintained that the more
developed sciences, versus sociology, construct abstract concepts. For
example, there are assertions about "mass" and "specific gravity" in
physics, about "bonds" and "valences of molecules" in chemistry, and
about "heredity," "natural selection" and "genes" in biology. They

argued that sociology's "immaturity" derives in large measure from its failure to use abstract concepts and theory. This approach taken by Willer and Webster has been updated by a variety of analyses pointing in the same direction (see for example Lauderdale, 1990; Phillips, 1972, 1979, 1985, 1988, 1990, 2001; Retzinger, 1991, 1995; Scheff, 1990, 1994, 1997; Wallerstein, 1980, 1991, 1998).

To illustrate further, Scheff's "part/whole" approach is based in part on joint work with Retzinger (1991, 1995; Retzinger and Scheff, 2000). It emphasizes a combination of moving up the ladder of abstraction from concrete concepts ("bottom-up strategy") as well as moving down from abstract ones ("top-down strategy"):

> In my earlier volume (Scheff, 1990) I specify a general approach to theory and method that I call "part/whole." This approach places equal emphasis on the smallest parts of a social system, the words and gestures in discourse, and the largest wholes, the institutions that exist within and between nations. In this view, understanding human behavior depends on rapid movement between the parts and wholes, interpreting each in terms of the other.
>
> My approach is similar to what is called morphology in botany, the study of the structure and function of plants. This approach looks at a single specimen in order to understand the species as well as studying the species in order to understand the specimen. Otherwise those details that are needed in explanation might be left out. Darwin's theory of evolution grew out of his observations of extremely small variations in the appearance of species living in separate regions. Had his method been more focused and "rigorous" (by current standards) in the form of an experiment or survey, he probably would have ignored these tiny details.
>
> Applying this method to the human sphere, I have focused on single concrete episodes of behavior: the inception of a marital quarrel at the interpersonal level, two world wars at the international level. I emphasize a "bottom-up" strategy, starting with a detailed examination of single events, as well as a "top-down" strategy, a bird's-eye view of many events in terms of abstract concepts. Part/whole reasoning requires that both strategies be used in conjunction (1994: 4-5).

Scheff's movement up and down the ladder of abstraction led him to the importance of examining human emotions as well as taking into account the complexity of human behavior, as he explains in a more recent work:

> When part/whole methods are applied to verbatim texts, the intricate filigree of even the simplest human transactions is revealed. Inevitably, crucial aspects of this filigree are emotions and bond-

oriented behavior. One important goal of the substantive chapters is to show that understanding the intricacy of human expressions is not a luxury, but an elementary requirement of human science. It is clear that societies (and the human relationships which constitute them) ride upon extraordinarily complex processes. Because emotional transactions are a vital part of human existence, and are usually omitted, the substantive chapters emphasize them, and their relation to behavior which is oriented toward maintaining the social bond. The part/whole method helps us to understand the relationship between human experience and the largest social structures (1997; see also Retzinger, 1991, 1995).

Without a reconstructed scientific method, as illustrated by Scheff's part/whole approach, we are constrained by traditional specialized orientations to avoid dealing with the enormous complexity of human relationships. More specifically, we are constrained to avoid taking into account "crucial aspects of this filigree" of human transactions, such as emotional processes.

Sociology's failure to develop systematic theories at a very high level of abstraction also derives from the relationship between the disciplines of sociology and philosophy coupled with the pragmatic stance of much of American sociology. As a discipline, sociology has in large measure distinguished itself from philosophy by emphasizing its empirical stance. That stance is seen as enabling it to confront the practical problems of everyday life. Mills saw this situation as follows:

> The ideal of practicality, of not being "utopian," operated   . . .as a polemic against the "philosophy of history" brought into American sociology by men trained in Germany; this polemic implemented the drive to lower levels of abstraction. A view of isolated and immediate problems as the "real" problems may well be characteristic of a society rapidly growing and expanding, as America was in the nineteenth century and, ideologically, in the early twentieth century. . .the practice of the detailed and complete empiricism of the survey is justified by an epistemology of gross description. . .(1943: 168).

Mills reveals the contradiction between ideals for practical action, on the one hand, and scientific procedures which tend to atomize problems and prevent the sociologist from understanding them, on the other hand. The very tools required for such understanding--abstract unifying theoretical concepts--come to be seen negatively as "philosophical" and are as a result avoided.

There are other equally deep causes for our situation. For example, we sociologists generally rely too much on ordinary language and fail to critically analyze our own practices and the social processes that underlie them. Our practice is guided by a disciplinary subculture that remains largely invisible to us. That subculture is nested within and largely shaped by the larger culture of our society in ways that we also do not see. Transforming sociology requires a critical stance to all three: to ordinary language and the assumptions it embodies, to the subculture of our profession, and to the culture or worldview of the larger society. Because ordinary language and our invisible subculture and culture permeate our practices, rectifying our situation is no easy feat.

Our perspective takes inspiration from two seminal critics of sociology, Alvin Gouldner and C. Wright Mills. Gouldner introduced the ideal of a "reflexive sociology" in his *The Coming Crisis of Western Sociology* (1970). There he presented this approach to the discipline as working "to transform the sociologist, to penetrate deeply into his daily life and work, enriching them with new sensitivities, and so raise the sociologist's self-awareness to a new historical level" (1970; see also Phillips, 1988). From this perspective we must somehow learn to apply our language of sociology to the language we use in everyday life, using the former to transform the latter. If we are doctors of a kind with specialized knowledge, then we must learn to heal ourselves.

Gouldner is more explicit about this relationship between sociological and everyday language in his response to a review of his book:

> The pursuit of hermeneutic understanding, however, cannot promise that men as we now find them, with their everyday language and understanding, will always be capable of further understanding and of liberating themselves. At decisive points the ordinary language and conventional understandings fail and must be transcended. It is essentially the task of the social sciences, more generally, to create new and "extraordinary" languages, to help men [sic!]] learn to speak them, and to mediate between the deficient understandings of ordinary language and the different and liberating perspectives of the extraordinary languages of social theory. . . .To say social theorists are concept-creators means that they are not merely in the *knowledge*-creating business, but also in the *language*-reform and language-creating business. In other words, they are from the beginning involved in creating a new *culture* (1972: 16).

Our own focus is on a scientific method which emphasizes using and linking abstract sociological concepts and then applying them to concrete phenomena. Following Gouldner, if we then proceed to teach this approach to others throughout society, we will be doing nothing less than changing culture.

Gouldner's idea is closely related to Mills' vision of "the sociological imagination":

> . . .that imagination is the capacity to shift from one perspective to another--from the political to the psychological; from examination of a single family to comparative assessments of the national budgets of the world; from the theological school to the military establishment; from considerations of an oil industry to studies of contemporary poetry. . .(1959: 7).

Mills wrote this in a book addressed not just to sociologists but to a general audience, believing that the sociological imagination could be widely developed throughout society. Gouldner and Mills together hold out to us a general direction not only for fulfilling "the promise of sociology" by changing sociology's paradigm but also for reviving and fulfilling the Enlightenment dream by changing our cultural paradigm. Yet if we are to move toward that dream, it appears essential that we go beyond the vagueness of Gouldner's and Mills' ideas and focus on what we sociologists can and should accomplish at this moment.

Current orientations to the scientific method within sociology are divided, as illustrated by (1) a traditional quantitative orientation emphasizing easily-measurable indices, questions of reliability and validity, statistical tests and prediction, and the context of verification, (2) a traditional qualitative orientation, concerned primarily with difficult-to-measure phenomena, that gets at situational context and is relatively unconcerned with statistics and prediction, and (3) a postmodernist perspective, generally opposing the idea of a general scientific method along with the existence of structures, and oriented to the momentary construction of reality as well as to the context of discovery. It is a division that reflects the tower of Babel within the discipline as a whole as well as throughout the social sciences. Our approach to the scientific method seeks to transcend these divisions between quantitative and qualitative approaches, and between postmodern constructivism and positivism.

Postmodernists are right to be skeptical about the positivist picture of science. Science is not a matter of putting in the neutral data and cranking out the truth via logical deduction. Nor is science a disembodied process that occurs independently of the interests and social conceptions of scientists. Yet we deny that the only alternative to positivism is postmodernist irrationalism. If science is only rhetoric and social constructivism, then so too are the postmodernist's analysis of science and social science--and that means we have little reason to believe them. We can reject the positivists' logic-of-science ideal without giving up the Enlightenment tenet that beliefs should be based on evidence and reasons. That evidence will not be incorrigible data that can be interpreted without theory. Those reasons will not be infallible and timeless. In our view, claims to good evidence and good reasons are empirical claims that have to be evaluated on the basis of all that we know about the natural and social realms. The social process influencing science can lead to raw rhetoric and pursuit of power, but it need not do so. Science is inevitably a collective enterprise and that very nature is its strength, for it requires the individual investigator to check what he or she believes against what others know. Of course, when investigators are locked in narrow specialization and are unreflexive about their own culture, strengths turn into straight jackets. That is precisely our current situation and the one we seek to eliminate.

We also seek to overcome the false dichotomy between quantitative and qualitative approaches, or between experimental and observational studies. Quantitative methods and experimental manipulation do not have a lock on good science. Much of molecular biology--science at its "hardest"--is largely nonquantitative; it produces not precise laws relating quantities but qualitative causal claims. Much of evolutionary biology, geology and astronomy are observational, not experimental, and qualitative rather than quantitative. Numbers are often a useful route to reliable results, but they are neither essential nor foolproof. What is important is that we be able to integrate our hypotheses in a web of theory and evidence and in so doing show that no other explanation is plausible. If quantitative evidence has no special pretensions, then neither is this true for qualitative evidence. Interpretation is not infallible or transparent, and any good qualitative piece of evidence has to be checked against what else we know about the social world.

We begin to defend our vision for sociology in the two sections that follow. In the first section our focus is on a historical examination of language. In particular, we trace the development of abstraction in language. A high level of abstraction is central to our reconstructed approach to the scientific method. This historical analysis will help us to understand the contrast between a traditional approach to the scientific method with its relatively low level of abstraction and our reconstructed approach. In the second section we sketch an interpretation of the scientific method that differs markedly from present practices but not from present ideals, building on our historical perspective. There we outline five elements of the scientific method, where defining concepts at a high level of abstraction emerges as part of a larger process. This has implications for all of the sciences and not just sociology and the social sciences.

LANGUAGE IN ORAL, LITERATE AND MODERN SOCIETY

The function of this historical perspective is to clarify the nature of our approach to the scientific method and not to stand on its own as a substantiated theory of what happened in history. It is a hypothesis about the past, and it is the kind of very broad hypothesis involving intangible phenomena as well as very long-term changes that is exceedingly difficult to test. Yet this volume centers not on theory but rather on interpreting the scientific method, and that interpretation should be assessed on the basis of its utility, as illustrated here and in the future. It is an approach designed to confront both ordinary or delimited research problems as well as the kinds of very broad problems confronted in this chapter.

Organisms, by contrast with physical structures, must interact with their environments to a fair extent in order to survive, granting that even physical structures cannot be completely isolated from all other phenomena.   And it is that interaction process taking place between organism and environment which is the basis for biological evolution. For what occurs amounts to a very slow "learning" process--using "learning" as a metaphor--based on that interaction. Not "learning" in the conventional sense as occurring within the lifetime of an organism and not tied to biological changes, but "learning," metaphorically, over many generations as a result of biological mutations which yield improved chances for adaptation to the environment. With the appearance of the human being and language, however, for the first time within evolutionary history we have the possibility of extremely rapid and far-reaching interaction and change in fundamental structures.

The ability of early human groups to interact rapidly--using language--with the phenomena within their environment appears to have been essential for their survival. Yet within an oral culture that language was largely limited to phenomena they could become aware of directly with their senses. Here we might think of Hamlet's "to be or not to be" soliloquy as the kind of abstract thinking which would get in the way of the rapid interaction with environmental dangers and opportunities which those early folk required for their survival. To illustrate the transition from oral to literate preindustrial society, we turn to a 1931-32 study of illiterate peasants in remote farming areas of Uzbekistan and Kirghizia, Republics in the former Soviet Union (Luria, 1976; see also Ong, 1982: 49-56).   A written language did indeed exist in those two isolated areas, but we can assume a heavy oral residue. Some questions asked for definitions, e.g., "Try to explain to me what a tree is." Typically respondents resisted such questions: "Why should I? Everyone knows what a tree is. You can look to see" (Luria, 1976: 86). As for the syllogism, subjects were told: "In the Far North, where there is snow, all bears are white. Novaya Zembla is in the Far North and there is always snow there. What color are the bears?" One response: "I don't know. I've seen a black bear. I've never seen any others.. . ." (104-108).

This journey from oral to literate culture has continued from its preindustrial beginnings to modern societies, which might well be called scientific or technological societies. They embrace the very abstract concepts of the sciences, as illustrated by the concepts of "organism" and "biological evolution," or the mathematical formula, $F = ma,$ or force equals mass times acceleration. Each of the concepts involved in that formula is extremely high on language's ladder of abstraction, just as are the concepts of organism and biological evolution. They deal with an incredibly wide range of phenomena from a falling apple to no less than the motion of the planets. Further, the concepts of the biophysical sciences do not remain isolated from one another but are tied together directly or indirectly in highly systematic ways. And this results in abilities to make accurate predictions about a very wide range of phenomena, predictions that have become the basis for rapidly developing technologies that we have come to label as the continuing industrial or technological revolution.

Granting our usage of abstract concepts in ordinary usage to an extent, we might question just how far we have moved away from emphasizing concrete concepts in our everyday usage of language. Figure 1-l, The Globe Metaphor for Levels of Abstraction, portrays the preceding analysis. The focus is on differences in the level of abstraction generally employed, where very high levels of abstraction may be found at both the North and South Poles and very low levels at the equator. The lower hemisphere has to do with the difference between oral and literate society, where both are portrayed by dots. The upper hemisphere contrasts the social sciences and their technologies, portrayed by dashes, and the biophysical sciences with their technologies, portrayed by solid lines. The illiterate peasants of Uzbekistan and Kirghizia are located in the lower right-hand quadrant, and their usage stays close to the equator or a low level of abstraction, granting that language does work in the same general way for us moderns as well. For both preliterate and literate society, language takes people up and down the ladder of abstraction. But us literates in the lower left-hand quadrant have learned to move much further up the ladder of abstraction, which happens to be movement toward the South Pole in Figure 1-

1. Their dots--by contrast with preliterates--extend to the South Pole's high level of abstraction, although most of those dots remain close to the low level of abstraction of the equator, suggesting our similarity to preliterate society.

Throughout the upper hemisphere the language of the sciences and their technologies also takes their users all the way from the equator to a high level of abstraction, depicted at the North Pole. But let us note that the dashes for the social sciences are denser near the equator, in common with the clustering within literate society, indicating a preference for language at a lower level of abstraction. It is only in the upper right-hand quadrant that usages at a high level of abstraction are not

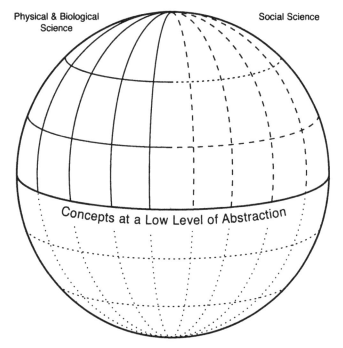

Figure 1-1. The globe metaphor for levels of abstraction.
(Adapted from Phillips, 2001, Figure 1-2, p. 22.)

secondary to usages at a low level. Those solid lines for the biophysical sciences and their technologies are meant to indicate their systematic integration of knowledge, where the abstract concepts at the North Pole build on and imply all of the knowledge located closer to the equator. By contrast, the lines of dashes for the social sciences and their technologies are meant to indicate limited integration of knowledge. This problem is linked to a failure of their abstract concepts to invoke the full weight of their more concrete concepts closer to the equator. And this contrast between the upper right and upper left quadrants reflects the rapid cumulative development and high credibility of the biophysical sciences and technologies, by contrast with the social sciences and their technologies.

The lines of latitude in all quadrants suggest the linkage among the lines of longitude, that is, among knowledge bearing on different kinds of phenomena such as sociological knowledge of the family, mental health, political sociology, economic sociology and the sociology of religion. In the case of $F = ma$ we have the phenomena of force, of mass and of acceleration, with the formula specifying their interrelationship so well that we can make precise predictions as a result. In this way, the lines of longitude and latitude together form a highly systematic web of knowledge that becomes the basis for developing effective technologies. By contrast, the lines of dashes for longitude and latitude within the social sciences are integrated only to a limited extent and have not yet formed such a web. Knowledge within the special fields of the biophysical sciences is integrated systematically or mathematically. Within the social sciences this occurs only to a very limited extent, as illustrated by the many Sections of the ASA dealing with social stratification but failing to give due recognition to that link.

Although we have focused on language up to this point, a deeper understanding of language requires that we examine briefly how language is related to the structure of modern society. Granting language's breadth, our understanding of it is limited unless we see it in relation to society as a whole and, in particular, to the change from preindustrial to modern society. We have already centered on this transition through our comparison in Figure 1-1 of oral society with literate society. There, we also compared the biophysical sciences and their technologies with the social sciences and their technologies, examining more closely the changes in society over the last four centuries. Yet a deeper understanding of the upper hemisphere of Figure 1-1 requires that we see language as a tool which may not only solve problems but which also may help to create them. This is illustrated in Figure 1-1 by the gap between the biophysical and the social sciences, yielding powerful biophysical technologies that can be turned toward destruction yet weak social technologies for confronting that problem. We have learned that biological evolution is not always an "onward and upward" affair, as illustrated by species like the dinosaurs whose failure to adapt to their environment led to their extinction. Language is our most powerful tool for addressing and solving problems, yet we might ask to what extent we have used it to confront and solve modern problems.

Returning to the Uzbekistani and Kirghiziani, we might note the balance they achieved: What possible use is there to creating a definition of a tree if one is not reading or writing about trees in situations far removed from one's immediate context? To what extent do we literates also have this kind of pragmatic balance among thought, feeling and action? This question speaks directly to the question of how language, the basis for our thought, has been used by us moderns in a one-sided way, paralleling our emphasis on the development of effective biophysical technologies by contrast with social technologies. We are all familiar with positive changes in society associated with the successes of technologies based on the biophysical sciences, changes which have yielded what has been called a "revolution of rising expectations" as modernization has proceeded. Yet all of these changes constitute only one side of the coin of modernization. The other side has to do with the limited achievements of the social sciences and their technologies, and the resulting imbalance between the two kinds of science portrays quite a different picture. We shall proceed to elaborate on this imbalance within modern society in preparation for the next section on the web approach to the scientific method.

However, the argument to be presented here is certainly open to debate, based on the specialized knowledge presently available within the social sciences. It is presented here as a hypothesis rather than as an analysis backed up by a thorough treatment of the relevant literature. Our purpose is to provide more of the context of what has been happening in modern society as a basis for examining the scientific method in the next section. Just as the web approach to the scientific method to be developed in that section is oriented to the complexity of human behavior, so must we orient ourselves to that complexity by opening up to the modern context within which the scientific method is located. Our argument may ultimately prove to be inadequate. The modern context may in fact prove to be different from what will be presented. Yet accepting that presentation is not essential for assessing the potential of the web approach to the scientific method in the next section. The utility of that approach should be evaluated on its own terms, whether on the basis of the illustrations to be put forward in Part Two or subsequent research exploring the fruitfulness of the web approach.

For some insight into language's failure to yield the progressive solution of social problems in modern society, we turn first to Simmel's analysis in his "The Metropolis and Mental Life":

> The deepest problems of modern life flow from the attempt of the individual to maintain the independence and individuality of his existence against the sovereign powers of society, against the weight of the historical heritage and the external culture and technique of life. . . .the metropolitan type   . . .creates a protective organ for itself against the profound disruption with which the fluctuations and discontinuities of the external milieu threaten it. Instead of reacting emotionally, the metropolitan type reacts primarily in a rational manner, thus creating a mental predominance through the intensification of consciousness. . .Thus the reaction of the metropolitan person to those events is moved to a sphere of mental activity which is least sensitive and which is furthest removed from the depths of the personality. . . .There is perhaps no psychic phenomenon which is so unconditionally reserved to the city as the blasé outlook...([1905] 1971: 324, 326, 329).

Simmel writes that "instead of reacting emotionally, the metropolitan type reacts primarily in a rational manner, thus creating a mental predominance through the intensification of consciousness." He is referring here the development of a modern imbalance between thinking and feeling, where the individual learns to protect his or her emotions. Freud would write of emotional repression in relation to this phenomenon. The result is the kind of imbalance between thinking and feeling which contrasts markedly with the balance we found in the oral-society orientations of the Uzbekistani and Kirghiziani,

Marx saw capitalistic society as alienating "man from himself, from his own active function, his life activity" ([1844] 1964: 125-127), and this is similar to Simmel's focus on the emotional withdrawal of the individual and the creation of a hard intellectual shell or blasé personality as a form of protection against the assaults of modern life. We moderns apparently have lost the balance among thought, feeling and action characteristic of the Uzbekistani and Kirghiziani, for we have learned to bury our emotions as a protective device. This is illustrated not merely by the blasé outlook of the city-dweller but by all of us moderns, for we are all the product of a literate society. Simmel continues his analysis of our emotional life:

> Money is concerned only with what is common to all, i.e., with the exchange value which reduces all quality and individuality to a purely quantitative level. All emotional relationships between persons rest on their individuality, whereas intellectual relationships

deal with persons as with numbers, that is, as with elements which, in themselves, are indifferent, but which are of interest only insofar as they offer something objectively perceivable. It is in this very manner that the inhabitant of the metropolis reckons with his merchant, his customer, and with his servant, and frequently with the persons with whom he is thrown into obligatory association. These relationships stand in distinct contrast with the nature of the smaller circle in which the inevitable knowledge of individual characteristics produces, with an equal inevitability, an emotional tone in conduct, a sphere which lies beyond the mere objective weighting of tasks performed and payments made. . . ([1903] 1971: 326-327).

Simmel once again points up the fundamental emotional lack we moderns illustrate. And it is held in place by the superficiality of relationships "which are of interest only insofar as they offer something objectively perceivable." This contrasts with our pre-modern relationships and their "emotional tone." Here, Simmel's concern also follows that of Marx: "A direct consequence of the alienation of man from the product of his labour, from his life activity and from his species-life, is that man is alienated from other men" (Marx [1844] 1964: 129). But granting the acuity of their analyses, what neither Simmel nor Marx discusses is the failure of the social sciences to deal with the problems in modern society associated with the successes of the physical and biological sciences, successes which have fueled the industrial revolution associated with the changes in society which they criticize. Further, neither one points up a key factor associated with those successes and failures: the enormous complexity of human behavior relative to the simplicity of physical and biological phenomena. And neither one suggests the role of linguistic levels of abstraction within this situation. This is not meant to suggest the failure of their contributions but only to suggest the limitations of those contributions for our understanding of the modern world.

Yet what about society's contemporary situation--including that of scientists--at the birth of the third millennium? For an illustration of our situation we might turn to Vidich's and Bensman's analysis of "Springdale," a small town in New York State, where large gaps developed between Springdalers' aspirations for success, friendship and self-determination and what they actually achieved:

The technique of particularization is one of the most pervasive ways of avoiding reality. It operates to make possible not only the failure to recognize dependence but also the avoidance of the realities of social class and inequalities. The Springdaler is able to maintain his equalitarian ideology because he avoids generalizing about class differences. . .Thus a new purchase is talked about only in terms of the individual who makes it, rather than the class style of the purchase...The realization of lack of fulfillment of aspiration and ambition might pose an unsolvable personal problem if the falsification of memory did not occur, and if the hopes and ambitions of a past decade or two remained salient in the present perspective...As a consequence, his present self, instead of entertaining the youthful dream of a 500-acre farm, entertains the plan to buy a home freezer by the fall...The greatest dangers to a system of illusions which is threatened by an uncompromising reality are introspection and thought...The major technique of self-avoidance is work. The farmer and the businessman drive themselves in their work almost to the point of exhaustion. . . (1960: 299, 303, 311).

The "technique of particularization" and the "falsification of memory" both point the Springdaler away from abstract thinking about earlier ideals and toward concrete thinking about his or her immediate situation. And as a result of these techniques of avoidance or repression, the Springdalers are able to achieve "some degree of satisfaction, recognition and achievement" (1960: 320). From this perspective we can understand a modern lack of balance between thought, feeling and action that we all share. It is the frustration accompanying an unfulfilled Enlightenment dream of a society that is able to confront and solve its fundamental problems. Social scientists, given the frustration associated with failing to achieve that balance in their professional work, experience a double frustration. All of us moderns, and particularly social scientists, nevertheless have to learn how to continue in life while living with these frustrations, which involve enormous gaps between our aspirations and their fulfillment. We are all much like the Springdalers who have also experienced such gaps. And the techniques we employ to achieve "some degree of satisfaction, recognition and achievement" also appear to be similar. For example, we sociologists appear to use the technique of particularization by hiding within our specialized Sections of the ASA, failing to open up to other knowledge. And we also appear to falsify memory by burying our earlier aspirations--which motivated us to enter the discipline--for fulfilling "the promise of sociology."

The Springdalers and us moderns differ from the Uzbekistani and the Kirghiziani in our imbalance between thought, feeling and action, where aspirations are repressed as a result of failures to fulfill them. Let us turn to Figure 1-2, which presents our examples of the Uzbekistani and Kirghiziani, Simmel's Berliners--illustrating the metropolitan mentality at the beginning of the twentieth century--and the Springdalers on a time line from preindustrial to modern society. This schematic diagram is a hypothesis designed to carry forward our view of the impact of the relative achievements of the physical and biological sciences and their technologies, on the one hand, and the relative failures of the social sciences and their technologies, on the other hand.

This graph of the invisible crisis of modern society centers on an accelerating gap between expectations or aspirations and the fulfillment of those expectations. On an absolute scale we might note increasing fulfillment of expectations. Yet we can also note the rapid acceleration of expectations—far outrunning their fulfillment—stemming from the

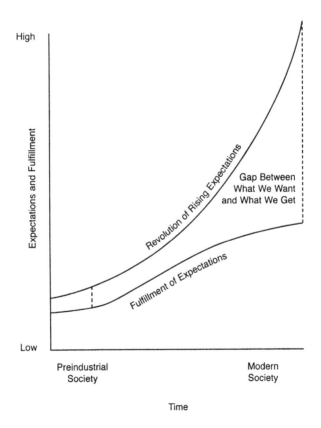

Figure 1.2. The invisible crisis of modern society.
(Adapted from Phillips, 2001, Figure 1.1, p. 20.)

increasing effectiveness of technologies based on the biophysical sciences. The Uzbekistani and Kirghiziani are located within early preindustrial society and experience a balance between aspirations and fulfillment. Metropolitans like the Berliners of the early 20th century, by contrast, have experienced a large gap between aspirations and fulfillment, and the Springdalers--like us moderns--have experienced by far the largest gap between what they want and are able to get. Those gaps are associated with the failures of the social sciences to confront and solve increasing problems involved within modernization. Following Figure 1-2 with its accelerating gap, we appear to be living on borrowed time.

Just as President Kennedy used metaphor so powerfully when he journeyed to Berlin during its blockade by the Soviet Union and declared, "*Ich bin ein Berliner*," can we sociologists declare no less vehemently, *Ich bin ein Uzbekistani*, *Ich bin ein Kirghiziani*, *Ich bin ein Berliner*, and *Ich bin ein Springdaler*? What is at stake for the sociologist is an ability to retain both the abstract thought of modern society without the imbalance between thought, feeling and action with which abstract thought has come to be associated. And it is that very repression of emotions which apparently makes it difficult for sociologists as well as moderns in general to confront fundamental problems. By claiming some degree of identity with the Uzbekistani and Kirghiziani, we are also becoming aware of the importance of their concrete ways of thinking and lesser degree of emotional repression, and hence greater balance among thought, feeling and action. And by claiming identity with the Berliners and Springdalers, we increase our consciousness of our sharing that emotional repression--and that greater gap between aspiration and fulfillment--characteristic of early industrial society. Overall, awareness of what we share with those earlier peoples helps us to open up to the long-term and relatively invisible processes depicted in Figures 1-1 and 1-2.

As we continue with our examination of modern society so as to provide a context for a subsequent focus on the scientific method, it is essential that we not neglect the institution of science. For that institution has proved to be absolutely central to the development of modern society. Thomas Kuhn--a historian and philosopher of science--has helped us to understand that institution with his influential analysis of revolutions within the physical and biological sciences (1962, 1977). This was nothing short of an intuitive application of the sociology of knowledge to explain dramatic achievements within those sciences. He identified three crucial components of change: preexisting subcultures or paradigms, often invisible to participants; anomalies or failures to solve problems within those subcultures; and the construction of new paradigms or subcultures that promise the resolution of those problems.

Kuhn's approach is illustrated by his analysis of Einstein's development of the special theory of relativity. The American engineers Michelson and Morley used an ingenious series of mirrors located miles apart to measure the speed of light as it ricocheted off one mirror after another. Newton's laws apply to the motion of light no less than to the motion of a boat on a river: the boat is slowed when it moves up-river against the current or across the river, and it is speeded up down-river. Similarly, following Newton, light should be speeded up in the direction of the earth's rotation and slowed as it proceeds in other directions. Not so, according to the precise experiments of Michelson and Morley. Contrary to Newton's laws of mechanics which had been widely accepted for hundreds of years, Michelson and Morley discovered that light travels at the same speed in any direction. Yet the physicists of Einstein's day, having lived their entire lives taking for granted the adequacy of Newton's laws of motion, generally remained unable to question those laws. Even after being presented with experiments which challenged those laws, generally they proved to be unable to question them seriously and, as a result, follow the ideals of the scientific method. Kuhn argued that it is not evidence alone which sways a community of scientists to reject an old theory in favor of a new one. Other factors as well play key roles, such as tradition, social hierarchy and the personality of the scientist. Kuhn's was an argument that followed the perspectives of the sociology of knowledge.

Einstein was able to challenge the prevailing paradigm or subculture of physical science by conceiving of an alternative paradigm, one based on a different way of thinking about motion (for a relatively recent account, see Holton, 1996). He started with the assumption that light travels at the same speed in any direction, thus accepting the conclusions of Michelson and Morley as a premise. And this led to a number of strange hypotheses which were involved within his special theory of relativity. That theory not only resolves Newtonian contradictions but it is able to make more accurate predictions of motion in all situations. Kuhn's analysis suggests that taking the first step of the scientific method requires some vision of subsequent steps. Einstein, for example, could challenge Newton's laws because he was able to conceive of an alternative theory that could account for observed contradictions. Extrapolating Kuhn's analysis of scientific revolutions, we can indeed begin to revive the promise of sociology and the Enlightenment dream if we can learn to see what is now invisible: contradictions within both our sociological paradigm and the cultural paradigm of modern society which holds our sociological paradigm in place. What we need in addition are alternative paradigms that promise to resolve those contradictions.

RECONSTRUCTING THE SCIENTIFIC METHOD: A WEB APPROACH

The following pages sketch an alternative paradigm for the scientific method as well as for modern society, paradigms which point toward resolving present-day contradictions within both. Following Kuhn, some alternative paradigm is essential if we are to begin to question our present approach to the scientific method, even if the alternative sketched here ultimately proves to be barren. The reader should be reminded that the utility of our own approach to the scientific method does not depend on the validity of the foregoing historical and linguistic analysis. Rather, that section was meant to clarify and illustrate our methodological approach, and it may succeed in accomplishing this even if it ultimately proves to be invalid. This volume represents a series of studies of published pieces where the authors take a second look at those publications with the aid of what we call a web approach to the scientific method. It is the approach used implicitly in the above section, and it will be outlined in this section. We believe in its possibilities for helping us sociologists--and other social scientists as well--to achieve both rapid substantive development and the rapid development of knowledge that can address effectively the basic problems of modern society.

Our approach to the scientific method has five components: (1) definition of the problem, (2) high level of abstraction, (3) low level of abstraction, (4) a web of knowledge, and (5) reflexive analysis within an interactive worldview. This approach follows sociological ideals for the scientific method that call for defining research problems on the basis of existing knowledge, openness to all relevant knowledge, testing abstract ideas or theory empirically and integrating knowledge systematically. Yet it is in fact a world apart from the way research is actually practiced within sociology and the social sciences. It is that practice which has yielded a tower of Babel within sociology, where knowledge is largely kept in the water-tight compartments presided over by the officers of fully forty Sections of the American Sociological Association. Linking the knowledge locked within those compartments requires abstract theoretical concepts like social stratification, which can bridge specialized areas of interest, such as the areas of sexism, racism, classism, ageism, ethnocentrism, prejudice, weightism, discrimination, homophobia, hegemony, power, elitism, credentialism, bureaucracy, hierarchy, authoritarianism, labeling and meritocracy. And such bridging can also open up the investigator to fundamental problems in society. This is much the way ordinary language works, but carried to a higher level of abstraction. Let us then consider in turn each of these five components.

Definition of the Problem

Successful inquiry requires a clear definition of the problem at hand. This may seem like a truism, but it is not. There are very different ways to conceive of defining a problem; those conceptions carry with them very different perspectives on the sociological enterprise. At issue is how we deal with complexity: do we ignore the complexity of social phenomena in an *ad hoc* and piecemeal manner? Or do we approach the complexity of social phenomena theoretically via abstract concepts? Also at issue is the depth of the problems that we take up. Do we content ourselves by ignoring the links between the specialized problems we take up and the fundamental problems in society? Or do we follow those links and open up to those basic problems? And equally at issue is our ability to confront those large problems. Do we remain helpless victims of them, or do proceed to solve them?

The piecemeal approach seems to dominate the profession. Yet even this appearance is deceptive, for apparently we cannot avoid making extensive theoretical assumptions in defining a problem to investigate. Those assumptions may be left unstated and even unknown to the investigator, but the complex nature of social phenomena means they must be there. The vocabulary we use, the way that vocabulary divides up the social world, the assumptions we make about causality--such as how parts relate to large wholes, the role of structural factors, whether causal relations are linear, reversible, or additive--are presupposed on how we define the problem. We can conduct research pretending that we need not decide such issues. However, in our view progress in research requires that we be explicit and defend such presuppositions.

As a case in point, let us focus on the broad, fundamental, long-term and dangerous problem depicted in Figure 1-2: the invisible crisis of modern society as reflected in an escalating gap between expectations and fulfillment. Within traditional methodology this is much too broad a problem: it must be broken down into pieces, with the pieces supposedly being put together at some future date. Yet let us recall Richard Lerner's statement at the beginning of this chapter:

> We have spent 100 years of reductionism trying to understand bio-
> logical processes by looking at the pieces. Now we're going to try
> to understand complexity, how the pieces work together.

Within Figure 1-2, for example, an understanding of the problem requires that we take into account both curves simultaneously, since it is
the two together which yield a gap. The upper curve lies in the domain
of cultural studies whereas the lower curve lies within the province of
social organization. Further, we were able to make sense out of and
unify illustrations bearing on illiterate Soviet peasants, Simmel's analysis of the metropolis and the study of Springdalers only by adopting a
very long-term perspective, one that reached far back to oral culture
and came far forward to contemporary society. For this, a piecemeal
approach will not do.

Our approach to the scientific method does not require a focus on
only those problems that are as fundamental and dangerous as the problem illustrated in Figure 1-2. The full range of problems presently of
interest to sociologists are open to this approach. Yet when we approach a given problem--say, the forces producing prejudice against
members of a minority group--that problem comes to be linked to other
problems because of the abstract concepts we employ. And as a result
we are able to open up to far greater difficulties than those apparent
within a specialized approach to the scientific method. For example,
such prejudice might be linked to patterns of social stratification--an
abstract concept--within modern society. Prejudice is certainly not a
small problem, but when we bring in social stratification as well then
we are dealing with the basic structure of society. This should not imply a neglect of the specialized literature on prejudice in favor of a
vague and general approach to that problem. We need not make a
choice between general problems and specialized problems. It all depends on the investigator's focus of interest, for general problems can
help us to understand more fully a specialized problem. And if one
centers on a general problem like the invisible crisis of modern society,
links with specialized problems can flesh out that general problem.

The studies within this volume range widely over the discipline, yet
they are all secondary analyses of published material. This should by
no means imply that our approach to research is limited to secondary
analyses. Rather, this is only one direction for using the scientific
method. Our rationale for such analyses is based primarily on our ability, with the aid of secondary analyses, to compare this approach to the
scientific method with the traditional one within the primary analysis.
For example, to what extent does the former suggest new insights? To
what extent is the former more credible? Another reason for secondary

analyses within this volume has to do with the importance of using concepts at a high level of abstraction, as was emphasized within the preceding section. Much of the process of social research has to do with data collection, and this takes away from time that might be spent on analysis. An individual doing a secondary analysis can thus afford to focus attention on abstract concepts and theory. Further, secondary analyses generally involve less time and funding. Those latter advantages are particularly important for a research direction that is new and as yet has limited credibility. Finally, secondary analyses can serve as markers which chart the development of a new approach to research: one can analyze one's own previous project, and then one can in turn analyze that secondary analysis, and so on.

Fundamental to an adequate definition of a research problem is both the commitment of the researcher to the importance of the problem as well as a review of relevant literature, including usage of key abstract concepts which employ that literature to examine the nature of the problem and point a direction for addressing it. As for that commitment, it appears that it is not just society as a whole that generally has lost faith in the credibility of social science for confronting the basic problems of modern society. We sociologists generally share that loss of faith, no longer believing in the Enlightenment dream or the promise of sociology. This is partly due to our lack of sufficient awareness of the complexity and invisibility of human behavior relative to other phenomena. Yet the regaining of that faith is a vital factor in developing the kind of research that dares to address the fundamental problems of society and make progress on them. As for seeing a problem in relation to prior studies, our own approach demands the use of theoretical concepts at a very high level of abstraction as a basis for reviewing the literature. Thus, we cannot proceed further in this discussion without introducing the sociological concepts we will require for defining the problem to be illustrated, namely, that of the invisible crisis of modern society. Here, then, we must turn to the next phase of the scientific method: the use of a high level of abstraction.

High Level of Abstraction

Abstract concepts are essential to progress in sociology. As we use the term, an abstract concept is not one that is far from reality. Rather, concepts are abstract when they allow us to explain diverse phenomena in diverse circumstances. We think such concepts are necessary for several reasons. Foremost is that if we are to overcome the isolating specialization in our discipline, we need a common language that can build bridges across our findings. Abstract concepts do just that. Yet they do more than build bridges. By connecting apparently diverse inquiries, abstract concepts promote an essential feature of the scientific enterprise: strengthening, refining, and testing work in one domain by incorporating its results into investigations in other domains. For example, Mendel's claims about a "unit of inheritance" and the biochemical study of nucleic acids were strengthened, refined, and tested in the 1940s when the abstract concept of a gene was applied to both. Finally, abstract concepts have another crucial feature--they are essential to developing theories as opposed to low-level generalizations based on ordinary-language concepts. Evidence, experiments, and statistical inferences are blind without theories identifying the relevant factors, confounders, and mechanisms (see Pawson, 1989).

As an illustration, consider Table 1-1, Elements of Behavior and Structuring of Behavior. It depicts a direction for understanding the invisible crisis of modern society--or any other research problem--in such a way as to confront the problems of complexity and invisibility. All of the cells or boxes are important for understanding any instance of human behavior, rather than any one particular cell or concepts used to illustrate that cell. Further, the concepts are defined very abstractly--as presented in the glossary at the end of this chapter--so as to avoid limitation only to certain periods or situations. Those definitions could easily have been different, given the divergence within the discipline. They were chosen so that the concepts could be used together fruitfully. For example, "Structuring of Behavior" emphasizes the degree of structure and includes both relatively structured phenomena (top and bottom rows) as well as situations (middle row). There are the patterned thoughts, feelings and actions of the individual (bottom row), the forces of culture and patterns of social organization within social structure (top row), and the momentary nonstructural thoughts, feelings and actions expressed in the situation (middle row). The columns have to do with different components of the behavior of the individual, metaphorically corresponding to "head," "heart" and "hand." These consist of beliefs or ideas, interests or aspirations, and action and interaction.

We can begin to understand the concepts simply from their positions within Table 1-1. For example, anomie comes to be seen as an aspect of social structure with an emphasis on individual beliefs, just as alienation is seen as an aspect of the structure of the individual with a focus on interests. We come to see both social stratification and addiction as aspects of action or interaction, with the former located within social structure and the latter within the structure of the individual. As for the situational concepts--label, relative deprivation and conformity--they range over, metaphorically, the "head," the "heart" and the "hand,"

ELEMENTS OF BEHAVIOR

	"Head": Beliefs, Ideas	"Heart": Interests, Aspirations	"Hand": Action, Interaction
Social Structures: Shared & Persisting Patterns	1 (anomie)	2 (cultural values)	3 (social stratification)
Situations: Momentary Behavior in a Scene	4 (label)	5 (relative deprivation)	6 (conformity)
Individual Structures: Persisting Behavior	7 (worldview)	8 (alienation)	9 (addiction)

CONSTRUCTION OF BEHAVIOR

Table 1.1. Elements of behavior and construction of behavior.

respectively. The concepts in Table 1-1--with the partial exceptions of worldview and addiction--are part of the contemporary sociological literature, fitting into the general framework of the discipline. For example, culture has to do with both "head" and "heart" at the level of social structure, whereas social organization has to do with the "hand" at that same level. What is different about this approach is its emphasis on the importance of all of the cells taken together that are depicted in Table 1-1--as illustrated by the concepts within those cells--for understanding any instance of human behavior [for a more detailed treatment of these concepts along with additional sociological concepts, see Phillips (2001).

We shall illustrate the basis for our definitions of the two concepts that presently are not widely used within the sociological literature: addiction and worldview. The concept of addiction--defined as the individual's subordination of individuality to dependence on external phenomena--carries forward Simmel's analysis of the problem of maintaining individuality as central to "the deepest problems of modern life." Whereas psychologists use the concept "habit" for the persisting actions of the individual, we sociologists have agreed as yet on no concept to inhabit this cell, hence our own usage of addiction. It refers not only to the phenomenon of biological dependence associated with substance abuse but also to any continuing action or interaction--such as watching TV, running or sexual behavior--which has become so compulsive or obsessive as to drown out the wide range of behavior we associate with the possibilities of the individual. As for the concept of worldview, it is defined as the individual's *Weltanschauung* or global outlook that is widely shared throughout society. According to its location in Table 1-1, a worldview is located within the beliefs or ideas of the individual, yet it has come to be there as a result of a socialization process transmitting cultural norms for what to believe to individuals throughout society. And just as culture serves as a broad and unifying structure for society, so does worldview serve as a broad and unifying structure for the individual.

By employing concepts from all the cells in an effort to understand the invisible crisis of modern society, we are illustrating a general approach to research methods where any given social problem--no matter how minute--can be approached with the full range of our sociological knowledge. Many other abstract sociological concepts can be added to these cells to help introduce that knowledge. Following our interpretation of Kuhn, it is useful to distinguish between the existing sociological "paradigm" or subculture which governs present usage of the scientific method and the alternative paradigm which we are introducing. Referring to Figure 1-1, our alternative paradigm emphasizes abstract concepts--lines of longitude up to the North Pole--no less than the bio-physical sciences. This approach contrasts with the middle-range emphasis within sociology. As a result, we are able to move toward solid lines of longitude where our abstract concepts come to carry the full weight of sociological knowledge. Further, our approach also parallels those sciences in its emphasis on linking knowledge within different specialized areas, moving us sociologists toward solid lines of latitude by bringing to bear multiple concepts on a given problem. Our own approach is not a mathematical one, but it is a systematic and pragmatic one in its effort to build on what the entire discipline has learned and using the result to focus on any given research problem.

Kuhn discovered, with the aid of his sociological orientation, that scientific revolutions were impeded by such phenomena as subcultural beliefs, hierarchies among scientists and deep personal commitments. This suggests that the paradigmatic approach within a science is itself tied to a worldview. Following our contextual approach to Table 1-1, we can see that worldview as linked to such phenomena as anomie, social stratification, labeling, relative deprivation, conformity to cultural values, alienation and addiction. As a result, we can begin to understand the origins within society as a whole of those forces that Kuhn discovered which stand in the way of scientific revolutions, pointing away from scientific ideals. For example, a stratified society would yield hierarchies among scientists, including patterns of relative deprivation and labeling in one scene after another. A society emphasizing situational conformity to cultural values and norms would pressure scientists to conform to the subcultural norms within their particular science. And a society yielding anomie, alienation and addiction would also yield individuals rigidly tied to personal commitments even if they flew in the face of scientific ideals. We label this *Weltanschauung* a "bureaucratic worldview" by contrast with an "interactive worldview."

Weber's conception of formal rationality helps to illustrate the ties between the bureaucratic worldview in general and its specific manifestation in the biophysical and social sciences. For Weber, modern bureaucratic organization is characterized by a formal rationality that (1) makes no assumptions concerning ends but only means to given ends, and (2) provides mechanical algorithmic rules to promote those ends. It is formal or bureaucratic rationality in the second sense that undermines current social science research (Kincaid, 2000). Perhaps the most unfortunate and widespread example of that influence involves the abuse of statistics. Social scientists (and many biophysical scientists as well) look to statistics for mechanical decision rules which it cannot deliver. Hypotheses that are statistically significant are

treated as well confirmed and those that are not significant are re-
jected--even though such conclusions are entirely unwarranted (Cohen,
1994). Explained variance or R^2 is taken to be a purely mechanical or
objective measure of explanatory power. Yet in fact high R^2 values
are compatible with minimal causal influence as measured by, say, a
regression coefficient and with a relation that is entirely spurious. The
bureaucratic worldview leads us to look for mechanical decision procedures where they cannot be found. It contrasts markedly with Weber's concept of "substantive rationality," where we would look beyond purely mechanical decision procedures so as to become sensitive
to a wide range of cultural values.

But if indeed our research methods are tied to our cultural paradigm, isn't it naive, if not phenomenally audacious, to think that we
can change that paradigm? However, it is within a bureaucratic
worldview that we approach change in an all-or-none way, but within
an interactive worldview we can take one step, pragmatically, toward
an interactive scientific paradigm. And that step might yield a step toward an interactive worldview, and so on. Gouldner and Mills have
given us a vision of this possibility. Let us recall Gouldner's emphasis
on a "reflexive sociology" and his words about extraordinary languages:

> At decisive points the ordinary language and conventional under-
> standings fail and must be transcended. It is essentially the task of
> the social sciences, more generally, to create new and "extraordi-
> nary" languages, to help men learn to speak them, and to mediate
> between the deficient understandings of ordinary language and the
> different and liberating perspectives of the extraordinary languages
> of social theory. . .(1972: 16).

Within our historical analysis we have traced the difference in levels of
abstraction between the Uzbekistani or Kirghiziani and us moderns, a
journey pointing us toward learning to use the abstract concepts of the
social sciences within our everyday lives. Mills joins Gouldner in envi-
sioning the possibility that all human beings can learn to develop a
"sociological imagination."

Yet can we ignore problems like anomie, alienation and addiction
which we Berliners and Springdalers have encountered, problems
which surely would stand in the way of moving toward thinking more
abstractly in everyday life? And in addition to our relatively intangible
or invisible problems there are the visible ones that command our attention from one moment to the next. Yet following Kuhn's analysis
of the scientific method, we humans can learn to solve even the most

complex and invisible problems. We can learn to use abstract concepts like those in Table 1-1 to help make those problems visible, just as ordinary language helps us to make visible the problems of everyday life. And we can well afford to have faith in a scientific method--granting that we lack certainty--that has proven its abilities in the case of the biophysical sciences and their technologies over the past four centuries. Granting the problems we sociologists face are substantially more complex and invisible, as yet we have learned of no biological barriers to our employing the same powerful scientific method that has worked so effectively in the past. Indeed, this is much the same as the argument of Auguste Comte. In our own times, however, it appears that our need for recapturing the Enlightenment dream and the promise of sociology is greater and more urgent than ever before.

More specifically, let us now turn to illustrating the application of the very abstract concepts in Table 1-1 to the problem of the invisible crisis of modern society. We might begin by seeing the growing gap between the two curves of Figure 1-2 as illustrating the kinds of fundamental contradictions within social structure that have to do with anomie. Probing the nature of the top curve of the revolution of rising expectations, we can see it as linked to cultural values: people-oriented values like "equality" and "freedom," and work-related ones like "achievement and success" and "material comfort" (Williams, 1970). The latter values are associated with the work ethic described by Weber ([1905] 1958) as well as with the increasing successes of the physical and biological sciences and their technologies. It is when we see those cultural values in relation to patterns of social stratification and bureaucracy that drastically limit their widespread fulfillment that we can understand not only the prevalence of anomie but also that of the alienation of the individual. All of these social structures and individual structures, including that of addiction, are held in place by an outer-oriented and bureaucratic worldview where the individual is torn apart by alienation, anomie and addiction. Of course other abstract structural concepts can help to fill out this picture, such as bureaucracy, group, norm, institution, self image and personality structure.

We have omitted from the above analysis of the problem its situational components. Without them, all of these structures remain reified: we are unable to understand the processes by which they are constructed within one scene after another. Also, it is not possible to understand the ways in which those structures in turn shape the momentary scene. Social stratification tends to produce alienation in the individual, but it works through situational phenomena like relative deprivation and labeling. For example, the individual in the metropolis of Berlin compares self to others who are wealthier, have more prestigious jobs, are younger or have more education. As a result, he comes to feel relative deprivation, just as the Springdaler might compare his achievements with those of others. They might then proceed to label others as successes and themselves as failures, thus fueling their feelings of alienation. Also involved in this behavior is conformity to such cultural values as "achievement and success," "material comfort" and material "progress." These situational concepts can of course be joined by other important situational concepts within the sociological literature, such as the definition of the situation, reinforcement, deviance and social interaction. Although we tend to think of situational concepts as concrete, in fact they are all very abstract in that they can refer to any past or present situation whatsoever. By learning to use them together with structural concepts, we can begin to understand how structures and situations come to be changed.

Low Level of Abstraction

Abstract theoretical concepts are essential. Yet we deny the assumption common to bureaucratic approaches that draw a sharp divide between the theoretical and the empirical, the abstract and the concrete. Both are essential. To paraphrase Kant, low-level empirical concepts without abstract theory are blind, abstract theory without empirical concepts is empty.

Moving down the ladder of abstraction is not a one-way process (Galison, 1987; Mayo, 1996). As numerous studies of the biophysical sciences demonstrate, the route from theory to observation involves diverse kinds and levels of interconnections. Raw data do not organize themselves and thus a theory of data is needed. Experiments must be designed and interpreted and thus a theory of the experiment is needed. These theories lie between theory at the fully abstract level and the data themselves; these theories often borrow from the theoretical resources of other domains. Thus Eddington's famous test of general relativity in 1919 involved physical understanding of telescopes and photographic plates, astronomical information about the sun's corona, and meteorological information about the effects of the atmosphere on the deflection of light.

This holistic picture contrasts with other common ways of thinking about the move from abstract to concrete--for example, with the idea of "operational definitions." Operational definitions are invoked in diverse ways in the social sciences. Sometimes they only ask that we relate theories to reality and evidence. That is a minimal demand no one can argue with. Yet taken too strictly even such a weak requirement may be implausible: many concepts in the natural sciences go for years without direct experimental ties to reality, gaining their plausibility by their theoretical role. Taken strictly, the requirement of operational definitions wants us to capture the meaning of a theoretical term by a set of operations. No finite set of measurements, however, will capture the content of theoretical terms--they can be measured in many different ways and take their meaning from their connections to other theoretical or abstract concepts. Moreover, measurement itself always requires theory. Searching for operational definitions that provide a mechanical, atheoretical tie to reality is misguided.

Unfortunately, sociologists have often tried to move down the ladder of abstraction with procedures that oversimplify the complexity of human behavior. A few sociological variables are identified and tests of significance or regressions are run. Implicitly, this appears to be an effort to imitate both the simplicity and predictive power of much of the physical sciences, as illustrated by the simple yet powerful formula, $F = ma$, or force = mass times acceleration. Yet Newton's law is tied to reality only via theories of mass, force, acceleration and how they are to be measured. Investigating variables without that further understanding is mistaken, both in physics and in sociology.

Herbert Blumer criticized this approach many years ago:

> influential personages with reference to the program, how such persons The objective of variable research is initially to isolate a simple and fixed relation between two variables...This is accomplished by separating the variable from its connection with other variables through their exclusion or neutralization...A difficulty of this scheme is that the empirical reference of a true sociological variable is not unitary or distinct. When caught in its actual social character, it turns out to be an intricate and inner-moving complex. To illustrate, let me take what seems ostensibly to be a fairly clear-cut variable relation, namely between a birth control program and the birth rate of a given people...For the program of birth control one may choose its time period, or select some reasonable measure such as the number of people visiting birth control clinics. For the birth rate, one merely takes it as it is...Yet, a scrutiny of what the two variables stand for in the life of the group gives us a different picture. Thus, viewing the program of birth control in terms of how it enters into the lives of people, we need to note many things such as the literacy of the people, the clarity of the printed information, the manner and extent of its distribution, the social position of the directors of the program and of the personnel, how the personnel act, the character of their instructional talks, the way in which people define attendance at birth control clinics, the ex-

pressed views of are regarded, and the nature of the discussions
among people with regard to the clinics…(Blumer, 1956: 688).

Blumer is here criticizing the simplifying assumptions, largely invisible, which lie behind what he calls "analysis of the variable" within
quantitative sociology. Granting the importance of moving down language's ladder of abstraction to concrete measurements of particular
factors, we sociologists should realize that we cannot learn much by
centering on only two variables within a complex context of factors
and ignoring the rest with some phrase like "other things being equal"
or *ceteris paribus*. Yet with a broader approach to the scientific
method we are in a position to open up to that "complex context of
factors." We can deal with both high and low levels of abstraction, as
illustrated by the globe metaphor in Figure 1-1. For example, there is
the little matter of cultural values and norms as well as patterns of social organization in society as a whole like social stratification and
bureaucracy. Quantitative sociologists generally see such considerations as interfering with the tools of measurement that we presently
have. They generally seek to isolate phenomena from their complex
contexts so as to yield measurements that prepare the way for using
mathematics to help us make predictions. By so doing, however, they
avoid a more pragmatic stance within which we might learn, a little at
a time, to understand phenomena more fully.

A Web of Knowledge

Implicit in the previous three features of scientific method is a
fourth: the idea that scientific understanding and investigation relies
on a web of belief. We saw that idea earlier in the claims that defining
a problem implicitly presupposes theory, that abstract concepts depend
on other information to tie them to reality, and that data do not speak
for themselves.

This holistic picture is at odds with the positivist conception of
science that took data as independent of all theory and that took the
rules of method of good science to be eternal truths known independently of our theories of the world. Social scientists generally accepted
this approach even while it was rapidly losing ground among philoso-
phers of science. Harold Kincaid's *Philosophical Foundations of the
Social Sciences* (1996) helps us to understand the enormous gap between a long-dead philosophy of science, which is still the basic orientation within sociology, and current philosophy of science that is the

basis for a much broader approach to the scientific method. Kincaid makes this orientation more explicit:

> Following Duhem (1954], Quine (Quine and Ullian, 1970) argued that hypotheses do not confront experience or evidence one by one. Rather, testing a single hypothesis requires a host of background theory about the experimental apparatus, measurement theory, what data are relevant, what must be controlled for, and so on. So, when experiments fail, they only tell us something is wrong somewhere. We can save any hypothesis from doubt by changing our background assumptions. Theories face the test of evidence as wholes (1996: 20).

If we go back to the globe metaphor in Figure 1-1 we can understand more clearly just what is involved here: the contrast within the northern hemisphere's lines of latitude between the dashes for social science and technology and the solid lines for physical and biological science and technology. Those dashes represent the isolation of hypotheses, concepts and fields of knowledge from one another, whereas the solid lines indicate relationships among hypotheses, concepts and fields of knowledge. Quine and Ullian argued that any test of a hypothesis invokes an entire "web of belief." They argued further that this web extends up and down language's levels of abstraction, illustrated by the lines of longitude in Figure 1-1:

> The analytic-synthetic distinction [attempted by logical empiricists] tries to separate the linguistic and factual components behind our beliefs. Some statements are directly tied to confirming evidence or experience; they are synthetic. Other statements gain their credibility from linguistic conventions and thus the empirical data can never refute them; they are accordingly analytic and a priori. Quine, however, denied that we could sharply divide evidence in this way, because testing is a holistic affair (Kincaid, 1996: 19).

Quine and Ullian along with Kincaid thus look to the entire web of solid lines of latitude and longitude depicted in Figure 1, implying the great deficiencies in the approach of the social sciences with its longitudes and latitudes made up of dashes.

Kincaid links this web approach to the work of Kuhn, who followed Duhem, Quine and Ullian and succeeded in expanding their depth and scope. For Kuhn, a great deal is involved in tying hypotheses to the world, such as metaphysical worldviews, research strategies, standards of good science, interpretations of scientific virtues, and much more. Here, Kuhn succeeds in alerting us, with his concept of paradigm, to a range of structures surrounding a hypothesis, as illustrated by the concepts of worldview and cultural values from Table 1-1. Thus, Kuhn brings into the research situation a sociological perspective. And Kincaid also follows Kuhn in the latter's reaction to postmodernist arguments about the limited worth of the scientific method. Kuhn states:

> Talk of evidence, of the rationality of claims drawn from it, and of the truth or probability of those claims has been seen as simply the rhetoric behind which the victorious party cloaks its power. . .(Kuhn, 1992: 9).

Kincaid's position here is much the same as that of Kuhn: the scientific method can be exceedingly valuable; it is not just another rhetorical device, even if it does not guarantee truth. In Kincaid's words, "empirical or observational evidence can still be the heart of good sense" (1996: 43).

Perhaps the best defense for the utility of a broad scientific method or a web approach within sociology is the demonstration of its effectiveness, as illustrated by the use of Figure 1-1 in helping us to understand the invisible crisis of modern society. Other illustrations appear within Chapters 3 and 4 of *Beyond Sociology's Tower of Babel: Reconstructing the Scientific Method* (Phillips, 2001). For example, there are studies bearing on Durkheim's analysis of anomie in his *Suicide* ([1897] 1966), such as Weber's *The Protestant Ethic and the Spirit of Capitalism* ([1905] 1958), Williams' analysis of major value orientations (1970: 452-504), Merton's essay on "Social Structure and Anomie" (1949) and his analysis of the rise of science in 17th-century England (1996: especially 231-232), and Horney's focus on contradictions among cultural values in her *The Neurotic Personality of Our Time* (1937). Similarly, those chapters invoke broad approaches--drawing on abstract sociological concepts--to the phenomena of alienation, social stratification and relative deprivation. Other analyses center on studies of revolution (Merton, 1949; Davies, 1962, 1971; Gurr, 1968; Skockpol, 1979; Tilly, 1978; Sztompka, 1993: 301-321; Michels, 1949), on Gandhi's techniques of *satyagraha* (Bondurant, 1965; Janis and Katz, 1959), and on emotions (Scheff, 1990, 1994, 1997; Retzinger, 1991; Lewis, 1971; Goffman, 1959; Elias, 1978). It is these kinds of illustrations that exemplify in brief the full-length studies in the present volume.

Reflexive Analysis within an Interactive Worldview

Let us recall once again Gouldner's emphasis on a reflexive sociology as a way to challenge our outer-oriented or bureaucratic worldview by applying the ideas of sociology to our own everyday lives.
Given the importance of the idea of reflexivity for our reconstruction
of the scientific method, Chapter 2 of Part One will flesh out that reconstruction by centering on reflexivity. To the extent that we can
broaden our vision so that we can learn to see ourselves as Uzbekistani
and Kirghiziani, we can come to realize our problem of having great
difficulty in thinking abstractly. And we can also gain optimism about
the future possibilities of gaining a balance among thought, feeling and
action, achieved in part by a balance between the effectiveness of the
social sciences and the physical and biological sciences. When we can
truly declare, *Ich bin ein Berliner*--following Simmel's analysis--we
can raise to the surface repressed emotions like shame, fear, guilt and
anger, learn to express ourselves and reach out to others, and develop
our individuality. And when we can see ourselves as Springdalers, we
can learn to emerge from hiding within techniques of particularization
and falsifying memory, procedures that keep us from seeing our deepest problems and confronting them. All these ways of challenging our
bureaucratic worldview--which imprisons our sociological paradigm--
can help to open us up to changing that sociological paradigm.

Applying our own methods and knowledge to ourselves involves
two interconnected tasks: identifying the social processes within our
profession and the social processes in the larger society that we reflect.
While that distinction is artificial, it helps us think about the myriads of
social processes influencing what we do and believe. Being aware of
such processes is an essential part of producing good social research.

Consider first the processes within the discipline of sociology.
Here we have much to learn. What causes and reinforces our isolating
specialization? What incentives and norms encourage the focus on
low-level empirical studies? How does the promotion, tenure, and
publication processes affect what we study, how we study it, and what
we take to be convincing evidence? How do funding sources and their
agendas influence what we do? What are the social networks and
status relations that influence our practice? And what do all these
various processes tell us about the reliability of our results?

Moving outside our discipline, by beginning to change our sociological paradigm we can also begin to change our bureaucratic worldview. More specifically, a shift in our understanding of how to use the
scientific method could enable us sociologists to handle more effectively the complex and invisible problems to be found within human
behavior. That in turn could yield increasing effectiveness in fulfilling
people-oriented values. And the result of this would work toward

changing the present stratification of the biophysical over the social sciences, yielding increasing support for the latter. Over time, such support could encourage sociologists to tackle effectively even such fundamental problems as alienation, anomie andaddiction. And through the understanding that this achievement was based on a change to an interactive worldview--where a bureaucratic one came to be seen as fostering those problems--powerful forces would develop for shifting the worldview and cultural paradigm throughout modern society to interactive ones. This would by no means put an end to the continuing achievements of the biophysical sciences and their tech-nologies, but it would work toward a better balance between the two. And it would also point toward a better balance between work-related and people-oriented cultural values.

Let us recall, however, that this theoretical analysis of what has been called "the invisible crisis of modern society" is no more than illustrative. It illustrates the reconstructed scientific method that holds together the diverse studies within Part Two of this volume. That very diversity attests to the potential of our approach. If we are able to build bridges enabling the authors within this volume to interact with one another, then why can't the discipline as a whole build bridges enabling sociologists within every field of sociology to interact with one another? Ours is an approach to the scientific method that enables us to address absolutely fundamental problems of modern society, just as the classical sociologists were able to do the same for their era. It requires us to confront the enormous complexity of human behavior, encouraging us to follow Mills' advice to shuttle far up and down lan-guage's ladder of abstraction. It also requires that we follow Gould-ner's advice to be reflexive, looking to nothing less than our own bu-reaucratic worldview. For it is that worldview which appears to hold in place a traditional approach to the scientific method that fails to fol-low scientific ideals. Yet that worldview can be changed to an increas-ingly interactive one just as our approach to the scientific method can be changed in the same direction.

This chapter has presented no more than an introduction to a recon-structed scientific method. We believe that this reconstruction can help us sociologists to fulfill "the promise of sociology," as expressed by such figures as Auguste Comte, C. Wright Mills and Alvin Gouldner. We have in mind the ability to achieve the rapid cumulative develop-ment of knowledge as well as the launching of increasingly effective procedures for solving even our most difficult and urgent social prob-lems. Chapter 2, with its focus on reflexivity, will complete our intro-duction to this reconstructed method. Although it will emphasize the-ory, it shares with the substantive chapters in Part Two the procedure of developing a secondary analysis of a previous publication. Our reconstruction of the scientific method is by no means limited to secondary analyses. Yet it has helped the authors of this volume to devote the time ordinarily spent in gathering primary data to the task of challenging procedures we have worked with for a great many years. We invite readers to let us know their reactions to this work and to test the utility of our approach within their own investigations. If there is in fact an "invisible crisis of modern society," then such investigations become an urgent matter.

GLOSSARY

The reader might note that this glossary is not put forward as an argument for the importance of these definitions over all others, for controversy over definitions within sociology is entirely legitimate. Rather, our approach to the scientific method calls for concepts at a high level of abstraction and also concepts that easily link systematically with one another. It is to these ends that we advance these definitions, which we view as helping to illustrate our approach.

Addiction: the individual's subordination of individuality to dependence on external phenomena

Alienation: persisting feelings of isolation from self, others, one's own biological structure and the physical universe

Anomie: the failure of society's norms or rules to guide the individual's actions toward the fulfillment of values or interests

Conformity: legitimate behavior as defined by norms and values for a given situation

cultural values: the widely-shared interests or ideals of a people

label: assigning an individual or group to a given linguistic category within a particular situation

relative deprivation: the individual's feeling of unjustified loss or frustration of value fulfillment relative to others who are seen as enjoying greater fulfillment

social stratification: a persisting hierarchy or pattern of inequality within a group

worldview: the individual's *Weltanschauung* or global outlook that is widely shared throughout society

REFERENCES

Blumer, Herbert. 1956. "Sociological Analysis and the 'Variable."
American Sociological Review 21(December):683-90.

Bondurant, Joan V. 1965. *Conquest of Violence*. Berkeley, CA: University of California Press.

Brown, Donald E. 1991. *Human Universals*. New York: McGraw-Hill.

Cohen, J. 1994. "The Earth is Round (p<.05)." *American Psychologist* 49:997-1003.

Davies, James C., (ed.). 1971. *When Men Revolt and Why*. New York: Free Press.

Davies, James C. 1962. "Toward a Theory of Revolution." *American Sociological Review* 6(February):5-19.

Duhem, Pierre. 1954. *The Aim and Structure of Physical Theory*. Princeton: Princeton University Press.

Durkheim, Emile. [1897] 1966. *Suicide*. New York: Free Press.

Elias, Norbert. 1978. *The History of Manners*. New York: Pantheon.

Forrester, Jay W. 1968. *Principles of Systems*. Cambridge, MA: MIT Press.

Forrester, Jay W. 1969. *Urban Dynamics*. Cambridge, MA: MIT Press.

Forrester, Jay W. 1971. *World Dynamics*. Cambridge, MA: Wright-Allen Press.

Freeman, Derek. 1983. *Margaret Mead and Samoa*. Cambridge, MA: Harvard University Press.

Galison, Peter. 1987. *How Experiments End*. Chicago: University of Chicago Press.

Goffman, Erving. 1959. *The Presentation of Self in Everyday Life.* Garden City, NY: Anchor Books.

Gouldner, Alvin W. 1970. *The Coming Crisis of Western Sociology.* New York: Basic Books.

Gouldner, Alvin W. 1972. "The Politics of the Mind: Reflections on Flack's Review of *The Coming Crisis of Western Sociology.*" *Social Policy* 5 (March/April):13-21, 54-58.

Gurr, Ted. 1968. "A Causal Model of Civil Strife." *The American Political Science Review* 62 (December):1104-1124.

Hempel, Carl G. 1965. *Aspects of Scientific Explanation.* New York: The Free Press.

Holton, Gerald. 1996. *Einstein, History and Other Passions.* Reading, MA: Addison-Wesley.

Homans, George C. 1964. "Bringing Men Back In." *American Sociological Review* 29(December):809-818.

Horney, Karen. 1937. *The Neurotic Personality of Our Time.* New York: Norton.

Janis, Irving L., and Daniel Katz. 1959. "The Reduction of Intergroup Hostility." *Journal of Conflict Resolution* 3 (March):85-100.

Kincaid, Harold. 1996. *Philosophical Foundations of the Social Sciences.* New York: Cambridge University Press.

Kincaid, Harold. 2000. "Formal Rationality and Its Pernicious Effects on the Social Sciences." *Philosophy of Social Science* 30 (March):67-88.

Kuhn, Thomas S. 1962. *The Structure of Scientific Revolutions.* Chicago: University of Chicago Press.

Kuhn, Thomas S. 1977. *The Essential Tension.* Chicago: University of Chicago Press.

Kuhn, Thomas S. 1992. "The Trouble with the Historical Philosophy of Science." Cambridge, MA: Department of the History of Science, Harvard University.

Lauderdale, Pat, Steve McLaughlin and Annamarie Oliverio. 1990. "Levels of Analysis, Theoretical Orientations and Degrees of Abstraction." *The American Sociologist* 21(Spring):29-40.

Lewis, Helen. 1971. *Shame and Guilt in Neurosis.* New York: International Universities Press.

Lundberg, George A. 1961. *Can Science Save Us?* New York: McKay.

Luria, Aleksandr Romanovich. 1976. *Cognitive Development* (edited by Michael Cole). Cambridge, MA: Harvard University Press.

Malotki, Ekkehart. 1983. *Hopi Time.* Berlin: Mouton.

Marx, Karl. [1844] 1964. *Early Writings* (translated and edited by T. B. Bottomore). New York: McGraw-Hill.

Mayo, Deborah. 1996. *Error and the Growth of Experimental Knowledge.* Chicago: University of Chicago Press.

Merton, Robert K. "Social Structure and Anomie." In Merton, *Social Theory and Social Structure.* New York: Free Press, 125-149.

Merton, Robert K. 1968. *Social Theory and Social Structure.* New York: Free Press.

Merton, Robert K. [1938] 1996. "The Rise of Modern Science." In Merton, *On Social Structure and Science* (edited by Piotr Sztompka). Chicago: University of Chicago Press.

Michels, Robert. 1949. *Political Parties.* New York: Free Press.

Mills, C. Wright. 1943. "The Professional Ideology of Social Pathologists." *American Journal of Sociology* 49(September):165-180.

Mills, C. Wright. 1959. *The Sociological Imagination.* New York: Oxford University Press.

Nietzsche, Friedrich. [1887] 1974. *The Gay Science* (translated by Walter Kaufmann). New York: Random House.

Ong, Walter J. 1982. *Orality and Literacy: The Technologizing of the Word*. London and New York: Methuen.

Pawson, Ray. 1989. *Measure for Measures: A Manifesto for Empirical Sociology*. London: Routledge.

Peirce, Charles S. 1955. *Philosophical Writings of Peirce*. New York: Dover.

Phillips, Bernard S. 1972. *Worlds of the Future: Exercises in the Sociological Imagination*. Columbus, Ohio: Charles E. Merrill.

Phillips, Bernard S. 1979. *Sociology: From Concepts to Practice*. New York: McGraw-Hill.

Phillips, Bernard S. 1985. *Sociological Research Methods*. Homewood, IL: Dorsey Press.

Phillips, Bernard S. 1988. "Toward A Reflexive Sociology." *The American Sociologist* 19 (Summer):138-151.

Phillips, Bernard S. 1990. "Simmel, Individuality, and Fundamental Change." In Michael Kaern, Bernard S. Phillips and Robert S. Cohen (editors), *Georg Simmel and Contemporary Sociology*. Dordrecht/Boston/London: Kluwer Academic Publishers.

Phillips, Bernard S. 1999. "Fire in the Cave: Sociology and the Invisible Crisis of Modern Society." Unpublished manuscript.

Phillips, Bernard S. *Beyond Sociology's Tower of Babel: Reconstructing the Scientific Method*. Hawthorne, NY: Aldine de Gruyter.

Quine, W. V. O. and J. S. Ullian. 1970. *The Web of Belief*. New York: Random House.

Retzinger, Suzanne. 1991. *Violent Emotions: Shame and Rage in Marital Quarrels*. Newbury Park, CA: Sage.

Retzinger, Suzanne. 1995. "Identifying Shame and Anger in Discourse. *American Behavioral Scientist* 38 (August):1104-1113.

Retzinger, Suzanne, and Thomas J. Scheff. 2000. "Emotion, Alienation, and   Narratives: Resolving Intractable Conflict." *Mediation Quarterly* (Fall): 71-86.

Roberts, Nancy, et al. 1983. *Introduction to Computer Simulation: The System Dynamics Approach.* Reading, MA: Addison-Wesley.

Sarasota Herald-Tribune. 2000. "Study Identifies Genes Specific to Aging Process." March 31, 4A.

Scheff, Thomas J. 1990. *Microsociology: Discourse, Emotion, and Social   Structure.* Chicago: University of Chicago Press.

Scheff, Thomas J. 1994. *Bloody Revenge: Emotions, Nationalism, and War.* Boulder, CO.: Westview.

Scheff, Thomas J. 1997. *Emotions, the Social Bond, and Human Reality: Part/Whole Analysis.* Cambridge, MA: Cambridge University Press.

Simmel, Georg. [1903] 1971. "Metropolis and Mental Life." In Simmel, *On Individuality and Social Forms* (edited by Donald N. Levine). Chicago: University of Chicago Press, 324-39.

Simmel, Georg. [1908] 1971. "Subjective Culture." In Simmel, *On Individuality and Social Forms.* (edited by Donald N. Levine). Chicago: University of Chicago Press, 227-34.

Skockpol, Theda. 1979. *States and Social Revolutions.* Cambridge, MA: Cambridge University Press.

Sztompka, Piotr. 1993. *The Sociology of Social Change.* Cambridge, MA.: Blackwell.

Tilly, Charles. 1978. *From Mobilization to Revolution.* Reading, MA: Addison-Wesley.

Vidich, Arthur, and Joseph Bensman. 1960. *Small Town in Mass Society.* Garden City, NY: Doubleday.

Wallerstein, Immanuel. 1980. "The *Annales* School: The War on Two Fronts." *Annales of Scholarship* 3(Summer):85-91.

Wallerstein, Immanuel. 1991. "Beyond *Annales*?" *Radical History Review* 49 (Winter):7-15.

Wallerstein, Immanuel. "Letters from the President, 1994-1998." International Sociological Association. Unpublished manuscript.

Weber, Max. [1905] 1958. *The Protestant Ethic and the Spirit of Capitalism.* New York: Scribner's.

Willer, David. 1967. *Scientific Sociology.* Englewood Cliffs, NJ: Prentice-Hall.

Willer, David, and Murray Webster, Jr. 1970. "Theoretical Concepts and Observables." *American Sociological Review* 35 (August):748-57.

Williams, Robin M., Jr. 1970. "Major Value Orientations in America." In Williams, *American Society, 3rd ed.* New York: Knopf, pp. 452-500.

Wrong, Dennis H. 1961. "The Oversocialized Conception of Man in Modern Sociology." *American Sociological Review* 26 (April):183-93.

Chapter 2

"Toward A Reflexive Sociology": A Second Look

Bernard Phillips

Although I wrote "Toward a Reflexive Sociology" in 1988, Alvin Gouldner's call for a reflexive sociology in 1970 has never been followed up in any systematic way. I hope that this volume--preceded by a book pointing in the same direction (Phillips, 2001, especially Chapter 5)--will contribute toward changing that situation. The concept can help us to examine the nesting of sociology's research paradigm within our broader cultural paradigm. And in this way we will be able to learn about the impact of the latter on the research process. Further, we can learn about how changes in our research paradigm can influence changes in our cultural paradigm. Chapter 1 presented the idea of reflexivity as one of the five components of a reconstructed scientific method. In Chapter 2, after some introductory remarks we proceed to three sections: a look at Gouldner's idea in the context of his work, an examination of "Toward a Reflexive Sociology," and a secondary analysis of that article based on our web approach. That secondary analysis will help to introduce the reader to the structure of the substantive chapters in Part Two, all of which are secondary analyses. Yet the focus of those chapters will be substantive, by contrast with the present methodological and theoretical emphasis.

I recall a conversation I had with Alvin Gouldner back in the early 1960s when we overlapped for a year at the University of Illinois' Department of Sociology in Urbana. He had already achieved a measure of fame and I was near the beginning of my career. We were having lunch and he advised me that the fruits of one's work come only after a very long period of effort, and that staying power is what is needed in a career. He appears to have been pointing toward the cumulative ideal of the scientific method, centering on the individual's ability to build on his or her own previous work. We might apply this idea to both Gouldner's work and my own. If his idea becomes important within sociology and social science at this time in history, he has not lived to see it happen. And with all of my own past efforts to criticize aspects of our traditional approach to the scientific method, if they bear fruit at this time this will be happening only at the end of my career. Yet perhaps an interactive scientific method--by contrast with a bureaucratic one--can work to speed up the cumulative process within sociology and the social sciences. Perhaps, if such a reconstruction takes hold, we will not have to wait so very long for cumulative development to take place. Perhaps such cumulative development will lead not only to great credibility for our discipline but also the kinds of changes in society which Gouldner envisioned.

When Gouldner's *The Coming Crisis of Western Sociology* (1970) appeared I was disappointed with the discipline's failure to respond to his call for "a reflexive sociology," especially since I was interested in the phenomenon of investigator effect (1966). Much later (1980) I wrote an article chiding system dynamicists--a group headed by Jay Forrester using a new approach to computer simulation--for failing to look at their own impact on the consulting process. And still later I wrote "Toward a Reflexive Sociology" (1988). The abstract of that article reads as follows:

Gouldner's call for a "reflexive sociology" in 1970 remains a largely unexamined idea, yet with the breakdown of functionalism's hegemony and the present ferment in theory its time may finally have come. In attempting to clarify and reconstruct Gouldner's idea, I begin with his concepts "background assumptions" and "domain assumptions," linking them with Kuhn's ideas. Employing levels of abstraction to approach Gouldner's material systematically, I proceed to develop and illustrate two contrasting background assumptions or world hypotheses: "stratification" and "interaction." Finally, I examine some methodological implications of these world views, centering on defining problems, ratio scales and images of measurement, sampling and multivariate analysis procedures (1988: 138).

My purpose here is not to focus on Gouldner's important concept, although I will begin with a brief look at it in relation to his work as a whole. Rather, it is to take a second look at that article I published back in 1988, emphasizing once again the weaknesses I see. Can the perspective of the web approach to the scientific method within this volume enable me to go beyond those weaknesses? Can it now yield insights unavailable at that time? Can that approach point a direction for the rapid cumulative development of our discipline? I claimed in that article that "Gouldner himself never followed up in any systematic way his call for a reflexive sociology. . . nor did he proceed to take his own advice--other than very sporadically--and turn the spotlight of analysis back on himself" (1988: 139). My central idea in this second look at that article is that I, too, was guilty of that same assessment, but that a web approach to the scientific method helps me to become reflexive. Reflexivity is one of the key elements of this reconstructed approach to the scientific method. It is crucial in opening up the scientist to questioning his or her basic worldview and cultural paradigm. Instead, we almost invariably bury our fundamental assumptions, thus avoiding large and threatening questions in favor of limited and highly specialized problems. I hope to illustrate here just how a web approach guides me toward a reflexive analysis.

REFLEXIVITY IN GOULDNER'S WORK

In reviewing Gouldner's work as a whole, John J. Stewart emphasizes his efforts to achieve both a fundamental critique of modern society and a direction for confronting modern problems:

Adopting an Enlightenment model of social inquiry, the entire corpus of Gouldner's work can be seen as a sustained attempt to show the Promethean character of humans who are the creators of their own world. In spite of the fact that social life has seemingly acquired an independence and dynamic apart from those who have created it, it is the role of the social scientist to indicate ways to remedy its constraining and oppressive features. In other words, sociology must concern itself not only with what is, but with what might be. Gouldner argues that the project for a "critical sociology" cannot stop at negativity--merely expressing a distaste for domination. Rather, a critical sociology should incorporate the insights of empirical social science if it is to avoid (1) abstract formulations as a philosophy of history in which some mythical subject (Reason, the Proletariat, the Party, or whatever) will usher in an era of liberation, or (2) a purely negative formulation that ultimately leads to a tragic pessimism where there are no counter-possibilities to social domination. . .(1984: 231).

Gouldner's early studies of leadership, strikes, bureaucracy and democracy (1950, 1954a, 1954b), his concern with technology (Gouldner and Peterson, 1962), and his efforts to develop an applied social science (1956, 1957, 1964a, 1964b) all illustrate his attempt to use empirical sociology both to uncover problems and to point directions for solutions. In his "The Metaphysical Pathos of Bureaucracy" he argued against those sociologists who "instead of telling men how bureaucracy might be mitigated, insist that it is inevitable. Instead of explaining how democratic patterns may, to some extent, be fortified and extended, they warn us that democracy cannot be perfect" (1955: 507). After the publication of his *The Coming Crisis* Gouldner does continue his interest in reflexivity, but only indirectly. He argued that "the first task of sociology and social theory is to create new communities for rational discourse by social theorists. . ." (1973: 78), later conceiving of a "New Class" of intellectuals who participate in a "culture of critical discourse" or a CCD (1979). Such critical discourse would, for Gouldner, be reflexive with respect to society's basic assumptions by challenging them. Gouldner also argued that all groups should be reflexive in examining their own assumptions critically instead of avoiding such a reflexive orientation. He suggests here that groups have a vested interest in the latter:

> Insofar as a theory. . .is linked more closely to the interests of some social groups rather than others, then it has an interest that it will refuse to put into question and will resist making focal. . .(1980: 314).

Let us look to how far Gouldner himself was able to proceed in moving toward a "reflexive sociology," beginning with his own description of its nature:

> . . .a Reflexive Sociology is concerned with what sociologists want to do and with what, in fact, they actually do in the world. . . .What sociologists now most require from a Reflexive Sociology, how-

ever, is not just one more specialization, not just another topic for panel meetings at professional conventions. . .The historical mission of a Reflexive Sociology as I conceive it, however, would be to transform the sociologist, to penetrate deeply into his daily life and work, enriching them with new sensitivities, and to raise the sociologist's self-awareness to a new historical level. . .A Reflexive Sociology means that we sociologists must--at the very least--acquire the ingrained habit of viewing our own beliefs as we now view those held by others. . . .

The character and quality of. . .knowing is molded not only by a man's technical skills or even by his intelligence alone, but also by all that he is and wants, by his courage no less than his talent, by his passion no less than his objectivity. It depends on all that a man does and lives. In the last analysis, if a man wants to change what he knows he must change how he lives; he must change his praxis in the world. . . .The core of a Reflexive Sociology, then, is the attitude it fosters toward those parts of the social world closest to the sociologist--his own university, his own profession and its associations, his professional role, and importantly, his students, and himself--rather than toward only the remotest parts of his social surround (1970: 487-490, 493, 504).

Perhaps like Auguste Comte's vision of sociology, Gouldner gives us a vision of a reflexive sociology with some suggestive directions but without filling in the blanks as to exactly what it involves or how to get there. His basic idea was not merely to follow Socrates' advice to "know thyself" but also to develop a vision for transforming self and society, confronting our most fundamental problems and suggesting that we should live that vision in our everyday lives. In his later work he indirectly suggested a means for moving in this direction through relationships among intellectuals who would develop a "culture of critical discourse." His "New Class" idea has been severely criticized for his thinking that intellectuals of all persuasions could somehow come together and act in such a critical way, yet his idea resembles that of widely-accepted ideas of how the scientific method should work. That concept has been defined in this volume as "a procedure for achieving deepening understanding of problems that builds on prior knowledge and is gained through patterns of social interaction." It is a community of scientists which fosters the scientific method. There is also Gouldner's emphasis on challenging one's own assumptions along with his vision of the importance of a positive direction for transforming self and world. In his *Coming Crisis* he attempted to do the former, but in a limited way. And his vision of a New Class, granting its vagueness and weaknesses, is at least an effort pointing toward the latter.

In reacting to a review of his Coming Crisis, Gouldner reveals a linguistic direction for moving toward a Reflexive Sociology:

> The pursuit of hermeneutic understanding, however, cannot promise that men as we now find them, with their everyday language and understanding, will always be capable of further understanding and of liberating themselves. At decisive points the ordinary language and conventional understandings fail and must be transcended. It is essentially the task of the social sciences, more generally, to create new and "extraordinary" languages, to help men learn to speak them, and to mediate between the deficient understandings of ordinary language and the different and liberating perspectives of the extraordinary languages of social theory. . . .To say social theorists are concept-creators means   that they are not merely in the *knowledge*-creating business, but also in the *language*-reform and language-creating business. In other words, they are from the beginning involved in creating a new *culture* (1972: 16).

It is language, then, which can make it possible for the sociologist to achieve fundamental change in self and world. Here again, Gouldner gives us an important hint about how to develop a reflexive sociology, but he remains unable to follow through in any systematic way, just as in the case of his other hints.

MY 1988 ARTICLE: "TOWARD A REFLEXIVE SOCIOLOGY"

Whereas Gouldner's *Coming Crisis* was written at a time when Parsonian structural-functionalism still was dominant within American sociology, the 1980s constituted a different era, and my article reflects the emerging breath of fresh air:

> . . .a previous consensus among many sociologists around a structural-functional perspective appears to have broken apart, in some measure due to the work of Gouldner, and no single theoretical perspective now dominates the scene. . .New ideas, such as those within ethnomethodology, neo-Marxist sociology, critical and phenomenological sociology, and the sociology of culture, suggest that

all of the most fundamental questions about theory and method we thought had been answered must be raised once again. What should be the nature of the scientific method, if it is indeed appropriate to speak of a science of human society? How significant should the study of the individual be for sociology? How are we to take into account the phenomenon of language? Can the discipline prove effective in developing theories of change and confronting fundamental societal problems? How are we to deal with the context--societal, historical and situational--within which a given human action is located? Is it possible to combine macro with micro sociology, and if so, how? (1988: 139).

In that article I attempted to make use of this atmospheric change by both clarifying Gouldner's idea and carrying it further. Gouldner's ideas of "background assumptions" and "domain assumptions" paralleled Thomas Kuhn's concept of "paradigm," with a domain assumption corresponding to a scientific paradigm and a background assumption corresponding to a cultural paradigm. And Gouldner also emphasized the importance of linguistic categories which we all learn as a basis for our learning these assumptions. Gouldner did not refer to Kuhn in his *Coming Crisis*, but this parallel helps us to understand how a Reflexive Sociology might be developed: questioning these paradigms while developing alternative ones. This combination of questioning coupled with developing alternatives meshes with Gouldner's own approach to both negating the existing situation and constructing a possible solution. In addition, I illustrated a contrast between two assumptions, "stratification" and "interaction," for three different "levels of abstraction," with the highest level corresponding to background assumptions and the lowest to domain assumptions. The lowest level, "persistence of inequality among individuals within a hierarchy of social categories in society as a whole," corresponds to a domain assumption prevalent in sociology. For the intermediate level I used the same definition but omitted "society as a whole" so that it could apply to interpersonal relationships.

For the highest level of abstraction I defined stratification as "the persistence of inequality among phenomena (as distinct from individuals) within a hierarchy of categories (as distinct from social categories)." This abstract concept is broad enough to include stratification in society as a whole, in smaller social contexts, and, in addition, between elements within the individual. To illustrate the latter, Simmel argued for the dominance of the intellect or rationality over emotions within the blasé city-dweller of modern society (1971: 326). This corresponds roughly to Marx's argument that industrial society has yielded emotional alienation for the worker, and also to Weber's claim that our society has produced "specialists without spirit, sensualists without heart." I then suggested that with an interactive versus stratified background assumption or cultural paradigm, we can follow Mills' advice--in the domain of sociological research--and shuttle far up and down language's ladder of abstraction. By contrast, a stratified cultural paradigm would separate that domain into three areas separating the work of Marx, Weber and Mills, with little communication among them. I contrasted an interactive approach with Merton's middle-range orientation (1968: 139-140), linking the latter with the discipline's lack of theoretical success.

I then proceeded to examine the methodological implications of an interactive background assumption or cultural paradigm, finding it to be valuable in several ways. For one thing, in common with a Reflexive Sociology it helps us to define absolutely fundamental problems for investigation, since a high level of abstraction enables us to examine basic assumptions. For another thing, it opens up to a dynamic image of measurement where the investigator interacts with the phenomena under investigation, and where that interaction must itself be analyzed along with those phenomena. Within a stratified cultural paradigm, by contrast, reality floats high above us, and our efforts at measurement yield imperfect measures which supposedly come ever closer to that truth. As for sampling designs, an interactive cultural paradigm can take us to a level of abstraction so high that there is little heterogeneity and, thus, can reduce the size of a sample to even N = 1. With respect to multivariate-analysis procedures, a reflexive sociology points toward moving up to a high level of abstraction along with change over time, situations where those procedures are relatively less needed. Overall, then, my example of a reflexive approach to sociology took me to a probe of two contrasting cultural paradigms, and the interactive one implied domain assumptions for doing sociological research which appeared to constitute an improvement over traditional domain assumptions.

A SECOND LOOK

Looking back at that 1988 article from the perspective of my present understanding of a web approach together with the cultural paradigm in which it is nested, my initial reaction is to open up the whole question of the nature of reflexivity or a reflexive sociology. Just as

Table 1 in Chapter 1 suggests the importance of taking into account as many of those nine categories as possible in looking at any phenomenon, so might we attempt this in examining the phenomenon of reflexivity. After all, one achievement of the web approach is its highly systematic approach, linking concepts dealing with social structures, individual structures and situations, all within a historical and problem-oriented framework. The idea of reflexivity directly contradicts a bureaucratic worldview and cultural paradigm, indicating an alternative worldview and cultural paradigm. More specifically, it seems to illustrate an interactive orientation, just as the reflexive individual attempts to be critical about absolutely fundamental assumptions about self and society. From this perspective, an effort to achieve reflexivity contradicts the basic forces within society and self, such as a bureaucratic approach that yields a narrow or specialized view of a given concept. And this perspective thus appears to support Gouldner's view that reflexivity is a key to the transformation of self and society. It follows Gouldner's orientation--and Kuhn's as well--to develop a direction that is both extremely critical of society as well as extremely constructive, by contrast with one-sided optimism or pessimism.

Let us carry this systematic approach to the concept of reflexivity a step further. It is in keeping with Gouldner's interest in both language and history that we examine his concept from a long-term historical perspective emphasizing language, just as we have done for the web approach in Chapter 1 of this volume. If we contrast the behavior of even the higher animals with the human being, we find a vast difference in their capacity to achieve what all of us have learned to do with the aid of language: examine one's own behavior in a previous situation from the perspective of being located in a different situation. Animals have memory to an extent, but orality enables us to remember to a vastly greater extent, and literacy succeeds in extending that ability considerably further. From this perspective we can see reflexivity in a much broader and more long-term way than Gouldner did or than I did in accepting and attempting to clarify his own definition. It appears more useful, instead, to see reflexivity as a characteristic of life in general, and also to see it varying greatly as we move up the scale of biological evolution. Beyond literacy--again following the general argument in Chapter 1--our ideals for the scientific method point to still greater reflexivity, since the researcher must become familiar with all previous relevant research in order to build on it.

From this perspective, Gouldner's call for a reflexive sociology suggests that we go beyond ordinary research procedures. In addition, what is required is what Gouldner also called for: the kind of research which questions not only domain assumptions or one's scientific paradigm but also background assumptions or one's cultural paradigm. Further, it is not just research which is involved, for the researcher's behavior in everyday life should also be understood with the aid of one's research paradigm, and it should succeed as well in questioning one's cultural paradigm. Still further, given these aims, the web approach nested within an interactive cultural paradigm appears to be a useful device for moving toward Gouldner's goal of a reflexive sociology. On the one hand, that approach includes reflexivity as one of its key characteristics. On the other hand, it is nested within an interactive cultural paradigm that appears to be congenial with a reflexive sociology. Of course, the utility of the web approach for achieving a reflexive sociology is at this point no more than a hypothesis. Yet it does provide us with a way of understanding reflexivity in a comprehensive way. And in addition it does yield a more specific direction than Gouldner provided that might in fact take us toward a reflexive sociology.

Our web approach, given our recognition that it is nested within a cultural paradigm that is everywhere in society and the individual, yields an insight which escaped me in my 1988 article: an understanding of the incredible difficulty of moving toward a reflexive sociology. I implicitly accepted the importance of doing so, and I proceeded to chide Gouldner for his own failures to move very far in a reflexive direction: "Gouldner himself never. . .proceed[ed] to take his own advice--other than very sporadically--and turn the spotlight of analysis back on himself," Yet, committed as I was intellectually to the importance of reflexivity, I did not embark on any reflexive analysis of myself in that 1988 article. In Gouldner's terms, I failed to engage in praxis, by contrast with at least some effort in the present article to do so. For example, my argument there gives little hint as to the importance of developing a reflexive sociology in relation to world problems, again by contrast with a web approach's illustration of the invisible crisis of modern society. And in that 1988 paper I accepted without question Gouldner's own description of a reflexive sociology, failing to see it in relation to a broader theoretical and historical framework.

Granting the great difficulty of moving toward a reflexive sociology, this analysis based on a web approach at least serves to clarify that direction in ways that I was unable to achieve in 1988. For one thing, it suggests the importance of a web approach to the scientific method--which includes a reflexive approach--as one way of moving toward reflexivity. That web approach includes a systematic approach to research, as outlined and illustrated in this volume, which was unavailable either in Gouldner's writings or in my own 1988 article. Would such an approach include the possibility of following Gouldner's vision of a reflexive sociology? Apparently so. That vision calls for a great deal, namely, an ability to confront the fundamental problems of the modern world by means of a transformation of self and society. A web approach to sociological research is seen here as nested within an inter-active cultural paradigm, opposing a bureaucratic scientific and cultural paradigm. This approach, then, equally calls for a great deal.

A web approach also helps us to understand the importance of a group effort in securing such fundamental changes. Gouldner's analy-sis of a New Class as instituting a culture of critical discourse appears to have been an indirect effort to move toward reflexivity, granting the arguments against this possibility. However, a web approach makes a group effort more viable, since it involves ideals which we are already committed to, namely, a community of scientists communicating with one another. The web approach, just like our traditional sociological research methods, is committed to such a community effort. However, those traditional methods have departed very far from that ideal, given a bureaucratic scientific method where knowledge is compartmental-ized within a large number of distinct areas. A web approach, by con-trast, would emphasize building bridges across such specialized areas, pointing toward the development of a genuine community of sociolo-gists.

Given the emphasis of a web approach on taking into account more of the complexity of human behavior, it points the investigator toward examining his or her impact on the entire research process. In "Toward a Reflexive Sociology" I examined several methodological implica-tions of Gouldner's idea: defining problems, ratio scales and images of measurement, sampling and multivariate analyses procedures. But I failed to devote attention to a phenomenon which calls into question every single piece of research conducted within a bureaucratic para-digm: the failure to examine the investigator's own impact on every stage of the research process. That would call for enlarging every in-vestigation to include a study of that impact. And to the extent that such a study deals with the crucial variables involved, it would have to get into the researcher's own worldview based on the prevailing cul-tural paradigm. Somehow I did not bring in what would have been a profound critique of traditional research, perhaps because--following Kuhn--I did not have an alternative research paradigm to replace the traditional one. Now, however, the situation is different. I am free to claim the deficiencies--based on the failure to be sufficiently reflexive and take into account investigator effect--of every single piece of published research in the social sciences. My ability to claim this is based on a vision of a reconstructed scientific method.

A web approach also points us more explicitly beyond the boundaries of sociology, for it is nested within an interactive worldview and cultural paradigm. In this way it points more clearly toward applied research on the basic problems of modern society, a direction that was important to Gouldner yet neglected in my 1988 article where my focus was on substantive or basic research. Sociology's division into forty distinct Sections also serves to separate sociologists primarily interested in understanding and solving society's problems from those interested in the cumulative development of substantive knowledge. Figure 1-3 suggests, following the web approach, that social science knowledge is the basis for social technology, and that effective social technologies will in turn encourage the further development of substantive or basic knowledge by giving the discipline more of the credibility it deserves. More specifically, the web approach should yield bridges connecting particular fields of basic research with particular areas of applied sociology, yielding mutual insights unavailable otherwise.

In addition, a web approach would support Gouldner's vision of developing an "extraordinary language" and teaching non-sociologists to understand and speak that language, a democratic vision similar to Mills' concept of the sociological imagination as a way of thinking and perceiving which we all should learn. This goes beyond the idea of a reflexive sociology to include the idea of a reflexive society. Here again, in my 1988 article I was unable to come up with this idea. For one thing, the nine categories within Table 1-1 provide a general framework for the individual's learning to think in more complex ways. Here, the individual would not be constrained to learn any technical vocabulary. For another thing, a technical vocabulary is illustrated in Table 1-1. There, individuals learning that vocabulary also learn to build on a great deal of sociological knowledge. If we take into account the metaphor of the individual as a quasi-scientist, then this approach transforms that into a metaphor of the individual as a scientist. Opposing the critiques of Gouldner's "New Class" as an elitist idea, this points toward the possibility of a truly democratic vision for modern society.

If I may be permitted to look back, reflexively, at the paper I have just written, I find that it is not so very different from my 1988 article. On the one hand, I grant that it carries substantially further an intellectual or "head" approach, to both understanding the enormous problems which reflexivity addresses as well as a direction for confronting them. And I also grant that it makes at least some inroads into what Marx and

Gouldner called "praxis.". Yet I still remain very largely a prisoner of the bureaucratic cultural paradigm and worldview so characteristic of modern society. What Gouldner's work and this paper achieve is primarily "head" progress toward a reflexive sociology and an interactive worldview and not "heart" and "hand" progress. "Head" progress is a very important step, yet it is only a step. Reflexivity coupled with an interactive cultural paradigm erect an infinite stairway for all of us, sociologists and non-sociologists alike. What remains is for us to climb that stairway, an ascent which requires heart and hand no less than head. Following Simmel, Marx and Weber, together with contemporary sociologists such as Scheff (1990, 1994, 1997) and Retzinger (1991, 1995); Retzinger and Scheff, 2000) along with Vidich and Bensman (1960), we moderns have all learned to bury heart and hand in favor of head. Following Gouldner, the task of climbing those steps lies before us in every scene of our lives. It is a question not just of how to work but also of how to live.

Scheff's and Retzinger's work during this past decade provide some specific guidance as to how we might proceed to become more reflexive in everyday life. For example, Scheff's part/whole approach--illustrative of a reconstructed scientific method--stresses the importance of both emotions and the social bond without losing sight of the intellect in addressing large-scale social structures:

> Because emotional transactions are a vital part of human existence, and are usually omitted, the substantive chapters emphasize them, and their relation to behavior which is oriented toward maintaining the social bond. The part/whole method helps us to understand the relationship between human experience and the largest social structures (1997: 1; see also Retzinger, 1991, 1995, and Retzinger and Scheff, 2000).

Scheff's approach is not merely programmatic. He goes on in his substantive chapters to provide illustrations of his approach. His substantive chapter headings read as follows:

3 Punishment, child development and crime: the concept of the social bond
4 Boy's talk, girl's talk: a theory of social integration
5 Origins of the First World War: integrating small parts and great wholes
6 Gender wars: love and conflict in Much Ado About Nothing
7 Microanalysis of discourse: the case of Martha Johnson and her therapist

8 Conflict in family systems

Beyond such substantive research, Scheff along with Retzinger emphasize the importance of relatively invisible behavior in everyday scenes which illustrate the phenomena of shame and anger. To give us guidance on how our research as well as our understanding in everyday life can proceed to make visible what is relatively invisible, Retzinger gives us cues for shame and anger (1991, 1995) which also appear in Scheff's Appendix (1997: 233-235). These cues include verbal markers for shame under the general categories of alienated (e.g., rejected, dumped, deserted), confused (e.g., stunned, dazed, blank), ridiculous (e.g., foolish, silly, funny), inadequate (e.g., helpless, powerless, defenseless), uncomfortable (e.g., restless, fidgety, jittery), and hurt (e.g., offended, upset, wounded). There are also verbal markers for anger (e.g.,cranky, cross, hot-tempered) and for shame-anger compounds (e.g., resentful, bitter, grudge). Retzinger also cites paralinguistic markers, illustrated for shame by vocal withdrawal or hiding behaviors as well as disorganization of thought (e.g., over-soft, rhythm irregular, silences). Examples for anger include staccato, loudness, heavy stress on certain words, and straining. The shame-anger combination is illustrated by whine, tempo up and down, and pitch up and down. There are also visual markers. For shame there is, e.g., hiding behavior (such as gaze aversion), blushing, and false smiling. For anger there is, to illustrate, brows lowered and drawn together, eyelids narrowed and tense, and lips pressed together.

This chapter along with the preceding one is limited in how far it takes us toward an understanding of a reconstructed scientific method. It is programmatic, just as so many criticisms of sociology's approach to the scientific method have been in the past. What is required in addition are illustrations of just how we can build on this framework to do the kinds of research which yield rapid cumulative development within the discipline along with a high degree of credibility. Part Two will be devoted to presenting a series of such illustrations from different fields of sociology. They are initial efforts to build on that framework, and we hope to follow them with other volumes containing other examples. Yet even such efforts will be insufficient to make the case for the potential of our reconstructed scientific method. What is required is that the reader try that reconstruction on for size. I believe that such efforts are important for the development of sociology at a time when its credibility is sharply limited even inside of the discipline. I also believe that at this time in history, given what I see as accelerating social problems, such efforts are urgently needed. They may show up an interactive scientific method as a completely useless idea, as a partially useful one, or as an incredibly important one. In any case we will learn more about the potential of the idea of reflexivity--incorporated within a reconstruction of the scientific method--for transforming the individual, sociology and society.

REFERENCES

Gouldner, Alvin W. 1950. *Studies in Leadership.* New York: Harper and Brothers.

Gouldner, Alvin W. 1954a. *Patterns of Industrial Bureaucracy.* Glencoe: Free   Press.

Gouldner, Alvin W. 1954b. *Wildcat Strike.* Yellow Springs: Antioch Press.

Gouldner, Alvin W. 1955. "The Metaphysical Pathos of Bureaucracy." *American Political Science Review* (June).

Gouldner, Alvin W. 1956. "Explorations in Applied Social Science." *Social   Problems* 3(1).

Gouldner, Alvin W. 1957. "Theoretical Requirements of Applied Social   Science." *American Sociological Review* 22(1).

Gouldner, Alvin W. 1964a. "Editorial: For Diversity in Social Science." *Trans-Action* 1(3).

Gouldner, Alvin W. 1964b. "Taking Over: The Problem of Succession in Organizations." *Trans-Action* 1(3).

Gouldner, Alvin W. 1970. *The Coming Crisis of Western Sociology.* New York: Basic Books.

Gouldner, Alvin W. 1972. "The Politics of the Mind: Reflections on Flack's Review of *The Coming Crisis of Western Sociology. Social Policy* 5 (March/April):13-21, 54-58.

Gouldner, Alvin W. 1973. *For Sociology: Renewal and Critique in Sociology Today.* New York: Basic Books.

Gouldner, Alvin W. 1979. *The Future of Intellectuals and the Rise of the New Class.* New York: Seabury Press.

Gouldner, Alvin W. 1980. *The Two Marxisms: Contradictions and Anomalies in the Development of Theory.* New York: Seabury Press.

Gouldner, Alvin W., and Richard A. Peterson. 1962. *Notes on Technology and the Moral Order.* Indianapolis and New York: Bobbs-Merrill.

Merton, Robert K. 1968. *Social Theory and Social Structure.* New York: Free Press.

Phillips, Bernard. 1966. *Social Research: Strategy and Tactics.* New York: Macmillan.

Phillips, Bernard. 1980. "Paradigmatic Barriers to System Dynamics." *Proceedings of the International Conference on Cybernetics and Society.* Cambridge, MA, October 8-10:682-688.

Phillips, Bernard. 1988. "Toward a Reflexive Sociology." *The American Sociologist* (Summer):138-151.

Phillips, Bernard. 2001. *Beyond Sociology's Tower of Babel: Reconstructing the Scientific Method.* Hawthorne, NY: Aldine de Gruyter.

Retzinger, Suzanne. 1991. *Violent Emotions: Shame and Rage in Marital Quarrels.* Newbury Park, CA: Sage.

Retzinger, Suzanne. 1995. "Identifying Shame and Anger in Discourse." *American Behavioral Scientist* 38(August):1104-1113.

Scheff, Thomas J. 1990. *Microsociology: Discourse, Emotion, and Social Structure.* Chicago: University of Chicago Press.

Scheff, Thomas J. 1994. *Bloody Revenge: Emotions, Nationalism, and War.* Boulder: Westview Press.

Scheff, Thomas J. 1997. *Emotions, the Social Bond, and Human Reality: Part/Whole Analysis.* Cambridge, MA: Cambridge University Press.

Simmel, Georg S. [1903] 1971. "Metropolis and Mental Life." In Simmel, *On Individuality and Social Forms* (edited by Donald N. Levine). Chicago: University of Chicago Press, pp. 324-39.

Stewart, John J. 1984. "Is a Critical Sociology Possible?: Alvin Gouldner and the "Dark Side of the Dialectic." *Sociological Inquiry* 1984:231-59.

Vidich, Arthur, and Joseph Bensman. 1960. *Small Town in Mass Society.* Garden City, NY: Doubleday.

PART TWO BUILDING BRIDGES

The studies presented in Part Two are efforts to illustrate how to build bridges connecting the fields within sociology's tower of Babel and, as a result, help to develop a discipline which is both rapidly cumulative and highly credible. These are initial efforts, with all of the failings that accompany the breaking of new ground. They represent no more than a small number of fields within sociology. And it is has indeed been difficult for us sociologists who have emphasized one aspect of the discipline for a great many years to see the implications of work done there for other fields. Sociologists who have mastered specialized literatures will of course have much to criticize about studies which martial only a limited portion of such literatures. Nevertheless, we hope that these studies will move our understanding of a reconstructed scientific method beyond the general statements and programmatic ideas put forward in Part One. We authors have become convinced of the importance of our efforts, granting our awareness of their shortcomings. Whether or not specialists in the fields under examination come to share our view remains to be seen. We hope that readers will help us to learn about the problems involved in our work. And we hope that they will embark on studies of their own which further test the utility of this reconstructed scientific method. We believe that the promise of sociology is not an impossible dream. And in these times of threatening social problems, we believe that we sociologists are confronted by an urgent responsibility to convert that dream into reality.

Introduction to Chapter 3

Whereas Jacobsen's 1969 doctoral dissertation was limited to the process of secularization, this secondary analysis with its broad concepts of "alienation," "bureaucratic order," "industrialized society" and "deviance," and its soul-searching reflexive orientation, transforms that study into a contribution to our general understanding of deviance. He opens up to the complexity behind the survey data he previously collected, including an understanding of the long-term change to industrial society, with the aid of a causal loop diagram. As a result, Jacobsen's data reveal a trend toward ever more deviance, bureaucracy, alienation and inconsistent socialization as we continue to move from preindustrial to modern societies. He links this conclusion to a number of other studies, including those bearing on the phenomena of anomie and social control. Yet this conclusion is not about an inevitable trend. Rather, it enables us to examine the forces which lie behind this trend with a view toward altering them. The causal loop diagram is a key tool which we can use for this purpose, for it helps us to confront the complexity of human behavior along with fundamental social problems in a highly systematic way. It enables us to convert theory from a vague enterprise into a focused procedure. Such causal loop analysis is a step toward the more systematic and powerful procedures of computer simulation, as illustrated by the work of Jay Forrester and others on "system dynamics." Jacobsen sees system dynamics as an important direction for social scientists who wish to confront the full complexity and dynamism of human behavior.

Chapter 3

The Process of Secularization: Toward a Theory-oriented Methodology[1]

Chanoch Jacobsen

INTRODUCTION

It is a salutary experience to have a senior scholar remind one of readings one should have studied in graduate school but neglected under the pressure of exam deadlines. This happened to me as I read Bernard Phillips' proposal for the Tower of Babel project. Particularly his reference to C. Wright Mills' call for reflexive sociology made me aware of past derelictions and errors of mine when studying for the doctorate. Not that my doctoral research was not reflexive: it was rather too reflexive. I had been active for some years in the Movement for Progressive Judaism in Israel, and was looking for a scientific explanation of the widespread rejection of anything religious by the Israeli public, hoping to find a way to check this extreme case of secularization. But I had overlooked or ignored some important points Mills had made on linking methods to abstract theory. As a result I failed at the time to see the broader problems in social theory of which the process of secularization is but an instance. Here, therefore, is a fresh look at that study.

THE ORIGINAL STUDY

My doctoral thesis was called "The Social Determinants of Secularity: An Empirical Study of Deviance from Religious Norms." It was a study of the process of secularization in nine American Christian denominations (1969; a summary is in Jacobsen, 1999:2-16). Although an empirical study, I had developed for it a theory of secularization. Following Weber, I postulated two bases for the legitimation of religious authority: tradition and rationality. Charisma I left out of consideration because with contemporary denominations it is an exception rather than the rule. Religious authority that is legitimized by tradition is always anchored in a social collectivity, and that has to be sufficiently integrated to maintain the tradition and perpetuate it. Thus the *integrative potency* of religions is a concept that may explain the extent to which they are undergoing a process of secularization. I measured integrative potency by two variables: the degree of involvement of church members in their congregation, and the amount of religious socialization that the members have had in the past. On the other hand, religious authority that is legitimized by rationality depends on the acceptance of the doctrine's validity. The chances that religious ideas will be accepted as rationally valid depend on their ability to explain satisfactorily that which its adherents want and need to know. I called this the *cognitive efficacy* of the religion's doctrine, reasoning that in today's fast-changing world religious doctrines have to be flexible as well as widely applicable to be cognitively efficacious. Flexibility was measured by the number of revisions their prayerbook had undergone in this century, and by the number of heretics per million adherents tried for doctrinal deviance in the last 140 years. Applicability was measured by responses to the statement: "Churches should stick to religion and not concern themselves with social, political and economic questions."

With these concepts I attempted to explain the variance among the denominations in the dependent variable, namely the degree of secularity of their congregants, as measured by how much members deviate from the norms of their church. Thus the thesis really was a study of deviance from religious norms: Why are they so commonly disregarded, despite church members' professed adherence to their particular faith?

Findings were rather less than conclusive. Three out of the four variables correlated negatively with the degree of secularity as hypothesized, but only flexibility was statistically significant (r=-.849). This was mainly due to the small sample size, which contained only nine denominations. More serious was the absence of any significant positive zero-order correlation between the four independent variables. I had to abandon my hypothesized path model (partial correlations) and substitute a hypothesis of cumulative impact (multiple correlations) of those variables on secularity. However, this changed neither the general theoretical framework nor the dearth of statistical significance in the findings.

In the data analysis I used Pearson's r, factor analysis and multiple regression. This was an error of misplaced precision.   Pearson's product-moment correlation coefficient and the factor analyses and regressions based upon it assume a linearity in the relationships between variables which is always questionable for sociological data. I might have used a less precise monotonicity coefficient, but that would have been unacceptable at the time.

A CRITICAL REVIEW

Though the thesis was approved and I duly received my degree, I see now that it contained some serious methodological flaws, even though the theoretical argument appeared fairly solid. The most glaring one is my attempt to explain a process with cross-sectional data, i.e., without taking into account the dimension of time. Of course I was aware that all processes evolve over time and that I really needed a longitudinal study, but considered that to get my degree in the foreseeable future that option was ruled out. That basic error led to others. Having left out the time dimension, there was no way to determine whether the process of secularization was gradual or sudden (I assumed it was gradual), whether there were any hidden delays in the process (I assumed there were none), or whether the rate of secularization was the same for all denominations (I had assumed it was). All these assumptions were implicit rather than stated. Even more damaging was the neglect of the possibility of feedbacks between variables in the process. In short, the basic mistake of seeing the outcome of a process as an indication of the process itself, both in theory and in the data analysis, led to an unrealistic picture of the whole issue.

At the time I did my doctoral research, I had little choice as far as methodology was concerned. Data collection had to be either longitudinal or cross-sectional. But new technologies have opened up ways of studying social processes more realistically now than was feasible then: by computer simulation. In particular, the groundbreaking work of Jay W. Forrester (1961) and his co-workers in what has come to be called System Dynamics (Richardson and Pugh, 1981; Roberts et al., 1983) offers an approach that is admirably suited to the complexity of social processes. A basic principle of this approach is that, rather than seeking the cause of social phenomena in forces exogenous to the system, one should analyze the system's endogenous feedback dynamics. To my mind, this is a very plausible and acceptable principle for sociologists. Constructing computer models to uncover these endogenous dynamics is not beyond anyone with even only a smattering of high-school algebra like myself.

Much of the work with System Dynamics has been concerned with the technique of building models and drawing inferences from them. That is its particular Achilles' heel: there is little guidance for thorough conceptualization. Although many of the problems modeled had a social character (e.g., Forrester, 1969; Meadows et al., 1972), there was little if any sociology underlying these models. Common-sense assumptions took the place of sociological knowledge. This has aroused much justified criticism. Forrester himself was noncommittal about SD's potential for sociology (Jacobsen, 1983), presumably because--like many others--he took much of its substance as self-evident and saw little added value in social theory. On the other hand, to reject the whole approach would be throwing out the baby with the bathwater, as there is much to be gained from SD, especially by sociologists who study social processes.

Many commonly used and widely researched sociological concepts are about processes: socialization, mobility, urbanization, social change, industrialization, to mention only a few. All these imply a time dimension in which these processes evolve. It matters a great deal how long they take to be felt, whether they are gradual or sudden, whether there are any delays involved and, if so, where and of what duration. Yet the passage of time is rarely treated as an independent variable, though it is clearly of central concern (Sorensen, 1978; Cohen, 1980). In empirical research there are good reasons for this, as longitudinal studies are costly, cumbersome, and usually prone to sample attrition.

Such considerations, however, do not apply to social theory. Even in the rare cases of theoretical sociology in which the time dimension is explicitly taken into account (e.g., Smelser's 1963 theory of collective behavior), the process is not described in time-specific terms, but as a sequence of events or phases. More often than not such phenomena are simplified and discussed at abstract levels, e.g., "industrialization leads to urbanization", or "bureaucratization leads to alienation," as if it did not matter what happens in-between or how long each phase in the sequence takes. Clearly, variations in rates of development are involved, but typically they are not even discussed, let alone systematically explained. This is a fundamental flaw in what passes for social theory, and other flaws follow from it. If the time dimension is disregarded, then so are delays and possible feedbacks with their positive or negative effects. Therefore, what is needed is just such an approach as that of System Dynamics, which views social processes as evolving within complex systems (Buckley, 1967), or what Phillips (2001) calls a web of concepts.

In the preliminary conceptualization phase of SD, modelers clarify the complex relations between theoretical concepts with "causal loop diagrams" (see below). In these diagrams, complex processes are charted over time, with their positive and negative feedbacks. This phase is by itself a useful and even essential exercise for anyone trying to explain a social process (Lenski, 1988), whether they actually go on to construct a model or not. But SD can do more for sociology than compel us to take a systemic viewpoint. It can enable us to implement the scientific method to the full by permitting replications and systematic experimentation with complete systems, and under strictly comparable conditions.

In what follows, therefore, I shall attempt to redesign my doctoral study along the lines of a system dynamics project. But to avoid the trap of abstracted empiricism and also tie in with the "sociological imagination" project within this volume, I will first try to link my original concepts to broader and more abstract ones from the sociological and psychological literature. Then, on the basis of that literature and analytic deduction, I shall develop a causal loop diagram showing how these concepts are related to one another and some of the feedbacks and delays that are involved.

A SECOND ATTEMPT

I had defined secularity in my thesis as "the proportion of a denomination's members who deviate from its important norms." Thus defined, secularity is a form of deviance from norms that are ordained by a religion, though typically without formal sanctions. Now, can any of the postulated antecedents to deviance of this kind be derived from or subsumed under the antecedents to deviance from norms in general?

One sociological concept that clearly fits both the argument of the thesis and social-psychological theory is socialization. If norms have been internalized through socialization, people receive autonomous rewards and sanctions by conforming or deviating, respectively. Thorough and consistent socialization makes them resistant to deviance, just as a lack of socialization makes them prone to it and more dependent on extrinsic rewards and sanctions (see also Kimberly's Chapter 4 in this volume).

How about involvement? It is the antithesis of alienation in more than one sense: normlessness, powerlessness, meaninglessness, isolation, self-estrangement (Seeman, 1959). Thus, if integrative potency depends on involvement, it also depends on the absence of alienation. Further, if integrative potency enhances traditional authority, the lack of integrative potency will weaken it. So it may be argued that acceptance of traditional authority will vary directly with the amount and quality of socialization to conformity to norms, and inversely with the degree of alienation.

Rational authority, as applied to conformity or deviance from norms, rests on the degree to which the norms "make sense" to the actor. In the limiting case of religious norms I had called this the cognitive efficacy of the doctrine which, so I had argued, depends on its flexibility and applicability. With regard to norms generally we cannot speak of doctrine, but we may speak of the definition of the situation, defined as "an individual's understanding of the momentary scene." That understanding may be either flexible or rigid, applicable or irrelevant. The amount of flexibility and applicability in the definition of a situation that is necessary to make sense will vary with the rate of social and environmental change. Rapid cultural and social changes such as exists in the contemporary world require ample flexibility and applicability. Thus, rational authority that defines situations rigidly with little regard to existential changes loses its legitimacy, and deviance is to be expected.

The pattern of social organization that relies most obviously on rational authority is bureaucracy. But bureaucratically defined situations are almost by definition rigid and thus irrelevant to many changed situations. Therefore, we may expect to see an inverse relationship between bureaucratization and rational authority in contemporary societies. The erosion of rational authority leads to deviance from norms whose legitimacy rests upon it, so that they will often be evaded or entirely disregarded, as indeed they are. We have thus broadened our theoretical framework and widened the theory and the scope of our interest from the specific process of secularization of religions to generic processes of increasing deviance, alienation, and bureaucratization. Note that in doing so we have reduced the number of concepts and raised them to a more abstract and inclusive level. Now I shall attempt to transform the hypothesized relationships into a causal loop diagram that depicts the whole process in logical sequence and shows where it will lead.

A CAUSAL LOOP DIAGRAM

Many of us have rightly been socialized to beware of causal inferences from statistical associations. That, however, has not prevented us from making tacit assumptions of causality in our theorizing. Causal loop diagrams are powerful tools for exposing such hidden assumptions and other logical errors. Since they deal with theoretical concepts and their relationships to one another, operational definitions of variables and mathematical prediction are not needed to construct such diagrams, yet they can be very helpful for clarifying complex theoretical processes.

In a causal loop diagram, the relations between concepts are depicted by directional arrows, with the arrowhead pointing to the affected concept. A plus or minus sign beside the arrow indicates that the hypothesized relationship is either positive or negative. The diagram shows direct relationships only: indirect relationships can be deduced by following the chain of arrows from one concept (node) to another. A causal loop diagram is called so because it is normal to find closed loops from some of the concepts to others which create either positive or negative feedback in the system, depending on the signs of the arrows.

A positive loop is one that drives each variable in the loop to its physical or logical limit. It is positive if it has an even number of minus signs, whose multiplication always gives a positive product. The net effect of a positive loop is to reinforce the process of change of each variable in the loop, a phenomenon known as a self-fulfilling prophesy or a vicious circle. A negative loop is self-regulating, driving the variables in it to a steady state by balancing their influence on one another. It is evidence of some mechanism of control, and may be recognized by the odd number of negative relationships in the loop.

After drawing arrows for the hypothesized relationships, we try to detect any logical feedbacks in the process. (The complete neglect of feedback was another flaw in the original theory, as it is extremely unlikely that there is none at all). For example, we have said that deviance increases due to a deficiency in rational authority for compliance, and that the lack of rational authority is due to bureaucratic rigidity and irrelevance. Now it is highly probable that deviance, even from informal norms, will frequently lead to an increase of bureaucratic rules, as the usual purpose of such rules is to attain uniformity and preclude exceptions. In other words, there is feedback from deviance to bureaucratization: a high level of bureaucratization makes for low rational authority. As a result, deviance increases, and as a result of *that* there is more bureaucratization and a further decline of rational authority. This loop has two negative relationships and is therefore positive. The one consoling point of such a prognosis is that the feedback is likely to be delayed, as bureaucracies are generally slow to react.

But the same positive feedback can also work in the opposite direction. A bureaucracy that is flexible and widely applicable to begin with will have the rational authority that makes for little deviance and no reason for growing bureaucratization on that score. Theoretically, either path is possible. For example, the dynamics of drug trafficking and of sociable cigarette smoking have the same positive trend, but in the first case it has resulted in increased deviance, and in the other in the institutionalization of a new informal norm (Jacobsen and Bronson, 1995).

We turn now to traditional authority which, as we have argued, increases with effective socialization. The difference between effective and ineffective socialization lies in the consistency with which role models demonstrate and reinforce the desired behavior (Bandura et al., 1963; Sewell et al., 1955). While it is possible for different role models to be consistent and effective, it is unlikely. The most consistent role models are the immediate family, who are the bearers of traditional authority. Thus, consistent socialization is directly affected by traditional authority, and we have another positive feedback loop (with zero negative relationships). This feedback also includes a delay, as it takes time for socialization to be inculcated and to be felt as acceptance of traditional authority and declining deviance.

Since the acceptance of traditional authority also makes for low alienation, and low alienation reinforces the acceptance of traditional authority, this feedback loop also is positive. There are two additional positive loops because, while authority of both kinds decreases deviance, both are also eroded by growing deviance. Thus there are five feedback loops in the diagram and, as all of them are positive, these processes will all be self-reinforcing and become stronger until they reach their physical or logical limit. Figure 3-1, however, is still incomplete. Other and more potent factors impinge on the delineated processes. What is it that drives bureaucratization, what causes alienation, and what affects traditional and rational authority? These questions have to be answered.

The basic reason for the growth of bureaucracies is not just the feedback from increasing deviance but, as Weber has pointed out (1947:58), the relative efficiency of bureaucratic administration, given the size and complexity of modern industrialized society. Alienation, too, is surely not to be explained solely or even primarily by a decline of traditional authority, but much more so by the individual's powerlessness in modern industrialized and bureaucratized society (Blauner, 1964).

To make Figure 3-1 more complete, therefore, we must add the exogenous concept of industrial society. The concept is exogenous because there seems to be no feedback from any of the nodes in the diagram leading to industrialization. Historically, of course, what *did* bring about that development was the rise of capitalism (Weber, 1930). However, as long as the majority of concepts are in the endogenous loops, this need not concern us further now.

Both traditional and rational authority depend basically on their legitimacy, i.e., on the fraction of those subject to their orders who agree that they are "right and proper" (Lipset, 1960:46). That fraction will vary according to whether prevalent cultural patterns are more traditional or more rational. Where a cultural pattern is dominantly traditional, many people will not legitimize authority if it does not fit the traditional pattern, even if it is backed by force. If the cultural pattern is mainly rational, majority opinion will depend on the validity of what I have called the definition of the situation.

The degree to which a cultural pattern is either traditional or rational is also an exogenous concept and for the same reason as industrialization: it affects the system as described, but is not visibly affected by it. Although these two concepts extend the theory well into the past, they must remain exogenous in our causal loop diagram because to deal with the historical trends that led up to them would require another article with separate diagrams. But at least every concept in the loops is now linked to a plausible cause.

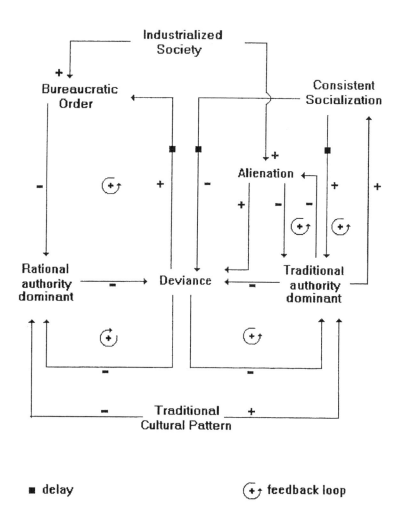

Figure 3.1. A causal loop diagram.

IMPLICATIONS

Where does all this lead, and how does it relate to the work of the Sociological Imagination Group? Assuming that Figure 3-1 is a realistic picture, the processes drawn show a disconcerting trend toward extremes. The direction of the trend depends on the initial conditions. In industrialized societies with rational cultural patterns it is toward more deviance, bureaucracy, alienation, and inconsistent socialization. The more industrialized the society, the more will these characteristics make themselves felt. Without industrialization (there are still such societies!) and with a traditional cultural pattern, the trend is toward the opposite: consistent socialization, more conformity, less bureaucracy and less alienation, but also a less productive economy, possibly with overpopulation and starvation.

The initial conditions in contemporary westernized society clearly point towards the first prospect. Deviance is becoming widespread in many areas of social life (Cohen, 1965; Gibbs, 1975; Simon and Witte, 1982; Jacobsen & Bronson, 1995). Bureaucratic control and the attendant alienation have also been documented (e.g., Whyte, 1956; Blau, 1970; Blauner, 1964), and rising divorce rates alone tend to make socialization more inconsistent (Goode, 1963).

This outlook can be frightening unless some mechanism of control is introduced into the system that checks these trends. What might such a control mechanism be, and how could it be activated? Formal control by law, inspectors and the like is inefficient and costly, as we know from our studies of patterned evasions (Jacobsen and Bronson, 1995). Informal control is largely inoperative in the anonymity and transience of urbanized life. That leaves only autonomous control as a possibility, but the lack of consistent socialization makes it difficult to inculcate.

Perhaps autonomous control through enlightened self-interest can be activated by a "protective custom" (Malarkey 2000), which would be a combination of traditional and rational authority. Maybe that will check the relentless striving for ever more intensive industrialization, much as ecological awareness is at last controlling the reckless despoliation of the environment. I am reminded of Skinner's controversial *Beyond Freedom and Dignity* (1971), and his unpalatable but plausible conclusion that we may have to forgo a part of our cherished values and privileges if we want to counteract the debilitating increase of deviance and maintain a livable society.

As for the Sociological Imagination Group, I have responded to the call for a more reflexive sociology by re-examining my doctoral study and found it wanting. Particularly so in my neglect of the time dimension in studying a protracted process, and in inferring from cross-sectional data the outcomes of such a process. As the honest confrontation of this flaw in theory as well method (not uncommon among sociologists) is but an initial step toward its correction, I suggested taking a further step toward a more theory-oriented research methodology with causal loop diagrams and dynamic simulation models.

Second, by regarding the process of secularization as one manifestation of the generic problem of the dynamics of deviance, this paper has built a bridge to the vast literature on criminal behavior, anomie and social control (Merton, 1949; Cohen, 1965; Rule, 1974; Janowitz, 1975; see also Kimberly, Chapter 4 in this volume). But beyond that, due to the logical necessity of stating the sources of the system's dynamics in a causal loop diagram, it has uncovered the historical antecedents of the presently widespread deviance from formal and informal norms, namely, industrial society and cultural patterns.

Third, I have used many items from Phillips' (2001) web of concepts: deviance, conformity, socialization, reinforcement, alienation, bureaucratization, definition of the situation, norms, and cultural pattern. Among the additional concepts I have used, traditional and rational authority tie in with Malarkey (2000) not only by the fact that the two types of authority are manifest in Toennies' concepts of *Gemeinschaft* and *Gesellschaft*, but also in that both pairs of concepts seem dichotomous, but really are ideal-typical poles with graduated degrees between them.

Finally, while I cannot accept Phillips' assumptions and his analysis of present trends in their entirety, I do agree with him that a dialogue between sociologists from different specialty areas for the purpose of agreeing on a common web of basic sociological concepts can result in a more convincing and cumulative theory of society than the Tower of Babel among sub-disciplines which we have now. But important as the dialogue is, it is only theoretical and, as Malarkey (2000) has aptly put it, theory without application is vain or meaningless. A theory is not scientific until it has been tested against reality and been found empirically adequate.

The dialogue can also be a step toward an alternative paradigm for a more scientific research methodology. Such a paradigm should improve the sorry reputation of sociology as little more than sophisticated verbiage (Lenski, 1988). I recommend System Dynamics simulation modeling because with it we can test the relationships between a whole web of sociological concepts simultaneously, and not just a selected few. Both the feasibility and the promise of this strategy have been demonstrated in our studies of patterned evasion (Jacobsen and Bronson, 1995), crescive legitimation (Jacobsen, 1999), and the dynamics of charismatic leadership (Jacobsen and House, 2001).

We can elaborate our causal loop diagram to bring the concepts to a less abstract level. If we then construct a simulation model from that diagram and compare the model's output to reliable time series of the relevant variables, we can soon see whether and how far the theory matches reality. That, in fact, is precisely what we did for our book, *Simulating Violators* (Jacobsen and Bronson, 1985). Over the years we tested the theory via the model against 15 data sets. The model reproduced on the average 81.5% of the variance in the 15 data sets, so that now we have grounds to claim empirical adequacy for the theory of patterned deviance.

The same method can be applied to other sociological theories and thus either make them convincing and cumulative or lead to discarding them if they fail to match reality. While it is unlikely that many sociologists will become expert at computer modeling, cooperation between the two fields is both possible and desirable. My personal experience is that it can also be mutually instructive. Sociologists will benefit from the advantages System Dynamics has to offer, and expert modelers will gain sociological insights. But even without going to the length of building a simulation model, a well thought-through causal loop diagram can, as we have seen, help immensely in unraveling the intricacies of complex social processes. I would encourage any readers young in mind and spirit to try it out on their pet theories. They will be surprised at the discoveries they will make.

NOTES

1. *Acknowledgment:* I am greatly indebted to the encouragement, challenge and help of Bernard Phillips. Without him, this paper could not have been written. I also wish to thank Thomas Scheff for his valuable criticism and suggestions. Responsibility for the final product rests with me alone.

REFERENCES

Bandura, A., D. Ross, and S. A. Ross. 1963. "A Comparative Test of the Status Envy, Social Power, and Secondary Reinforcement Theories of Identificatory Learning." *Journal of Abnormal and Social Psychology 67:*527-534.

Blau, P. M. 1970. "A Formal Theory of Differentiation in Organizations." *American Sociological Review, 35:*201-218.

Blauner, R. 1964. *Alienation and Freedom.* Chicago: University of Chicago Press.

Buckley, W. 1967. *Sociology and Modern Systems Theory.* Englewood Cliffs, NJ.: Prentice-Hall.

Cohen, A. K. 1965. "The Sociology of the Deviant Act: Anomie Theory and Beyond." *American Sociological Review, 30:*5-14.

Cohen, B. P. 1980. *Developing Sociological Knowledge: Theory and Method.* Englewood Cliffs, NJ: Prentice-Hall.

Forrester, J. W. 1961. *Industrial Dynamics.* Cambridge, MA: Wright-Allen Press.

Forrester, J. W. 1969. *Urban Dynamics.* Cambridge, MA: MIT Press.

Gibbs, J. P. 1975. *Crime, Punishment and Deterrence.* New York: Elsevier.

Goode, W. J. 1963. *World Revolution and Family Patterns.* New York: Free Press.

Jacobsen, C. 1969. "The Social Determinants of Secularity: An Empirical Study of Deviance from Religious Norms" Unpublished Ph.D. thesis, University of Wisconsin, Madison. Microfilm copies are available from University Microfilms, 300 North Road, Ann Arbor MI 48106.

Jacobsen, C. 1983. Personal interview with Jay W. Forrester.

Jacobsen, C. 1999. *Social Dynamics: Theory and Research.* Haifa: Technion, Israel Institute of Technology.

Jacobsen, C. 1999. "The Process of Crescive Legitimation: Theory, Simulation Model, and Three Empirical Tests." *Adaptive Behavior 7(3):*249-261.

Jacobsen, C., and R. Bronson. 1995. "Computer Simulation and Empirical Testing of Sociological Theory." *Sociological Methods and Research* 23:479-506.

Jacobsen, C., and R. Bronson. 1985. *Simulating Violators.* Baltimore MD: The Operations Research Society of America.

Jacobsen, C., and R. J. House. 2001). "Dynamics of Charismatic Leadership: A Process Theory, Simulation Model, and Tests." *The Leadership Quarterly, 12:75-112.*

Janowitz, M. 1975. "Sociological Theory and Social Control." *American Journal of Sociology,* 81:82-107.

Kimberly, J. C. 2002. "Small Group Processes and the Legitimization of Societal Stratification: From Experiments to the Operation of Groups in Natural Situations." In Phillips, Kincaid and Scheff (eds.), *Toward a Sociological Imagination: Bridging Specialized Fields.* Lanham, MD: University Press of America, Chapter 4.

Lenski, G. 1988. "Rethinking Macrosociological Theory." *American Sociological Review 53:*163-171.

Lipset, S. M. 1960. *Political Man.* New York: Doubleday.

Malarkey, J. J. 2000. "Toennies' Community and Society: Discovering 100 Years of Continuity and Change in Community Theory." Unpublished paper.

Meadows, D. H., D. L. Meadows, J. Randers, and W. W. Behrens. 1972. *The Limits to Growth.* New York: Potomac Associates.

Merton, R. K. 1949. "Social Structure and Anomie." In Merton, *Social Theory and Social Structure*. New York: Free Press, pp. 125-149.

Phillips, B. 2001. *Beyond Sociology's Tower of Babel: Reconstructing the Scientific Method*. Hawthorne, NY: Aldine.

Richardson, G. P., and A. L. Pugh. 1981. *Introduction to System Dynamics with DYNAMO*. Cambridge, MA: MIT Press.

Roberts, N., D. Andersen, R. Deal, M. Garet, and W. Shaffer. 1983. *Introduction to Computer Simulation.*. Reading, MA: Addison-Wesley.

Rule, J. B. 1974. *Private Lives and Public Surveillance: Social Control in the Computer Age*. New York: Schocken.

Seeman, M. 1959. "On the Meaning of Alienation." *American Sociological Review* 24:783-791.

Sewell, W. H., P. H. Mussen, and C. W. Harris. 1955. "Relationships among Child Training Practices." *American Sociological Review* 20:137-148.

Simon, C. P., & A. D. Witte. 1982. *Beating the System: The Underground Economy*. Boston: Auburn House.

Skinner, B. F. 1971. *Beyond Freedom and Dignity*. New York: Alfred Knopf.

Smelser, N. J. 1963. *A Theory of Collective Behavior*. New York: Free Press.

Sorensen, A. B. 1978. "Mathematical Models in Sociology." *Annual Review of Sociology*. Palo Alto, CA: Annual Reviews, Inc.

Weber, M. 1947. *The Theory of Social and Economic Organization*, (ed. by Talcott Parsons). New York: Free Press.

Whyte, W. H., Jr. 1956. *The Organization Man*. Garden City, NY: Anchor Books.

Introduction to Chapter 4

Kimberly is able to tie his long-term and extensive contributions to the analysis of small groups to large-scale patterns of social stratification in American society. This involves his tying together exchange-based small-group theory and external status theory, also located within the literature of small groups. As a result, he is able to derive directions for policy-oriented research pointing to the creation of a more humane society. Using the web approach to the scientific method was crucial to his ability to solve the problem of how to combine those two small-group theories. For one thing, it oriented him to emphasize very abstract concepts as a device for linking phenomena. For another, it is oriented to concepts at a macroscopic level no less than concepts at a microscopic level. There is also its focus on the importance of moving far down language's ladder of abstraction to concrete data, by contrast with model building which often fails to examine its concrete implications. And its systematic approach meshes with the systematic orientation of the small-groups literature. Further, the web approach points toward understanding long-term change in society as a whole, an orientation that is generally absent from that literature. To illustrate this temporal contribution of the web approach, a single small-group goal can be related to a host of cultural values, such as equality, freedom, democracy and the worth of the individual. Those cultural values change over long periods of time and, as a result, alter the nature of that goal. Without this understanding, we would tend to see small-group behavior as isolated from its context within society.

Chapter 4

Small Group Processes and the Legitimization of Societal Stratification:

From Experiments to the Operation of Groups in Natural Situations

James C. Kimberly

INTRODUCTION

We recently developed a general theory of the operation of small groups (Kimberly, 1997, 2000[1]). The theory takes into account all of the basic processes which occur in groups and attempts to relate them to one another so as to explain the development, stabilization, orderly change and disintegration of groups. To our knowledge this is the only work since Homans' (1950) work which attempts to develop a general model of group operation (we use theory and model interchangeably when referring to general theories). The model grows out of exchange theory, but it is not simply a rational model. It includes--in addition to goals and productive structures--affect structures of trust, attraction, and influence. It is the only model we know of which permits the integration within the group leader of a "bureaucratic" type of authority growing out of the productive structure with a "charismatic" type of authority growing out of trust and attraction.

The challenge to small group researchers is to take some of the knowledge they have amassed and attempt to extend it to natural situations. We use the term "natural" advisedly. By the term we mean combinations of theoretically defined processes. We do not mean concrete reality. Combinations of processes take us closer to concrete reality, but at that level there will always be some "noise". Within the context of attempting to extend small group theories to natural situations, there is the question of the level of processes to which one attempts to make extensions. One might attempt to develop a more complex theory of group behavior or make an extension to a more macro level. In this paper, we attempt to do both. We try to show how our small group theory and another theory, which we call the theory of external status, can be combined in natural groups. We do this through specifying certain variable states of the group structure itself as conditions affecting the operation of the two theories.

The theory of external status focuses on inequality processes in small groups (Berger, Cohen and Zelditch, 1966; Ridgeway and Berger, 1986; and Berger, Zelditch, Anderson and Cohen, 1972). We attempt to specify the conditions which determine when our model and when the external status model is the stronger in the operation of natural groups. Then we attempt to show how the two theories may be related to societal stratification. This involves a discovery that they make up a complex, integrated theory that helps explain legitimization and de-legitimization of the societal stratification structure. This combination and integration of the theories at the societal level is the major focus of the paper.

We also have another purpose. At one point, we were simply comparing our small group theory and societal stratification in general. We discovered that one can use the comparison to suggest directions for applied research. More specifically, we found that small group processes in the context of societal stratification processes suggested directions for applied research that might make society more humane. We want to make very clear that these suggestions cannot be justified entirely by scientific work. They involve value judgments which can in the long run only be accepted or rejected by members of the society.

In summary, we have three purposes: 1) to attempt to combine our model of group operation and the external status model in a way that moves us toward the operation of natural groups; 2) to attempt to combine the two theories in explaining the legitimization of the societal stratification structure, and 3) to attempt to show how a comparison of group processes in our model with societal stratification processes suggests directions for applied research.

As we proceed, we shall from time to time make comparisons of our concepts and theories with how they might occur and operate in a feudal society.

Before turning to our first objective, let us comment on how this paper relates to the methodology advocated by the Sociological Imagination Group (see Chapter 1 of this volume). Two of the principles of that methodology are to use very abstract, interrelated concepts to locate important research problems and to formulate theories so that they take account of as many of the abstract concepts as possible. It also includes formulating the type of specific data which would test the theories in the context of all of the concepts which apply. We had always attempted to see the conceptual similarities between inequality in small groups and societies by viewing both very abstractly as social systems and by formulating what we thought was a similar exchange process in both systems. Seeing the conceptual similarities helped us connect positions in groups and occupations in societies. We had suspected that distributive justice processes at the two levels were similar. Empirical work by House and Hawkins (1975) on distributive justice in occupations had shown that the justice theory which is a part of our small group theory applied to at least in part to that level. While this is in keeping with a third principle of the methodology of using very abstract concepts to connect components the small group and the society, it did not permit us to make a firm connection between inequality in the group and societal stratification. The number of concepts was too limited.

It was the immersion in a set of very abstract, interrelated concepts about societal stratification, namely, stratification itself, anomie, comparative reference groups, relative deprivation, distributive justice, and alienation and data relevant to all of them which eventually led us Della Fave's (1980, 1986) work on the legitimization of societal stratification. Della Fave had used something like the methodology advocated by the Sociological Imagination Group. He had brought together Mead's concept of the development of a generalized other, equity and distributive justice theory, and one component of external status theory. It was when we found his theory which, in effect, uses group processes in attempting to explain the legitimization of societal stratification, that we knew we had found a significant problem. An earlier experimental test of the theory by Stolte (1983) had not supported it. It was Stolte's use of the distributive justice theory which is a part of our small group theory to attempt to explain his negative findings that led to the insight as to how groups might be involved in both the legitimization and de-legitimization of societal stratification structures. Thus, moving down the ladder of abstraction, a fourth principle of the methodology, to concrete data, helped us reformulate Della Fave's theory, and the abstract, interrelated concepts and data related to them convinced us we were probably right. For example, the data relating to anomie, which nowadays encompasses reference group processes and relative derivation; distributive justice; and alienation all seemed to support our reformulation. We will see this later. The abstract, interrelated web of concepts also led to the further insight that the value-orientation of equality contained a component, namely, equality of opportunity, which would condition the legitimization and de-legitimization process.

We can mention here some of the other connections of our work to the abstract, interrelated concepts advanced by the Sociological Imagination Group. When we consider our small group theory, we relate its concept of a group goal to societal values. This involves a number of value-orientations. We also relate equality norms in the expressive structure of instrumental groups to the societal equality value-orientation (see Williams, 1970, Chapter XI, for a complete treatment of value-orientations in American society). In defining authority in the group, we relate a component of authority to the concept of bureaucracy. Finally, when we consider the distributive justice theory our small group theory involves, we relate that theory to the concepts of situation and reinforcement.

We turn now to our first objective, that of attempting to show how our theory and the external status theory can be extended to some degree to natural groups. We will consider our theory first.

THE GENERAL THEORY OF GROUP OPERATION: INSTRUMENTAL GROUPS

We present here our model of group operation as it applies to instrumental groups. It also applies to expressive groups, but we do not treat them in this paper (see Kimberly, 1997, for application of the model to expressive groups). We go into it to the extent that we do because it is necessary to understand the theory and because the theory is an example of integrating theories and findings in a whole area of specialization which is divided by many sub-specializations.

The theory of group operation is based on an exchange theory model. Basically, this model holds that inequality in instrumental groups represents "payment" for the differential skills members bring to the group and employ in pursuing attainment of the group goal. Viewed from this perspective, the inequality structure of the group consists of rewards. These are prestige, power and economic rewards (see Homans, 1961, 1974; Blau, 1964 and Emerson, 1962, 1972 I and 1972 II for general theories of exchange).

We have developed this exchange model in a number of ways (Kimberly, 1997, 2000). We make authority another inequality reward, but once developed, authority profoundly affects the whole group structure. The explanation we advance for the development of authority is as follows. Authority arises in the group when some member demonstrates that he or she can further attainment of the group goal by controlling and coordinating the productive behavior of the members, allocating new members to productive positions and allocating economic rewards to members. In time, he or she comes to be given rights, subject to clear limits approved by the group members, to change the group goal and the productive structure of the group. This is a form of bureaucratic authority. This is a connection of our theory to the abstract concept of bureaucracy in the web of concepts advocated by the Sociological Imagination Group.

We digress here briefly to discuss the formation of the group goal. We argue that agreement on a goal can be obtained if members can agree that the goal can be seen as instrumental to the values they hold. They do not have to share the same values. They need only accept one another's values for espousing the group goal. This would apply in both volunteer groups and work groups in organizations. In the latter case, there could be values adopted by the organization which workers might not share, and they might pursue the goal for different values on which they agree. For example, there could be a variety of values that may motivate the formation of say a volunteer group to attempt to repeal the death penalty in a state or a team of construction workers in a construction corporation. We cannot go into it here, but in the volunteer group the motivation involved would be intrinsic (concerned primarily with goal-attainment) and in the case of the work team the motivation would be extrinsic (concerned primarily with values placed on inequality rewards; see Kimberly, 1997:54-64).

We view individual values as specifications of societal values (Williams, 1970: Chapter XI). For example, some individuals in a group attempting to repeal the death penalty in a state might be motivated by the value placed on the individual personality in our society. (Williams, 1970:495-498). They might see this value as prohibiting the taking of life. Others might be motivated by a general moral orientation or humanitarian mores based on religious belief (Williams, 1970:461-464) Many might also be motivated by the value of individual achievement but probably would not offer this as a reason for participating in the group. Certainly, most, if not all, would probably hold and advance as a motivation for participating in the group the value of individual freedom (Williams, 1970:479-484). They would need such a value to go against the prevailing opinion concerning the death penalty. In general, we hold that in groups societal values take the form of concretizations of relevant societal values which members bring to the group. (Kimberly, 1997:7-8).

Now let us return to the description of our development of the exchange model of group operation. The person who acquires authority is usually the most skilled member of the group. The degree of skill a member possesses defines the dependence of the group on him or her because level of skill is, at least roughly, correlated with the number of persons available from outside the group who would be able to replace him or her. Because of the group being differently dependent on members, different amounts of prestige and power develop and different amounts of economic rewards are allocated to them. Prestige and power develop automatically from evaluations made by group members. All of these rewards serve to bind the members to the group. The authority person usually receives instead of prestige, deference to his or her instructions. He or she has the most power and usually receives the most economic rewards. In a recent new development of the theory (Kimberly, 2000), we argue that in integrated groups, which we define below, the members put their power in abeyance so as not to interfere with the control that has been granted to the authority person. This occurs only if the authority person is performing adequately.

We have also developed the model so as to incorporate structures of trust, attraction and influence. Trust derives from the performances of members and the authority person. Members receive equal trust if they perform adequately in their positions. Each is doing what is expected, and fulfillment of expectation generates trust. The authority person receives equal trust for adequately performing his or her authority activities. However, over time, he or she acquires the influence necessary to persuade the members to go beyond the limits set on his rights to change the group goal and the related productive structure. This influence develops as follows. When adaptation to the environment is first required and changes not within the scope allowed to him or her are needed, he or she uses her power to make the changes. If the changes result in adaptation, there is an increase in trust by the members, and an expectation that the authority person will adapt the group in the future begins to develop. The increase in trust leads to an increase in attraction to the authority person. He or she becomes the most attractive person in the group.

It is the increase in attraction that leads to influence. The general theory explaining the causal connection of attraction to influence is cognitive balance theory, especially as formulated by Newcomb (1955, 1959, 1968). According to Newcomb, if two persons who are attracted to one another disagree about some matter of relevance to them both, cognitive imbalance is created for both of them. In such h a situation, the persons will attempt to reach agreement, which will restore cognitive balance for both of them. They will attempt to influence one another concerning the disagreement. When attraction is differential, that is, when one of the two people is more attracted to the other than the other is to him or her, the person who is less attracted will usually influence the person who is more attracted. In short, the less attractive person's position will come to be agreed upon. This occurs because the more attracted person will be under greater psychological pressure to achieve agreement and reach a state of cognitive balance. Thus, In group in which an expectation that the authority person will adapt the group has developed, in any disagreement with a member, the authority person will always influence the group member.

The above description is our development of the exchange model for an instrumental group. We define now what we mean by an *integrated group*. Throughout the remainder of the paper, whenever we refer to our theory or model, we shall mean *a group that is integrated as defined by theory*. In such a group, the productive positions are filled in terms of skill, and an authority person has emerged because he or she has demonstrated ability to further attainment of the group goal in the ways described above. We need to develop the theory a little further here to elaborate somewhat on what is included in the authority person's rights to change the group goal and productive structure. There is an additional right included with these. This is the right to change the rules concerning the allocation of economic rewards to positions. Briefly stated, the right is limited to a given kind of change, specifically, to the right to adjust the differences in the amount of economic rewards allocated to positions. This refers to the differences between the amounts allocated to the different position, which may be larger or smaller. Such changes must not violate the *rank order* of positions based on their difficulty and the required level of performance.

Furthering attainment of the group goal gives legitimacy to the authority person. The productive positions within the group vary in difficulty, and members receive prestige, power and economic rewards in terms of the dependence of the group on them as was explained above.

Justice exists for group members because the productive positions are filled by the authority person in terms of skill. For the theory defining justice in groups in this way, see Kimberly, 1962, 1966, 1967, 1970, 1972, 1977. For empirical work related to the theory, see Kimberly and Crosbie, 1967; McCranie and Kimberly, 1973; Margolin, Kimberly, and Whitt, 1992; and Kimberly, McCranie, Whitt and Wiest, 1993. For a brief review of these works and additional empirical work relevant to the theory, see Kimberly, 1997. This theory is central to the problem of legitimization of the stratification structure and is described later. Justice is increased by the authority person by allocating economic rewards on the basis of position difficulty and performance. As noted above, members' power is put in abeyance in deference to authority when the authority person's performance is adequate. This includes maintaining justice through his or her allocations.

The structures of trust, attraction and influence described above have come into being. Trust results from adequate performances of all members. It leads to an attraction structure in which the authority person, because of expectations he or she will adapt the group, is the most attractive person. This, in turn, leads to him or her being influential.

This completes our description of an *integrated group*. We need to present here elements of the expressive structure of instrumental groups. There are always found in instrumental groups some norms which define ways in which all members are considered equal. These are specifications of societal equality norms. One value involved is the belief that everyone has value and should be treated that way. (Williams, 1970:475-476) Common courtesy is an example. Another societal value that finds expression in small groups is equality of opportunity (Williams, 1970:477).   In the group, this value may take the form of periods being set aside in which all members are asked by the authority person to make suggestions concerning the operation of the group.   Equality norms found in groups are thus concretizations of societal values.

We did not note this above, but some trust is based on members' conformity to such norms. Equality norms apply equally to everyone including the authority person.

We now make a new elaboration of the theory. Legitimate authority and justice make possible the trust, attraction and influence described earlier. This structure of trust, attraction and influence constitutes a condition which makes it possible for equality norms to multiply. The new norms will be based on known norms but not necessarily societal norms. They may be suggested by work organizations or similar instrumental groups and specifically adapted to the group.   The increase in such norms leads to an additional increase in the structures of trust and attraction. This occurs because equality is rewarding. We suggest that the increase in trust and attraction, in turn, leads to a reduction in the degree of inequality which the productive positional structure produces. Such a reduction would have to occur through a reduction of the difference between the amount of prestige, power and economic rewards different positions receive. The rank order of positions would have to be maintained in order to maintain justice. Thus, increased equality outside of the positional structure reduces overall inequality. The authority person's prestige, power and economic rewards will be reduced somewhat, but the trust and attraction which derives from the expectation he or she will adapt the group will remain the same, and he or she will remain influential. The existing structure of authority will be maintained because it is deeply rooted in structural needs, for example, control and coordination of productive behavior and the right to make limited changes in the productive structure of the group, that is, in its goal and productive positions.

Thus, as argued earlier, the theory of group operation is not purely an exchange or rational behavior model. It includes the affect structures of trust, attraction and influence and systematically relates them to the productive structure. In an integrated group two modes of authority merge in the same leader. He or she has both bureaucratic authority in the form of control over the productive structure of the group and charismatic authority in being the most trusted, attractive, and influential member of the group.

This conception of an instrumental group is partially a result of the fact that the theory applies to a modern class society. We can speculate how the conception would have to be modified for a feudal agrarian society. In our theory we treat instrumental and expressive groups separately. In a feudal society the two would be largely merged. In a modern class society, expressive groups tend toward maximum equality. In feudal societies, the expressive component probably would involve more inequality in itself because of its merger with the instrumental structure. We shall not go into any detail as to how the expressive component would differ from our conception of it because that would require us to present our whole theory of expressive groups (for the theory of expressive groups, see Kimberly, 1997). However, equality as we know it in modern societies is a historical development. In American society it takes three forms. First is the idea that all persons have value and should be treated that way. Second is our formal equality represented by our legal rights. Finally, there is equality of opportunity which has resulted from the impact of freedom, especially in the form of economic freedom, and individual achievement and success on the equality-orientation (see Williams, 1970:475-478, for this conception of the equality value-orientation).

In feudal societies, there was no conception of the equal value of each person. Legal rights contained no form of equality except for persons in the same social status. In fact, legal rights defined forms of inequality. Thus, our treatment of expressive structures in groups would be quite different in such societies. There would be new elements to the group structure. In the lowest estate, traditional norms concerning the authority of different types of members, for example, different sexes and ages and persons holding different kin statuses, would affect the authority structure. Authority would not be based so much on furthering goal-attainment. The traditional norms would probably account for this. Inequality within the expressive structure would probably be aligned with the authority structure, so that only behavior among persons with the same status would show signs equality in the first sense mentioned above. In the two higher estates, legal statuses within the nobility and clergy would largely structure the operation of groups. The strong emphasis on inequality within the two estates might increase the degree of inequality within expressive structures beyond that found in the lowest estate (as we shall see, external status theory presents a somewhat similar picture of groups, but in modern societies).

In modern societies, equality serves to some extent as a buffer against the extreme inequality in agrarian societies. For example, Lenski (1966:286) has estimated that in agrarian societies the ruling classes constituted 2 percent of the population and received 50 percent of the income. In our society, it takes 20 percent of the population to reach 50 percent of the income (see Kerbo, 2000:63-67, for a brief discussion of agrarian societies).

THE EXTERNAL STATUS THEORY

The exchange model we have presented contrasts with the external status model which focuses on the development of inequality in groups. (see for example Berger, Cohen and Zelditch, 1966; Berger, Fisek, Norman and Berger, 1977; and Webster and Foschi, 1988). The theory is equally as abstract as ours. The two theories differ in that the theory of external status does not take into consideration a division of labor and the positional structure it involves. According to the theory, group members' prestige and power derive from external statuses such as age, sex, and race. In experiments, researchers have generally used fictitious tasks which appear to have but really do not have a solution. For example, is there more white or black area in a larger rectangle made up of smaller rectangles of black and white. Actually the white and black each constitute 50 percent, but this is not apparent because of the arrangement of the inner rectangles. The subjects are told the task requires a certain kind of ability. For example, contrast sensitivity, which is fictitious. As this example makes clear, subjects do not work on different parts of a task. Rather, all offer solutions to the same task.

In the *typical* experiment, subjects are made aware that they have different external statuses, for example age, sex, or race. Each subject gives an initial and a final solution. On a large percentage of trials after his or her initial solution, the subject is told his or her partner disagreed with his or her solution. They are not told each other's final decisions, and no feedback as to the correct answer to the task (which would, of course, be bogus) is given. Most experiments show that under these conditions, the subject with the low external status, for example, female when the partner is described as male, shifts to her partner's initial decision on the final solution on most of the disagreement trials. In short, influence occurs. This is taken as an indication that the subjects are using the external statuses to assess ability at the task and of the emergence of power and prestige differences based on the ability differences. There are studies involving natural groups with findings which parallel those of the experimental studies. Cohen and Zhou (1991) found that gender in R and D groups in organizations affected evaluations of group members. Umberson and Hughes (1987) using data from a national probability sample found that physical attractiveness affected achievement and psychological well-being. This suggests that attractiveness resulted in success in many groups.

The theory has been extended to authority (See, for example, Ridgeway and Berger, 1986 and Ridgeway, Johnson and Diekema, 1994) The extension holds that external statuses become a part of what Berger and colleagues call referential structures. These are structures in the larger society in which certain types of external statuses become associated with high social status generally. There are two types of such structures: categorical, such as age, sex, and race; and a structure in which it is believed some people have high ability generally. The latter type of referential structure serves to confirm and strengthen the categorical referential structures. High statuses in such structures lead to a member of the group becoming the authority person. Generally, two categorical statuses are assumed to activate the referential structures. In short, multiple categorical statuses are taken as indications of ability relevant to exercising authority which is defined in terms of dominance behavior in the group.

Berger, Webster, Ridgeway and Rosenholtz, (1986) say that task characteristics can indicate ability. They define a task characteristic as behavior which indicates task competence, for example, factual, confident, relaxed behavior which is non-threatening. An experiment by Sev'er (1989) shows that when the external status (black) of one juror is low and a task characteristic (confidence) is high and the another juror's external status is high (white) and a task characteristic (confidence) is low, the first juror prevails with subjects watching a video of the two jurors arguing. In short, confidence overcomes the status characteristic of race. Since high actual ability is likely to produce high confidence, we think this experiment raises question of the extent to which the theory of external status applies in natural groups.

CONDITIONS UNDER WHICH THE EXCHANGE MODEL AND THE EXTERNAL STATUS MODEL OPERATE STRONGLY

We want to consider first the conditions under which the external status theory and its extension to authority are likely to operate strongly. We propose that both the status and the authority components of the theory tend to operate strongly whenever the group goal tends to be *non-operational,* that is, when it is not possible to assess goal-attainment clearly; or when the effects of members' performances in different positions on an *operational goal* cannot be clearly assessed. The latter condition would obtain when the level of skill required in the positions and the level of performance of the persons in them is impossible to assess directly. A basic condition preventing such assessment is *a lack of consensus on the definition of positions.*

Non-operational goals and a lack of consensus on definition of positions tend to occur together because when the goal is not operationalized, it is not possible to specify what should be done in different positions in order to attain it. We suggest this situation tends to occur whenever existing knowledge is not sufficient to define the goal so that its attainment can be measured. It is likely that these conditions existed in the R and D groups studied by Cohen and Zhou (1991) where gender was found to affect evaluation of group members.

We further propose that a lack of consensus on definitions of positions can occur even when the group goal is operationally defined. This would tend to occur whenever attainment of the group goal is not the primary source of motivation for participation in the group but attainment of inequality rewards is. Ridgeway (1981, 1982) has shown that demonstrating group-motivation (which would focus on goal-attainment) as opposed to self-motivation (which would focus on inequality rewards) tends to break down the operation of external statuses. We treat the two types of motivation and refer to them as intrinsic and extrinsic (Kimberly, 1997:54-64).

Thus, lack of knowledge, which prevents operationalization of the group goal and clear definitions of positions, or the existence of extrinsic motivation, which prevents clear definition of positions in spite of operational definition of the group goal, appear to be the fundamental conditions in natural groups for the development of both status and authority on the basis of external statuses. Conversely, many natural groups do have operational goals and clearly defined positions and, consequently, the amount of skill the different positions require and the levels of members' performances in them can be assessed. When the latter conditions obtain, the process which occurs concerning both internal inequality (prestige, power and economic rewards of members) and authority (viewing it as a position) is the exchange process.

In actuality, most groups probably present varying degrees of the conditions described above which affect whether an exchange or external status process operates in creating and maintaining inequality. When the group goal is largely operationalized and positions are clearly defined to a large degree and the amount of skill required and the level of performance in them can be assessed to a high degree, the exchange process operates much more strongly than the external status process. The reverse is true. When operationalization of the group goal is very limited and/or positions are not clearly defined, the external status process operates much more strongly than the exchange process.

The authors of the theory of external status have also developed a theory of distributive justice (Berger, Zelditch, Anderson and Cohen, 1972). It is part of the external status perspective in that it considers statuses external to the group. Briefly stated the theory holds that what the authors call local comparisons suffer from a lack of a standard frame of reference. The authors give the example of two skilled mechanics. The first makes $4.30 an hour and the second makes $3.52 an hour. From the comparison it is not clear whether the first is appropriately paid and the second underpaid or the second is appropriately paid and the first is overpaid. Once the mechanics learn that skilled mechanics typically make $4.30 an hour it is clear that the first mechanic is appropriately paid and the second is underpaid. What the mechanics have done is to use what the authors call a referential standard. The full standard would include *two generalized individuals*, for example, mechanics, who have two states of a characteristic, for example, skilled and unskilled, with which are associated two states of a *goal object*, for example, hourly wages. Both the characteristics and the goal objects confer prestige (the consumatory value of goal objects is excluded from the theory). It would be necessary for the two ranges of hourly wages not to overlap for the full standard to be useful. The full standard would apply, for example, to skilled and unskilled mechanics.

We want to consider next how this theory relates to our conception of an integrated instrumental group. There is built into our general theory a theory of inconsistency between skill and position. Thibaut and Kelly's concept of comparison level (1959: Chapter 6) can be applied to these types of inconsistencies. One's comparison level for a given position is the reward-cost outcome he or she expects in the position. In our theory, we show that misallocation to positions in terms of skill puts individuals below their comparison level if it is assumed that the comparison level is that for positions which are consistent with the individuals' skills. While Thibaut and Kelly present the concept largely in terms of a relationship with another person, it is clear from the examples they give in discussing it that they would apply it to the more complex relationships a social position involves as we have done in our theory. The comparison level is determined by past experiences in similar positions as well as what the individual knows about the rewards and costs of other similar positions. In particular, it is only positions which the individual feels he or she has the ability to obtain that affect his or her comparison level (Thibaut and Kelley, 1959:85).

There is a question as to how often referential structures involved in the external status theory will be employed in the case of an integrated instrumental group. In order to judge the justice of allocations of members to positions, group members would have to reach consensus on the amount of skill each position requires and what is an adequate level of performances it. There will be strong bonds of attraction among members. This should lead to consensus on the required levels of skill and performance. Consensus on skill and performance requirements should be more powerful than external referential structures. We do not rule out the operation of the latter entirely. They will probably serve to modify the local standards over time, but we think they will only to a limited extent affect the local standards developed by the group members. Surely, referential standards are something the authority person will have to be very knowledgeable about, and he or she will have to justify the reward structure of the group in terms of the specific positions in the group as opposed to similar ones outside of the group. The group consensus on the reward structure should help him or her. We think that referential standards will have a weak effect as long as consensus on local standards is high and a strong effect if con-

sensus on position definitions and, consequently, on the skill and performance levels required is low. Again, it appears that the operation of
external statuses is weak when consensus on the instrumental structure
of the group is strong.

The presentation of these two very abstract theories and the factors
which qualify their operation sets the stage for making an important
point. One way we get from simple to complex theories is to demonstrate the conditions under which different simple theories work and
then to specify when variation in these affects the strength with which
each theory operates. At that point, one has a complex theory which is
closer to a natural situation.

THE RELATIONSHIP OF EXPERIMENTAL
WORK TO NATURAL SITUATIONS

Because not many small group researchers have attempted to extend theories tested in experiments to more natural situations, the view
that experiments are artificial and cannot be generalized to natural
groups has developed. Let us consider what may be involved here.
Theories abstract unitary processes from the real world. In the real
world, these are interconnected with other unitary processes. Abstraction permits study of a single process. Experiments are ideal for this
purpose. Initially, they are designed to assess one theory at a time.
Variables that may affect the theory being studied are controlled by
randomly assigning subjects to conditions. Experiments isolate theories
so we can understand them. Each experiment is a test and only one
test of a theory. Positive findings help confirm the theory.

Part of the way we get from the experiment to the natural situations
is through building into theories scope conditions. These define the
conditions under which the theory applies and these have to be created
in the experiment when the theory is tested.. We have specified the
conditions under which the exchange model of group operation and the
external status model should apply. The former applies when there is
complete consensus on the productive structure of the group and the
skills and performances it requires. The latter applies when there is no
consensus on these factors. When the scope conditions for a theory
fully exist in a natural group, the theory should fully apply. However,
as we have seen, any theory will apply in a context of other theories
which are also operating. Earlier, we pointed out that the exchange
model and the external status model often operate simultaneously.
Thus, in a natural situation, the operation of theories are often weaker

or stronger. What we must move toward is combinations of theories which we understand. This will take us closer and closer to complex natural situations (see Webster, 1994, for a complete treatment of experimental methods).

We hope to demonstrate further in this paper another way abstract theories combine so as to move closer to the natural world. Specifically, we hope to show that to understand the legitimization of the societal stratification structure, we have to combine components of both of the exchange model of groups and the external status model in the context of Mead's (1934) theory of the development of the self and a generalized other. We have to do this in a way that permits the operation of one theory to affect one another directly, not simply to vary with variation in scope conditions affecting their operation. Field and survey studies often can be very important in trying to understand how to combine theories in terms of how they affect one another.

The life sciences demonstrate the view we are presenting. The real world for medicine is the human body in which many structures and processes affect one another.   Basic research seeks to discover how very abstractly defined processes, often in combination, affect the complex operation of the human body. To take a current example, life scientists appear to be on the verge of discovering how to instruct embryonic stem cells to make any specialized cell in the human body. This research will involve learning how to use DNA to instruct a cell as to what to type of cell to become. Our understanding of DNA is a very abstract understanding. We know it tells stem cells to specialize. What we are seeking is the process by which DNA does this. Once we know this, we may be able to regenerate almost any part of the human body. Such regeneration will vary from body to body, perhaps being successful in some and not in others. However, enormous advances can come when sufficient fundamental processes are understood. Such understandings come both through experiment and highly controlled observations which analytically dissect unitary phenomena we wish to understand. The objective is to put the phenomena back together once they are understood so that we move closer to the natural world.

THE STRATIFICATION STRUCTURE OF
THE UNITED STATES

We shift now to our third objective which is to show how the comparison of our group model with the stratification structure suggests possible directions for applied research. This will also provide some sense of the nature of the stratification structure. This will be useful when we turn to our last objective, a new formulation of an existing theory of the legitimization of the stratification structure.

Stratification structures in modern industrial nations center about the occupational structure. We draw primarily on Beegley's (2000) description of the stratification structure of the United States. The public is able to rank occupations in terms of their standing. They assign scores using a nine-point scale. According to Beegley (2000: Chapter 2), the prestige of occupations results from the amount of skill they require. Education is a good indicator of skill. Income varies by occupation. The prestige hierarchy produces deference to those above and derogation of those below oneself. Such deference and derogation results in society-wide patterns of domination and subordination. Others in occupations which rank close to one's own are treated as equals, and intimate interaction occurs with them. Racial-ethnic status and gender as well as skill affect the occupations people obtain.

Patterns of class identification are highly related to occupation. White male workers in white-collar occupations with the highest scores view themselves as middle-class. White male workers in blue-collar occupations with the lowest scores view themselves as working-class. White male workers in the middle section of prestige scores divide themselves into two groups. Those with similar scores identify as either middle or working class depending on whether their jobs are white- or blue-collar. Unemployed women appear to identify with a class using their husband's occupation. Employed married women appear to identify with a class by either using their husband's occupation or by combining their own and their husband's occupations. The explanatory variables appear to be primarily the extent to which women support gender equality and support women working. It appears to be those who support both equality and working who combine their own and their husband's occupation in identifying with a class. The most recent data show that employed wives employ the status sharing in class identification. Only about 5 percent of the population see themselves as lower class and about 4 percent as upper class. Patterns of identification vary by race and class. These patterns correlate with the occupational distribution of the groups. Class, race or ethic identification segregate most neighborhoods of most U.S. cities. Class identification defines people with whom one shares a life-style and with whom one wishes to intimately associate, for example, friends, neighbors, or marriage partners.

Income and wealth show great inequality in the U.S. (Beegley, 2000: Chapter 7). The basis of wealth is ownership of income producing assets, primarily stocks and bonds, business assets and real estate. In 1995 the top 1 percent of wealth holders owned 37 percent of the wealth, the next 9 percent owned 31 percent, and the bottom 90 percent owned 32 percent.

In feudal societies the basis of wealth was land ownership. In the fourteenth century in France the church owned approximately one-third of the land. In the sixteenth century in France it is estimated that the nobility owned 20 percent of the land. The basis of wealth was in the hands of the first two estates in feudal societies, the church and the nobility (Kerbo, 2000:66-67).

Income, as opposed to wealth, is also very unequally divided in the United States. In 1997 the quintile distribution was 3.6 percent for the lowest quintile, 8.9 percent for the second quintile, 15 percent for the middle quintile, 23.2 percent for the fourth quintile and 49.4 percent for the highest quintile. Thus the three lower quintiles had a total of 27.5 percent of the income.

In a review of feudal societies, Lenski (1966:228) estimated that the governing class usually was about 2 percent of the population and received about 50 percent of the income. In the United States income is somewhat less extremely unequal. It takes the upper 10 percent of income receivers to reach approximately 50 percent of the income. In a democracy people are supposed to rule through elected representatives (Beegley, 2000: Chapter 6). However, in the 1996 presidential election, only 49 percent of the adult population voted, and voting is related to income levels. In 1996 the percent registered was 48 percent for people with incomes under $10,000 and 82 percent for people with incomes over $75,000. The percent of people voting varied from 33 percent to 74 percent for the same income levels. Politically, money creates power. This is because of the high cost of winning. In 1996 the average amount spent by winners in the Senate races was $4.7 million. Losers spent an average of $2.8 million. In the House races, the average spent by winners was $700,000. Losers spent an average of $300,000. In the 1996 election, contributions were as follows: business $454,674,000; labor $49,258,000 and ideological/single issues sources $29,346,000. In a modern class society, the financial elites attempt to control the governmental bureaucracy which has considerable power. In feudal societies, by contrast, the church and the nobility ruled by decree.

Money creates access. The major way of maintaining and increasing wealth is through influence on tax law bills. Any benefit of tax law to corporations benefits the wealthiest 10 percent of the population. They hold 85 percent of all corporate stock. Sometimes tax law bills benefit individuals through the insertion of special rules which apply only to a small class of persons.. Thus command of wealth becomes based in law in modern class societies. The emergence of a much more powerful governmental bureaucracy is a new feature of such a society. Beegley (2000:149-150) suggests that this type of political structure leads to anomie where middle-class voters accept benefits to the rich and powerful in return for limited protection for themselves.

COMPARISON OF SOCIETAL STRATIFICATION WITH THE OPERATION OF INEQUALITY IN THE GENERAL THEORY OF INSTRUMENTAL GROUPS

We now compare the picture of societal stratification just presented with the operation of inequality in the general theory of instrumental groups. The societal stratification structure has a strong concentration of economic goods at the top leading to strong influence over government which is the authority structure of the society. In more specific terms, power, based on economic goods, is concentrated at the top. This power results in strong control of the authority structure. The prestige structure is loosely connected to these two structures reflecting the occupational structure which in turn is roughly connected to the distribution of skills relevant to it.

In the small group, the authority person's role corresponds to that of the wealthy and the government in the society. The productive positions would correspond to occupational strata. There are not sufficient positions or persons in the same position for persons in small groups to approximate anything like classes.

The processes in the group would be like the societal processes if attainment of the group goal produced money, and the authority person kept a vast amount of it for him or herself. The money the authority person did not keep for himself or herself would be extremely unevenly divided by the authority person with very large amounts going to one or two members in the more difficult positions and very small amounts going to the rest of the members. This allocation would be discrepant with the prestige and power due to members because of the difficulty of their positions and their performances in them. It would be considered unjust by the members. In an attempt to retain the members in the easier lower positions, the authority person might increase the amounts going to such members somewhat but would still retain a large amount for the one or two members high in the structure and for himself or herself. Failing to maintain justice would make his or her authority at least partly illegitimate and create a measure of negative attraction toward him or her. This would offset the attraction based on the extra trust in him or her resulting from expectations that he or she would adapt the group in the future. The loss of the extra attraction would result in loss of his or her ability to influence members concerning needed changes in the group structure that future environmental conditions might require.

Thus, were a group to be structured and operate like the society, it would likely disintegrate if most of the group members had any other options. This comparison is very useful in that it tells us what aspects of the society need to be considered to understand how its inequality structure operates. One of the major things that is immediately apparent about the society and its operation is that the way its inequality structure operates is obscured by the lack of information about its operation. Partly this is a result of its great size and partly it is a result of secrecy created by persons high in the economic and political structures. (Cf. Kerbo, 2000: Chapter 16).

This comparison also led to a new insight about the *integrated group*. This insight was described prior to the comparison. It was suggested the legitimacy of authority and the existence of justice for members make for harmonious relationships which lead to an increase in equality norms which define ways in which members are equal. The equality norms, in turn, lead to a reduction in the amount of inequality produced by the productive positional structure.

This comparison also provides an unusual opportunity to develop what we can only call a utopian conception of the good society. Here we clearly leave objective science behind because we now will be considering some of the things which our objective work on small groups suggests might make a more humane and satisfying life for all members of the society. Thus, we are making suggestions for applied research. Such research seeks to determine ways of obtaining valued outcomes. The valued outcomes ultimately have to be decided by the members of the society themselves.

What does the small group model suggest? The authority person in the small group must further attainment of the group goal. The legitimacy of the national government to the extent it exists is based partly on electoral processes. Since only half of the population now votes for the executive branch, one certainly may wonder about its legitimacy. The legislative branch more nearly reflects local concerns and contributes to the legitimacy of the government. Together the two branches, structured by the constitution, legitimate the judicial branch. Something like the acceptance of a variety of values in defining the group goal is represented by the compromises that the government makes as it formulates and implements national policies. The success or failures of these policies as perceived by the population also partially determines the legitimacy of the government. What does not exist at the group level is massive control of the authority person by persons outside of the group who provide him or her with money to be used to get group members to select him or her as the authority person (we have already shown that the authority person could not maintain legitimacy if he tried to grow wealthy at the expense of group members). Clearly, if meaningful campaign finance reform were passed it would go a long way toward making the government more legitimate.

With regard to the economic inequality which exists in the society, not being an economist, we are unable to determine how much capital accumulation is sufficient to keep the economy healthy. If a third of all wealth is required, it would seem preferable that it be more widely distributed among members of the society so that groups with diverse points of view could help make investment decisions. One thing we can say about the distribution of wealth is that it may be a factor in what appears to be a growing rejection of the legitimacy of the present political economy. There is clear evidence that skilled workers, unskilled workers and unskilled supervisors hold anti-capitalistic attitudes (Wright, 1997). We will discuss this evidence in the final section of this paper.

In the small group the allocation of persons to positions is probably better than is the allocation of persons to occupations in the society. This is because there is so much more knowledge of what the positions in the small group require. This comparison raises the question of what might be the effects of improving the allocation of persons to occupations in terms of skill and performance. For one thing relationships between classes might be more respectful. After all, if everyone is doing a job well, they deserve a general respect (Cf. Davis and Moore, 1962; Homans, 1961). Present laws against discrimination in hiring and firing do something to move in this direction. The great difficulty here is information. The occupational structure is enormously complex and for most people this complexity would be an information overload. The theory developed and furthered by Berger, Cohen and Zelditch, (1966) tends to explain how persons use various status characteristics as short-hand for ability at tasks even though the status characteristics may have nothing to do the with the tasks. Della Fave (1980,1986) has suggested people tend to use primary resources such as prestige, power, wealth to attribute deservedness to the holders. In our terms, holding a given occupational position with at least one primary resource visible (prestige, power or economic rewards) can lead to attributions of skill and performance commensurate with the occupation's demands (this process is considered in the last section of the paper where we consider legitimization of the stratification structure).

It would be very difficult to entirely break this process down. But perhaps in some way the more unjust allocations of persons into occupations could be reduced. That unjust allocations are widespread is shown by a study by Umberson and Hughes (1987), which used data from a national probability sample surveyed in 1978. It showed, using appropriate controls, that physical attractiveness was related to personal and family income, education, and occupational prestige. If appearance has such a wide-spread effect, it seems clear that anything which could be taken to indicate the justice of one holding a given occupation is apt to be very powerful. The work of Berger and his associates has generated research aimed at understanding how to break up the process of using very limited knowledge to make judgments about skill and performance (see Kimberly, 1997:75-102, for reviews of some studies). More such research is needed. Actually, knowing more about this process would be very beneficial to employers.

We should note here that the theory of group operation we are using clearly takes into account market processes of supply and demand of persons. Changes in these variables affect replacements for groups and, consequently, affect the distribution of prestige, power and economic rewards within groups. As long as such changes do not disturb the fundamental rank order based on position difficulty and performance, they can be accommodated by groups.

If we can create a more legitimate national government and a more just occupational structure, according to what happens in groups, there should be greater trust between classes and there might be an increase in attraction among members of the different classes. This would probably not be a desire for intimate relationships, but there might be a greater human concern for people across class boundaries. This could take the form of greater emphasis on equality in the sense of every person having value and deserving treatment in those terms. This could lead to greater economic support for those at the bottom of the stratification structure.

Given a more legitimate national government and greater trust of it, we would expect the government to have greater influence with the population. Conversely, the greater human concern of the population for members of different classes just mentioned, could lead to the government placing greater emphasis on forms of legal equality.

THE LEGITIMIZATION OF THE STRATIFICATION STRUCTURE

In preparation for this paper we explored anomie theory which has been combined with reference group theory and relative deprivation theory (see Passas and Agnew, 1997), distributive justice theory (see Miller, 1999), alienation theory (see Kohn, 1983), and findings related to all of them. However, it was the problem of how the social stratification structure is legitimated which provided the best connection between small group theory and societal stratification. A theory of the legitimization of the societal stratification structure by Della Fave (1980, 1986) provides an excellent opening for the systematic connection of both our theory and the external status theory to societal stratification processes. We are deeply indebted to his work and Stolte's (1983) attempt to evaluate it. Della Fave's work helps us connect the two theories to societal stratification through Mead's (1934) work relating to the development of the self. Stolte's work helped us see the connection of our theory to the problem of legitimization. This problem is important because if a stratification structure is largely legitimate, certain negative consequences of stratification tend to be minimal. These consequences are anomie and the social disorder to which it may lead and the alienation of individuals from work and society.

The theory of external status involves components which attempt to connect the society to small groups. As we have seen, status characteristics cause attributions of ability, being high in a categorical referential structures reinforces a referential structure involving high social status and high ability in general at the societal level and causes acceptance of dominance in groups. Referential structures involving generalized actors, status characteristics and goal objects are used to assess justice in the small group and also in larger structures in the society. However, the external status theory is not an exchange model and lacks concern with the division of labor and the positional structure of the group with which our theory is fully concerned. We shall show that it is this concern with the division of labor in the group which permits us to systematically connect the two theories within the process by which the societal stratification structure is legitimated.

We recognize that different methods of legitimization are employed in different types of societies. For example, in feudal societies the basic method of legitimization was legal ideology which was supported often by a religious ideology (Kerbo, 2000:53-56). We shall argue that in a class society like the United States, there is a complex sociological process which involves a combination of both a part of our theory of small groups and the external status theory along with the social-psychological process of the development of the self and a generalized other (Mead, 1934:141-149). We shall also see that this process is affected by the value-orientation having to do with equality in society.

In his theory of legitimization, Della Fave (1980) attempted to connect the person to the stratification structure of the society and to show how the person comes to view the structure as legitimate. Drawing on Mead (1934:141-149), he argued that we become aware of ourselves because we realize that our gestures produce in others the same effect they do in us. This lets us take the role of others and anticipate their reactions to us or some third party. The self develops as we associate what others expect of us and how they react to us. In this process, as self-evaluation develops, there develops a generalized other consisting of significant others, that is, those who meet our needs. As we mature this generalized other expands and becomes more diverse as we interact with persons who are strangers. We come to define a norm of justice by associating our self-evaluation and the self-evaluations of others, which define our contributions, with the rewards we and the others obtain. Justice exists when self-evaluations and rewards are in line. In the stratification structure, rewards consist of money, power and prestige. These are the primary resources of the structure. We extend the generalized other by means of status ascription. Such ascription is based on very limited knowledge of persons very far above and below us in the stratification structure (Della Fave draws on Berger, Cohen and Zelditch, 1966). We usually know only a little about such persons such as some or all of the primary resources they command. We assume that contribution is aligned with the primary resource or resources.

As described earlier, Berger and his associates (see Berger, Fisek, Norman and Zelditch, 1977, and Ridgeway and Berger, 1986, for central formulations) have shown that when provided only with status characteristics such as age, sex, or race, subjects in small groups make judgments as to who has the greater task ability always in line with who has the higher status characteristic, *regardless of the type of task skill involved.* They have also shown that acceptance of domination in groups occurs when two or more status characteristics, for example, age and education, are high. They believe two status characteristics tap societal referential structures. The categorical structure reinforces a referential structure having to do with high social status and high ability in general. The experiments related to their research always severely limit knowledge of persons to the status characteristic or characteristics. This makes their theory a relevant theory for Della Fave to have used (although he only used the first formulation described above) with respect to persons about whom we know little. The possible explanatory mechanisms in the theory are cognitive balance and/or reinforcement theory. The weight of the evidence seems to come down on reinforcement theory because when given both high and low status characteristics for the same person, subjects appear to average them in making decisions about the person's ability. This implies the subjects are using all information available in an attempt to solve the task. Thus, it is the reward of successful task solutions that is sought (see Kimberly, 1997:72-108; 139-145 for reviews of some of this work and also for an attempt to integrate it with exchange theory generally).

Della Fave believes the sense of objectivity that we attribute to the generalized other reinforces the tendency to perceive the stratification structure as legitimate in the way he specifies. Stolte (1983) conducted an experiment concerning Della Fave's theory. He put subjects into two networks, one in which three subjects out of four could bargain for exchanges of hypothetical resources with only the fourth subject and one in which everyone could bargain with everyone else. He predicted that the subjects limited to a single other for bargaining (which made them low power relative to the single subject who could bargain with any of the three of them) would have lower scores on self-efficacy, which they did, and also, if Della Fave's theory were correct, see their terms of exchange as equally fair. They saw their terms of exchange as less fair, which called Della Fave's theory into question (Stolte predicted self-efficacy would be equal and perception of the terms of exchange would be fair in the network in which everyone could bargain with everyone else, and this proved to be the case). Stolte thinks our theory of distributive justice in small groups may explain his finding. It will be remembered that this theory is a part of our theory of group operation. The most general statements of this theory along with relevant empirical findings are found in Kimberly (1997:154-175). Some of the theory's predictions concerning how the inconsistencies of skill and position with which it deals may lead to attempts to change group structure and, by implication, larger group structures in organizations are found in Kimberly (1962, 1966, 1967, 1970). We do not consider these processes in this paper.

In its simplest sense, what the theory says is that because of the general tendency to assign persons to positions in which they have the skill to perform adequately, persons learn to expect the rewards and costs that go with such positions. Rewards are those the inequality structure of the group provides, namely, prestige, power and economic rewards. These vary with the difficulty of the position and the level of performance expected in it. The variation in rewards results from the fact that difficulty of position and level of performance tend to be correlated with the number of persons competent to perform in the position who are available outside of the group. In short, the more difficult the position and the higher the level of performance expected, the harder it is to replace a person, and the more inequality rewards he or she must receive to retain him or her. Part of inequality rewards are based on position, which defines the person's responsibility, and part are based on performance, which defines how well the person carries out his or her responsibilities. Costs are based on effort which the performance entails.

A reward-cost expectation develops (people subtract costs from rewards and rewards must exceed costs) for positions which are in keeping with the person's skill. This conception of a reward-cost expectation tied to skill is based on Thibaut and Kelly's (1959:81-97) conception of an expectation for a reward-cost outcome. He defines the comparison level as the reward-cost outcome one expects in a given relationship. We have applied the comparison level concept to social positions. Thibaut and Kelley (1959:85) specified that only reward-cost outcomes the person feels he or she is able to obtain affect the comparison level. This is similar to our position that the reward-cost expectation is related to skill.

This is another point at which we can relate our work to two additional concepts in the web of concepts. These are situation and reinforcement. We argue in our theory that over time persons average in some way the rewards received and costs incurred in similar positions requiring a given level of a skill and subtract the generalized costs from generalized rewards, that is they generalize a reward-cost outcome from situations involving use of the skill. They then come to expect to obtain that reward-cost outcome in any positions in which they use the skill. Of course, reinforcement is central to both our and Thibaut and Kelley's theory. .

Let us return now to our theory of inconsistency of between skill and position. Here we want briefly to show what happens when a person is allocated to a position which is *too easy* or *too hard* for his or her skill. In the first case, which we shall call *high skill-easy position*, the component of prestige, power and economic rewards based on position decreases because the position is easy. While the high skill person may increase performance at first, over time it will decrease because boredom sets in. Thus, the other component of prestige, power and economic rewards based on performance also decreases. The overall effect is a general decrease of rewards. Costs increase because of the boredom. Thus, rewards decrease and costs increase and the reward-cost outcome is worse than it would be in a position consistent with skill.

Consider now the other case, namely, *low skill-hard position*. In this case, rewards based on position increase because the position is hard. Rewards based performance decrease because the person cannot perform adequately in the position. Thus, in general, rewards tend to remain at the same level overall, one base of them increasing and the other decreasing. However, the costs increase greatly because of the person's low skill. This is intensified by the fact that low-skill persons tend to weight costs heavier than rewards. In short, they focus on avoiding costs as opposed to obtaining rewards (Thibaut and Kelley, 1959:97). Thus, again, the reward-cost outcome is worse than it would be in a position consistent with skill.

That the type of inconsistency we have been discussing operates at structural levels above the level of the small group is shown in a study by House and Hawkins (1975). They studied education (skill) and occupation (position) in a small community. Using survey data, they found that persons with low education (low skill) and high occupation (hard position) showed effects of psychological strain when age and motivation were treated as intervening variables. Persons over 45 showed strain. This strain they suggested was due to the fact that education is less likely to change after 45, cementing into place the inconsistency. Persons low on extrinsic motivation (low concern for money and prestige of occupation) showed strain. This they explain by the fact that it is likely that persons who do not value money and prestige are less likely to feel that their struggle to compensate for educational deficiencies has been worth the effort. These findings strongly suggest that communities and work organizations, which consists of occupations, are affected by the type of inconsistencies with which our theory deals. This study is important because at the level of the stratification structure we are dealing with occupations

Let us return now to Stolte's experiment. He argues that the expectations for rewards and costs we employ in our theory of distributive justice become a part of the self. Since the subjects were all college students, he thinks they probably had relatively equal conceptions of their bargaining ability which was tied to the rewards and costs they expected to incur in bargaining situations. In the experiment those whose bargaining opportunities were restricted probably felt their rewards and costs fell below what they expected. Hence, they felt little self-efficacy. They also felt their terms of exchange (which were related to the power structure of the network) were unfair.

Della Fave (1996) modified his theory to attempt to take into account Stolte's finding. He says persons lower in the stratification structure constantly have to accept unequal exchanges if they are to meet the needs of life. Being forced to accept unequal exchanges along with enforcement of dominant standards in the culture, such as production standards enforced by employers, academic standards enforced by teachers, technical efficiency standards and verbal proficiency standards, leads to the idea that rewards are distributed according to equity or justice norms and that a person knows where he stands with regard to exchanges and standards. Somehow this process also leads to the notion that mental work is superior to manual.

We do *not* think that being forced to accept unequal exchanges would create any sense of equity or justice. Just the converse, we think it would create a sense of injustice in each case in which an unequal exchange was forced upon the person. Stolte's experiment itself shows this. If we assume that college students feel they have a certain amount of bargaining ability, those prevented from using it by having their exchange possibilities limited should have felt their situation unfair. This appears to be exactly what happened. The way to think about the reward-cost expectations that people develop as they perform in social positions and the relations they involve is that the reward-cost expectations constitute the people's conceptions of what they are capable of and what they deserve for it. This corresponds very closely to Mead's conception of self-evaluation. As we shall see later, people at the lower reaches of the stratification structure in all probability do not feel their situations are just. We think this is a result of acquiring, as they move out of the family into school and later into first occupations, conceptions of what they can do. If later they find themselves in situations where they are not allowed to use these skills, they feel it is unjust.

The enforcement of standards that Della Fave discusses *are* probably part of people learning what is fair. The standards probably fairly place limits on the positions to which persons are entitled. So by defining skill, they reinforce the development of reward-cost expectations congruent with skill. Della Fave also decomposed the self-evaluation concept so that it did not include self-esteem. He argues that those low in the stratification structure can and do gain self-esteem from comparing themselves only at their own level which prevents relative deprivation and lets them obtain self-esteem from meeting the standards that obtain in their own work and the standards the work leads to in their life styles. Thus he argues the very thing that permits them to acquire self-esteem also commits them to work roles and the way of life they involve and labels them as inferior. This is in keeping with findings that self-esteem is roughly equal for black and white and poor and affluent children (Della Fave, 1986:483).

We think this is a process that occurs. Davis (1996) analyzed data from a representative sample of college graduates. He found that for 56 percent of male students (the 56 percent were in certain academic areas), that grade-point average (GPA) affected career decisions more than quality of college. He was able to show that a measure of subjective confidence was more strongly associated with GPA than with college quality. Since GPA is higher if the student attends a less difficult college, he suggests that relative deprivation is at work. His argument is that the student compares with others in his own college; comparison is local. He found that going to a lower quality college and attaining a higher GPA, leads to higher-level career choices. He also found that the student attending a higher quality college and attaining a lower GPA reduces the level of his career choices. It is this latter effect that is like Della Fave's suggestion that persons lower in the stratification structure reduce their aspiration level so as to attain self-esteem.

Research by Koln and associates (1983) examined national probability samples of men in the labor force in 1964 and 1974. They found (1983:64, 83-93, 155-161, 180-186) that alienation in the sense of feelings of powerless and self-estrangement existed at the bottom of work organizations, at the bottom of the societal stratification structure and at the bottom of the class structure. This suggests that there are feelings of much injustice among those at the bottom of these structures. That aspiration has not been relinquished by these people is suggested by the fact that normlessness also occurs consistently with alienation suggesting that a process of anomie is occurring (for the latest on the state of anomie theory, see Passas and Agnew, 1997).

Let us turn now to how people assess the legitimacy of people in positions which are very high above or below their own. Della Fave suggests that it is here that the external status processes comes in operation. He argues that if we know a person is high or low on one or more of the primary resources of prestige, power and economic rewards, we assume that they that they deserve their position. We think this certainly occurs. However, we think it occurs only for persons who feel their own position is just. If they find themselves in a position they feel is unjust, we think it is much easier for them to wonder if persons above them deserve the positions they have and if those below them do not deserve higher positions. What we are suggesting is that experiencing injustice in the work they do, people come to suspect that others do not deserve what they have or what they lack. The implication here is very powerful. It is that if there is much injustice in a society, justice in general is called into question. That we may be entering a period when the political economy we have may be coming into question is suggested by the data we consider next. Kluegel and Smith

(1986:119-122) surveyed a 1980 national probability sample of all persons over age 18 in the United States. They found that persons felt that occupations at the bottom of the stratification structure received too little income and that those at the top received too much income. In short, it appeared that they felt the income structure needed to be lowered at the top and raised at the bottom.

Income is one of the rewards which rests both on the difficulty of position, which involves the skill required, and the level of the person's performance. Inconsistency can involve only an income which does not meet reward-cost expectations. In this case, the position may be correct in terms of the person's skill, so this may be an inconsistency arising from a source other than position allocation. We treat economic reward allocation separately from position allocation in our work (Kimberly, 1997, 2000).

A recent study by Wright (1997) employs data from a 1980 random probability sample of adults in the labor force who were currently employed in the United States. It appears that anti-capitalistic class consciousness has developed in this country. It includes the skilled-labor category. Because this is such a powerful indicator of feelings of illegitimacy of the stratification structure, we review it briefly here.

Wright defines class structure in terms of ownership, authority and skills. Owners he breaks into capitalists (10 or more employees), small employers (2 to 9 employees), and petty bourgeoisie (0 to 1 employees). Employees he classifies by authority and skill. There are three categories of authority: manager, supervisor and no authority. There are also three categories of skill: expert, skilled and unskilled. In order to get as pure a working class category as possible, he used a relative expansive criterion for authority, moving persons toward the management end of the scale and a relatively expansive criterion for skill, moving persons toward the expert end of the scale.

He defines employees in terms of nine cells in a 3 x 3 matrix. On top is skill, ranging from left to right, expert to skilled to unskilled. Vertically there is authority, ranging from the top to bottom, manager to supervisor to no authority. He measured class consciousness with a five-item scale containing Likert-type questions answered strongly disagree, disagree, don't know, agree and strongly agree, for example, "Corporations benefit owners at the expense of workers and consumers." This is an anticapitalist statement. All questions were of this form. Responses were scored -2 and -1 for disagree responses, which indicated a procapitalist view and +1 and +2 for agree answers which indicated an anticapitalist view.

He found three distinct coalitions among the class positions. Capitalists (score -2.17), expert managers (-2.62), expert supervisors (.073), skilled managers (-0.68), and unskilled managers (-1.09) constituted a capitalistic-class coalition. Small employers (score +0.35), petty bourgeoisie (+ 1.08), experts (+ 0.16), and skilled supervisors (+ 1.30) made up a middle-class coalition. Skilled workers (+2.67), unskilled workers (+2.66) and unskilled supervisors (+1.56) made up a working-class coalition. If employees alone are considered, the scores from the unskilled worker cell to the expert manager cell are monotonic decreasing. All other rows and columns are also, except for the cell involving skilled manager. These coalitions are significantly different from one another at the .001 percent level. Thus, it appears that the relatively pure working-class coalition consisting of skilled workers, unskilled workers and unskilled supervisors are clearly anticapitalist.

Wright's findings are in keeping with Kohn et al.'s (1983) findings of alienation consistently at the bottom of work organizations and the society as a whole. It is also in keeping with Kluegel and Smith's (1986) finding that the American people want the range of income inequality reduced by lowering the top and raising the bottom of the range.

All of these studies tend to support the importance of our view that persons develop reward-cost expectations that they associate with occupations in which they can perform adequately. Once such expectations are violated by placement in an occupation which requires either more skill or less skill than they have, it seems likely they may come to suspect the legitimacy of the whole stratification structure. This should break down the external status process. It seems that the type of inconsistency which is probably most prevalent in our society is high skill-low position. The types are relative to stratification level. They can exist at a high or low level.

We have brought together two fundamental processes involved in stratification. One is a process involving the consistency of a person's occupation with his or her skill. The other is a process involving the attribution of contribution congruent with limited knowledge of another's status. In particular such attribution tends to involve assuming contribution is congruent with any of the major resources, namely, prestige, power or economic rewards. We are predicting that the latter process occurs only if the person's own skill and occupation are *consistent*.

We think that Della Fave is correct that Mead's conception of how self-evaluation and evaluation of others in a generalized other develops is correct. We argue that the other two processes, the status consistency theory from our own exchange model and the external status theory developed by Berger and associates are fundamentally connected. When reward-cost expectations are violated by incorrect placement in an occupation, we argue that the process involving attributing congruent contributions to persons in distant occupations about which one knows little breaks down. Put another way, *when one's skill and occupational position are inconsistent, that fact becomes a condition for stopping the external status process in which persons in distant positions are assumed to deserve their positions.* Should there be enough persons whose skills and occupations are inconsistent, the whole structure of stratification may become illegitimate. We suspect this is why an anticapitalist class consciousness is developing in this country.

We must now qualify the prediction of this theory because of the value context in which it probably operates. The value-orientation involved is that equality (Williams, 1970:472-479). As noted earlier, equality appears to occur in three different forms in our society. One form is the idea that every person has value and should be treated that way. Another form is the formal equality demonstrated in our legal rights. The third form is the one that concerns us. It involves a compromise with the values of freedom, specifically economic freedom, and the values of success and individual achievement. These values have resulted in equality of opportunity as a third form of equality (Williams, 1970:475-478).

Findings by Kluegel and Smith (1986) relate to this. They developed two scales. One measured support for inequality. The other measured support for equality. The scales were derived from data obtained from all persons in the national probability sample. The two scales correlated -34. The authors argue that the low correlation suggests a substantial portion of the respondents agreed with both types of statements in the two scales. The say this suggests doubts about the justice of economic inequality leads people to adopt beliefs supporting more equality rather than rejecting beliefs that advocate the necessity of income inequality. Thus, it appears that there is a tendency in our society not to let feelings concerning equality overcome a belief that inequality is necessary.

This means we should predict that if a person feels strongly about a need for inequality, he or she will tend to believe in the existence of equality of opportunity. This belief, in turn will lead to an assumption that those much higher or lower in the stratification structure than himself or herself, have earned what they have. This would counter the effect of inconsistency of their own status, should it exist. Thus, the belief in the existence of equality of opportunity is a variable which will mute the operation of the de-legitimization process. The belief becomes a condition specifying when the process of de-legitimization will occur.

Our development of the work of Della Fave and Stolte, of course, must be tested. This could be done by a survey of persons in the occupational structure in which the consistency of their statuses is assessed. This would involve whether they feel their skill is consistent with the demands of their occupation. Additional information should be obtained concerning whether their prestige, power, and economic rewards are what they expect and whether the effort their performance requires is what they expect. The latter questions would serve to confirm whether the person's assessment of the appropriateness of his or her skill was correct. Such a study should also involve the assessment of occupations very distant their own in terms of whether persons in them deserve their occupations in terms of their skill and performance. A strong association between inconsistency in one's own occupation and assessments that those higher or lower do not deserve their occupations, that is, that persons high do not deserve the occupations they have and that those low deserve a higher occupations, would support our formulation of the process of de-legitimization. A control would have to be built into the study in terms of a measure of the belief in equality of opportunity and whether this is associated with conviction that most persons deserve the occupations they have.

An assessment could also probably be modeled in an experiment. Subjects could work on part of a complex task of middle difficulty, and their conceptions of their skill related to the task could be manipulated. Consistency and inconsistency between their perceived skill and their task could be created. Then they could be asked to assess the skill and performance of persons working on much harder and much easier parts of the overall task. Again an association between inconsistency of their own situation and doubt that those working on the harder and easier tasks have appropriate skill, that is that those working on the harder the task deserve an easier task and that those working on the easier task deserve a harder one, would support the theory. Also again beliefs about whether or not there was equality to attain the tasks in the experiment would have to be created.

Anomalous results in the survey could be examined in the experiment. We would see a possible interplay between survey and experiment. We think we have shown how two small group processes which are very different and which operate at under different conditions at the small group level can be extended to occupations which make up the societal stratification structure. We have also shown how the two processes can be systematically related to one another so as to explain legitimization and de-legitimization of the stratification structure.

SUMMARY AND CONCLUSIONS

Let us review what we have done. We presented two fundamental small group theories which explain inequality in groups in very different ways. We have tried to show when one theory operates more strongly than the other. This involved identifying the variable structural conditions of the group which explain this.

We have described the American stratification structure and attempted to show how comparing the exchange-based small group theory with it suggests important directions for policy-oriented research aimed at creating a more humane society.

Finally, we have systematically related the exchange-based small group theory to the external status theory (which Della Fave used) in a way that explains when societal stratification legitimization and delegitimization occur. We have kept the context of Mead's conception of the development of the generalized other as a basic structure for the formulation of the theory.

The methodology of the Sociological Imagination Group has come into our work in a number of ways. We have shown how very abstract conceptions of groups and societies as systems and conceptions of similar processes in them enabled us to connect groups and the society; how immersion in abstract, interrelated concepts related to stratification helped us discover an important research problem, that of the legitimization of the societal stratification structure; how moving down to concrete data helped us see how to reformulate the theory which lacked support; how the interrelated concepts and related data allowed us to make an initial assessment of the reformulation; and finally, how the interrelated concepts helped us see that a component of the equality-value orientation conditions our reformulation of the theory. When we discussed the development of group goals in the exchange-based theory, we had an opportunity to show how a host of societal values might enter into the definition of a single group goal. We also showed how societal equality norms enter into the expressive structure of instrumental groups. In a later section, where we discussed the justice component of our theory of group operation, we had occasion to relate the concepts of situation and reinforcement to the idea that reward-cost expectations develop which are generalized from many similar situations involving the use the same skill. We also were able to relate the part of Della Fave's theory which deals with how those lower in the stratification structure obtain self-esteem to additional work on relative deprivation.

Finally, in comparing our concept of an instrumental group in our society to such a group in a feudal society, we saw how the more profound inequality the latter society severely limited expressive behavior to persons of the same status. We pointed out that equality is a modern development in societies and to some degree limits the degree of stratification within them.

We feel we have only made a beginning in relating our small group work to larger social systems, but we hope we have offered some guidance as to how it might be done.

NOTES

1. This paper was presented for the author at a working session of the Sociological Imagination Group at the annual meetings of the American Sociological Association in Washington, D.C., August 2000. It presents new developments in the theory and makes clearer its logical structure. Much of the empirical work related to the theory appears in Kimberly,(1997).Copies of the paper may be obtained from the author at the Department of Sociology at the University of Nebraska-Lincoln, NE 68588-0324, or by requesting them at jbkimber@email.msn.com.

The present paper is a result of working approximately a year and a half in the context of the Sociological Imagination Group, the leaders of which are the editors of this volume. Our first effort which was shared at the August, 2000, meetings of the American Sociological Association in a working group session chaired by Bernard Phillips. This is the paper cited above. It was an attempt to develop the small group theory and to make its logical structure clearer. This did not suggest firm ways of connecting the small group theory to the web of very abstract, interrelated concepts employed by the Sociological Imagination Group because we focused on demonstrating the theoretical integration we had developed in the small group area. We decided to examine the small group theory in the context of societal stratification. This involved an exploration of anomie theory which has been combined with reference group theory, relative deprivation theory (see Passas and Agnew, 1997), distributive justice theory (see Miller, 1999), alienation theory (see Kohn, 1983), and findings related to all of them. In a first paper, we were able to compare inequality processes at the two levels but were not able to firmly connect them. However, it was our immersion in both very abstract, interrelated concepts related to stratification and concrete data related to them and critiques by Bernard Phillips of the first paper and an earlier version of this paper which led to the present paper. His critiques caused us to search for a firmer theoretical connection of the processes at the two levels. We focused on Della Fave's (1980, 1986) theory of legitimization of the stratification structure.   It employs an external status theory.   It was upon reading Stolte's (1983) experimental work on Della Fave's theory that we came to see that the external status theory and the distributive justice theory which is a part of our small group theory could be systematically related to one another so as to explain legitimization.   As we argue in this paper, this is a major step forward in understanding legitimization.

REFERENCES

Beeghley, L. 2000. *The Structure of Social Stratification in the United States*. Boston: Allyn and Bacon.

Berger, J., B. P. Cohen and M. Zelditch, Jr. 1966. "Status Characteristics and Expectation States." Pp. 29-45 In J. Berger, M. Zelditch, Jr., and B. Anderson (eds.), *Sociological Theories in Progress, Vol. I.* Boston: Houghton-Mifflin.

Berger, J., M. H. Fisek, R. Z. Norman and M. Zelditch, Jr. 1977. *Status Characteristics and Social Interaction.* New York: Elsevier Scientific Publishing.

Blau, P. 1964. *Exchange and Power in Social Life*. New York: Wiley.

Cohen, B. P., and X. Zhou. 1991. "Status Processes in Enduring Work Groups." *American Sociological Review* 56:179-188.

Davis, K., and W. Moore. 1945. "Some Principles of Stratification." *American Sociological Review* 10:242-249.

Della Fave, L. R. 1980. "The Meek Shall Not Inherit the Erth: Self-evaluation and the Legitimacy of Stratification." *American Sociological Review* 45:955-971.

Della Fave, L. R. 1986. "Toward an Explication of the Legitimation Process." *Social Forces* 65:476-500.

Emerson, R. M. 1962. "Power-dependence Relations." *American Sociological Review* 27:31-41.

Emerson, R. M. 1972. "Exchange Theory, Part I: A Psychological Basis for Social Exchange." In J. Berger, M. Zelditch, Jr., and B. Anderson, (eds.), *Sociological Theories in Progress, Vol. II..* Boston: Houghton-Mifflin, pp. 38-57.

Emerson, R. M. 1972. "Exchange Theory, Part II: Exchange Relations and Network Structures." In J. Berger, M. Zelditch, Jr., and B. Anderson,(eds.), *Sociological Theories in Progress, Vol. II.* Boston: Houghton-Mifflin, pp. 58-88.

Homans, G. C. 1961. *Social Behavior: Its Elementary Forms.* New York: Harcourt, Brace and World.

Homans, G. C. 1974 *Social Behavior: Its Elementary Forms.* Rev. ed. New York: Harcourt Brace Jovanovich.

House, J. S. and E. B. Hawkins. 1975. "Why and When is Status Inconsistency Stressful?" *American Journal of Sociology* 81:395-412.

Kerbo, H. R. 2000. *Social Stratification and Inequality: Class Conflict in Historical, Comparative, and Global Perspective.* Boston: McGraw-Hill.

Kimberly, J. C. 1962. "An Experimental Test of a Theory of Status Equilibration." Unpublished Ph.D. Dissertation, Duke University.

Kimberly, J. C. 1966. "A Theory of Status Equilibration." In J. Berger, M. Zelditch, Jr., and B. Anderson (eds.), *Sociological Theories in Progress, Vol. II..* Boston: Houghton-Mifflin, pp. 213-226.

Kimberly, J. C. 1967. "Status Inconsistency: A Reformulation of a Theoretical Problem." *Human Relations* 20:171-179.

Kimberly, J. C. 1970. "The Emergence and Stabilization of Stratification in Simple and Complex Social Systems." In E. O. Laumann (ed.), *Social Stratification.* Indianapolis: Bobbs-Merrill, pp. 73-101.

Kimberly, J. C. 1972. "Relations among Status, Power, and Economic Rewards in Simple and Complex Social   Systems." In Berger, J., M. Zelditch, Jr., and B. Anderson, (eds.), *Sociological Theories in Progress. Vol. II..* Boston: Houghton-Mifflin.

Kimberly, J. C. 1977. "Inconsistency among Components of Stratification and Cognitive Consistency and Reward-cost Process." In Hamblin R. L. and J. H. Kunkel, *Behavioral Theory in Sociology: Essays in Honor of George C. Homans.* New Brunswick, NJ: Transaction Books, pp. 385-407.

Kimberly, J. C. 1997 *Group Processes and Structures: A Theoretical Integration..* Lanham, MD: University Press of America.

Kimberly, J. C. 2000 "A General Theory of Group Operation" (Part of "A Method of Constructing Complex Theories" ; paper presented to the Sociological Imagination Working Group at the annual meetings of the American Sociological Association, Washington, D. C., August, 2000).

Kimberly, J. C. and P. V. Crosbie. 1967. "An Experimental Test of a Reward-cost Formulation of Status Inconsistency." *Journal of Experimental Social Psychology* 3:399-415.

Kimberly, J. C., with contributions by Edward W. McCranie, H. P. Whitt, and J. H. Wiest. 1993. "The Social Psychology of Status Inconsistency: Status Structure and Psychological Processes." In Hodge, R. W., and H. Strasser (eds.), *Change and Strain in Social Hierarchies*. New Delhi: Ajanta Books International, pp. 73-115.

Kluegel, J. R., and E. R. Smith. 1986. *Beliefs About Inequality: Americans' Views of What Is and What Ought to Be.* New York: Aldine DeGruyter, pp. 73-115.

Kohn, M. L., and C. Schooler, with contributions by J. Miller, K. A. Miller, C. Schoenbach and R. Schoenberg. 1983 *Work and Personality: An Inquiry into the Impact of Social Stratification.* Norwood, N.J.: Ablex Publishing Corporation.

Lenski, G. 1966. *Power and Privilege.* New York: McGraw-Hill.

Margolin, L., J. C. Kimberly and H. P. Whitt. 1992. "Status Effects on Acceptance of Influence." *Sociological Perspectives* 35:451-473.

McCraine E. W., and Kimberly, J. C. 1973. "Rank Inconsistency, Conflicting Expectations and Injustice." *Sociometry* 36:152-176.

Mead, G. H. 1934, *Mind, Self and Society.* Chicago: University of Chicago Press.

Miller, D. 1999. *Principles of Social Justice.* Cambridge, MA: Harvard University Press.

Newcomb, T. M. 1955. "An Approach to the Study of Communicative Acts." In Hare, A. P., E. F. Borgatta and R. F. Bales (eds.), *Small Groups.* New York: Knopf, pp. 149-163.

Newcomb, T. M.   1959. "Individual Systems of Orientation."   In S. Koch (ed.), Psychology: *A Study of a Science, Study I., Vol. 3.* New York: McGraw-Hill., pp. 384-442.

Newcomb, T. M. 1968. "Interpersonal balance." In Abelson, R. P., W. J. McGuire, T. M. Newcomb, M. J. Rosenberg and P. H. Tannenbaum (eds.), *Theories of Cognitive Consistency.* Chicago: Rand McNally.

Passas, N., and R. Agnew (eds.). 1997. *The Future of Anomie Theory.* Boston: Northeastern University Press, pp. 384-442

Ridgeway, C. L. 1981. "Nonconformity, Competence, and Influence in Groups: A Test of Two Theories." *American Sociological Review* 46:333-347.

Ridgeway, C. L.1982 "Status in Groups: the Importance of Motivation." *American Sociological Review* 47:76-88.

Ridgeway, C. L., and J. Berger. 1986. "Expectations, Legitimization, and Dominance Behavior in Task Groups." *American Sociological Review* 51:603-617.

Ridgeway, C. L., C. Johnson, and D. Diekema. 1994 "External Status, Legitimacy, and Compliance in Male and Female Groups." *Social Forces* 72:1051-1077.

Sev'er, A.   1989   "Simultaneous Effects of Status and Task Cues: Combining, Eliminating or Buffering?   *Social Psychology Quarterly* 52:327-335.

Stolte, J. F. 1983. "The Legitimization of Structural Inequality: Reformulation and Test of the Self-evaluation Argument." *American Sociological Review* 48:331-342.

Thibaut, J. W. and H. H. Kelley. 1959. T*he Social Psychology of Groups.* New York: Wiley.

Umberson, D., and M. Hughes. 1987. "The Impact of Attractiveness on Achievement and Psychological Well-being." *Social Psychological Quarterly* 50:227-236.

Webster, M., Jr. 1994. "Experimental Methods." In Foschi, M., and E. J. Lawler (eds.), *Group Processes and Structures: Sociological Analyses*. Chicago: Nelson-Hall, pp. 43-69.

Webster, M., Jr., and M. Foschi (eds.). 1988 S*tatus Generalization*. Stanford: Stanford University Press.

Williams, R. M., Jr.   1970. *American Society: A Sociological Interpretation*. New York: Alfred A. Knopf.

Wright, E. O.   1997 *Class Counts: Comparative Analysis in Class Analysis*. New York: Cambridge University Press.

Introduction to Chapter 5

Kincaid applies a highly systematic and logical analysis to the 1967 work on stratification and occupational mobility by Blau and Duncan. His approach encompasses a range of theoretical and methodological orientations and assumptions involved in that work and raises questions rarely raised within the literature of sociology. His focus is on the importance of paying attention to the entire theoretical context within which a given proposition is located, and also to shuttle far up and down language's ladder of abstraction. As a result, he is able to criticize the limitations of the occupational attainment literature along with related literatures, functionalist perspectives and certain quantitative procedures. He finds the recent work of Tilly as going beyond the work of Blau and Duncan in important respects, since Tilly does not simply treat social stratification as a piecemeal variable in common with the orientation that Mills called abstracted empiricism. And Tilly does indeed shuttle up and down language's ladder of abstraction. Yet a web approach can improve on Tilly's functionalist orientation. It enables us to bring to bear social psychological processes that lie behind patterns of discrimination and more fully explain its persistence. Kincaid proceeds to cite a variety of studies that can be brought to bear to achieve such a fuller explanation. These include work by Scheff on shame, Van Ausdale and Feagin on young children and Howard on self-mutilation. A web approach opens up as well to a great deal more research than these few examples illustrate.

Chapter 5

Explaining Inequality

Harold Kincaid

One of the more sophisticated and sustained research traditions in sociology is found in the work on stratification and occupational mobility, exemplified in the work of Blau and Duncan (1967). That work purports to explain "the foundation of the stratification system in our society." This chapter analyzes this research tradition and recent attempts to go beyond it from the perspective outlined in Chapter 1.

Section 1 below outlines the relevant elements from the sociological imagination perspective and how I interpret them. Section II outlines the main claims and methods of the occupational attainment literature. Section III discusses various ways this work fails theoretically to explain social structure, fails methodologically to provide compelling evidences, and what the perspective of this volume implies about how these limitations might be overcome. Section IV looks at extant attempts to rectify these limitations and suggests ways they might be improved.

SECTION I: RELEVANT ASPECTS OF THE SOCIOLOGICAL IMAGINATION

Three key ideas from the sociological imagination tradition will be used here: the "web" approach to scientific method, the idea of "moving up and down the ladder of abstraction," and the notion that scientific investigation ought to be "reflexive." All have been explicated in Chapter 1. This section expands on that explication and outlines the specific understanding that I apply in the rest of the discussion.

The web concept claims that all empirical testing takes place within the context of a web of background knowledge, yet instead of ignoring that complex context it should become part of the research process. The more extensive and varied the total web we take into account, and the more its pieces are tested against each other, the stronger the resulting product. It is these diverse evidential relationships that are crucial, and no set of isolated propositions can substitute for this richness.

Several important morals follow for assessing social research. A first is that there is no inherent difference between quantitative and qualitative research, experimental and observational: with the right background knowledge qualitative, observational data can be compelling and quantitative experimental evidence can be entirely unpersuasive without it. A second related moral is that scientific inference is never a purely mechanical or logical matter--data plus rules of logic are not enough to produce determinate results. Procedures that are claimed to be purely logical are often disguised substantive empirical assumptions.

The idea of "moving up and down the ladder of abstraction" rejects what Mills called abstract empiricism and grand theory. Abstract empiricism is the atheoretical compiling of data and listing of variables taken directly from ordinary language. Grand theory invokes abstract concepts without systematic ties to concrete phenomena and concepts. Avoiding both requires balancing the need for high-level theory that organizes diverse phenomena and concrete connections to particular phenomena.

Studying variables chosen and described without theory is likely to lead to error in the following ways. Assume that we want social research that produces full causal explanations. Proceeding atheoretically means potentially missing causes of three different types: confounding causes, complicating causes, and structural causes. A confounding cause is one that leads to spurious connections in the data. Without a theory to identify possible causal factors, no purely statistical technique will identify such confounders. A complicating cause is one that would add further causal factors to a putative or already established causal model. Such causes are often categorized as part of the "error term" in atheoretical approaches. Doing so however means less complete explanations--part of the causal story is unknown--and less confidence in our evidence--the unknown causes may in fact be confounders.

Perhaps most importantly, proceeding without invoking the general categories of abstract theory leads to missing structural causes. A structural cause as I use the term is a cause that makes other causal relations possible--it is a more fundamental or underlying cause. For example, the genetic system of an organism is a structural cause that makes possible the causal relation between signaling molecules and cellular response. Eschewing abstract categories and theories makes identifying such structural causes difficult, leads to less than full causal explanations, and deprives research of those connections to other results that increase credibility.

My argument shall be that standard work on stratification poorly balances the need for abstract theory and concrete ties. As a result it misses the sort of causes just described. Showing how it does so is crucial to seeing how such work can be improved.

The third distinctive component from the sociological imagination tradition is that social research should be "reflexive." By this is meant that successful research requires an awareness of the historical, sociological and psychological processes influencing the research itself. In short, we need to apply sociology to the practice of sociological research. Doing so in the stratification case will suggest that some standardly used research tools have a large rhetorical rather than substantive justification.

SECTION II: THE STRATIFICATION RESEARCH TRADITION

There are three key elements to the occupational attainment tradition in stratification research: what it claims to explain, the basic kinds of models in it invokes, and the kind of evidence it adduces on their behalf. I begin with Blau and Duncan's version of these three elements and them move on to later developments in the tradition.

Blau and Duncan are explicit that their goal is to explain stratification: "the understanding of social stratification in modern society is best promoted by the systematic investigation of occupational status and mobility" (p. 5). They do not define stratification narrowly but take it in the usual sociological sense that connects it with class, status, and power. Facets of stratification associated with class and status are based on occupational structure: "the hierarchy of prestige strata and hierarchy of economic classes have their roots in the occupation structure; so does the hierarchy of political power and authority." (p. 7) Thus their basic explanatory goal is a complete explanation of stratification in the full bodied sense.

The models they build to achieve this goal essentially involve occupations and the variables that influence assignment of individuals to those occupations. US occupations are divided into 17 different categories. Blau and Duncan then ask how individuals are sorted to those categories. Their basic model "dissects the process of occupational mobility by tracing the interdependence among four determinants of occupation achievement, two of which refer to a man's social background (father's education and father's occupation), and two of which refer to his own training and early experience that prepare him for his subsequent career (education and first job)" (p. 402). Since on their view occupational status and mobility best explains stratification, these variables are essential to it as well.

One important thing to note about Blau and Duncan's matching process is that it results, in their words, in "achievement." Individuals are matched to positions in large by their ability to perform the relevant function. Efficiency assures that on average the best people are assigned to the appropriate tasks: "the achieved status of man, what he has accomplished in terms of some objective criteria, becomes more important than his ascribed status" (p. 430); this results from "a pervasive concern with efficiency." (p. 430).

Blau and Duncan support their models with data from a survey of a large national sample of men. They analyze their data with regressions and path analyses (to separate direct from indirect effects). They evaluate how well their regression models fit the data by two criterion: tests of significance and percent explained variance. The former concerns the odds of seeing the sample correlations when no correlations are present in the population. Explained variance concerns how accurately their sample independent variables predict their sample dependent variables. Blau and Duncan do note that these criteria have their failings--any correlation in large enough sample will be significant and explained variance isn't always a good indicator of causes. Nonetheless, they invoke both to show that their specific model of mobility is well supported.

Developments after Blau and Duncan move in at least two directions. Occupational scales and path analysis continues, but further variables concerning individual traits indicative of skills are included. Jencks et. al (1972), for example, find surrogates for IQ and include that in the regression equations. In certain respects the Bell Curve is an extension of this development. Economists also extend related models with an added emphasis on human capital, i.e. investments in human skills, and a particular concern with effects not just on occupational status but income (Becker 1975). All this work adopts the same criteria of success as Blau and Duncan--statistical significance and explained variance--though without the hesitations that Blau and Duncan expressed.

A second direction for this tradition of stratification research adopts new statistical methods, namely, log linear analysis. Doing so allows them to avoid the hierarchical gradational model of occupations and to just look at probabilities of moving from one category to another. This work generally finds noticeably greater affects for ascriptive processes than did Blau and Duncan or Jencks et. al.

SECTION III: NARROWNESS OF VISION

No doubt much careful work has gone into the occupational attainment tradition and our understanding has been improved. Yet I want to argue that the its data is not as solid and that its explanation not as deep as they might be. Important causes of the three sorts mentioned earlier have been excluded. Adding them in could make for more credible results. In this section I describe how.

One consequence of the web approach to scientific method noted earlier is that inference from data to hypotheses is never a purely logical or formal matter. Inference always must be made against the background of and with the help of what else is known. Trying to treat scientific inference as purely logical is thus likely to make for uncompelling results because mechanical rules are being asked to do more than they can. A paradigm instance of this error is the use of statistics, particularly significance testing, in the social sciences (they are not alone in this error).

Blau and Duncan are no exception to this generalization. They invoke statistical significance as a criterion of acceptability for their favored models. But statistical significance cannot do want they want, especially if they want to use it in arguments with others who believe that the causal variables studied have greater or less importance than Blau and Duncan attribute to them. Blau and Duncan's significance tests tell us the probability of seeing a correlation of the observed size in our sample when there is no correlation at all in the population. Someone who thinks the relations between education and attainment are weaker than Blau and Duncan conclude can argue as follows: I believe the true correlation in the population is X, where X is less than the amount observe in Blau and Duncan's sample. The probability of seeing Blau and Duncan's sample correlation when the true correlation in the population is X is also less than .05. In short, the competing hypothesis can claim statistical significance as well. At this point statistical significance does not decide between competitors and further and different kinds of evidence is called for. Such evidence might include case study evidence, historical evidence, longitudinal studies, and so on. It is only by ignoring the web of testing that Blau and Duncan can act as if the statistical evidence is decisive.

Here is also an example where the reflexivity of the web approach pays benefits. If we take a historical and sociological look at the practice of significance testing, it is much easier to appreciate its limitations. Current statistical practice in the social sciences (and similar story can be told for the natural sciences) is a hodge-podge of the very different theoretical approaches of Fisher, Neyman and Pearson, and Bayesians. Much of current practice would be endorsed by none of these three approaches. Through an interesting historical and sociological process (see Gigerenzer et. al 1989) the current rhetoric of significance tests (McCloskey 1985) established itself as a powerful force, one of dubious merit.

I want to move now from these more methodological issues to substantive theoretical weaknesses. To set up these issues, let's recall the basic elements of the status attainment explanations. They work this way: A set of relevant individual traits are identified. Then it is claimed that there is some process assigning individuals to positions because they have those traits. There are important issues about the nature of that matching process which I shall get to later. At this point, however, I want to assume the matching process is unproblematic and focus instead on the presuppositions of this sort of explanation.

On the web view adopted here, what counts in good explanation is not a purely formal or logical matter. One way this fact surfaces is that explanations have a pragmatic or contextual nature. If we think of explanations as answering a question, these contextual features are obvious. If I ask why Adam ate the apple, my question is ambiguous until further parameters are spelled out: Do I want to know why he ate it rather than threw it? Do I want to know why Adam rather than Eve ate the apple? Do I want to know why Adam ate the apple rather than the nearby pear? In each question there is a different implicit contrast class. It is this contrast class that is set by context or pragmatic factors in an explanation.

The occupational attainment explanations ask why an individual obtained the occupation that he or she has. They answer by appeal to individual traits and a matching process. In other words, they are asking this question: Why did individual I1 get occupation O1 rather than O2...On? However, this is not the only question we might ask. We might instead ask why did individual I1 get an occupation from the set O1...On rather than set On+1...m? The first question takes the distribution of occupations as given, the latter does no--t it asks why there is one distribution rather than another. Occupational attainment theory answers the first, but that leaves the second question unanswered.

Another way to see the point is via this homey example. We have a pen full of different dogs. Each day a truck drives up and dumps bones into the pen. Canine warfare ensures. After the fighting is over, we can ask why each individual got their respective bones, some big and some little. We can answer with the individual traits of the dogs. But that is not the only answer or a full explanation. What is missing? Missing is the size distribution of the bones on the truck. Identifying the relevant traits of our canine competitors tells us nothing about this fundamental question.

So the now hopefully obvious point is that the occupational attainment research tradition does not explain important aspects of social structure but instead takes them as given. The types of occupations and their relative status, authority, rewards, and so on are taken as given and left unexplained.

This is unfortunate for two reasons. First, it means the occupational attainment tradition misses confounding and complicating causes. This can occur in two seemingly obvious ways: by ignoring race and sex. Blau and Duncan's work as well as Jencks et. al completely leaves out gender. Their results are based on a sample composed entirely of men. That means the effects they identify are not entirely accurate. The factors that they claim influence education will do so less in the population at large, for at the time of their sample women received less education than men--gender here is a complicating cause. The influence of education on occupational status will also be misestimated, for discrimination against women with education equal to that of men will reduce the total influence of education. In this case gender is again a complicating cause--it intervenes between education and occupation as it were.

The other reason to regret that structure is presupposed is that it leaves us with incomplete explanations--ones that ignore important structural causes in my terminology. This criticism is not new to me, though I have given it a more general framework than is usually the case. Critics usually remark that there is no place for power or social structure and leave it at that. But the really interesting question is how to bring social structure in and what that involves. We discuss this issue in the last section.

Another substantive weakness of the status attainment literature is its functionalism. Blau and Duncan defend the view that it is objective rational standards that by and large account for who is assigned to what positions in the status hierarchy; those objective standards assure that those individuals with the best traits for a given position occupy that position. Here they are continuing the functionalist tradition of Davis and Moore (1945), even though they do not explicitly endorse a thorough going functionalism about social organization in general.

Of course functionalism as a general theory of society has been criticized for its conservatism, for ignoring conflict, for the unfalsifiability of its claims, and so on. No doubt there is something to these criticisms. Yet they are at such a level of generality their force and the positive remedies they suggest are obscured. Assessing Blau and Duncan's more specific functionalist thesis in the concrete can thus be of value.

We must ask two crucial questions of Blau and Duncan's functionalist thesis: individuals assigned to positions are the best among what reference group and by what criteria are they the best? The neoclassical economic model resting in the background would answer the first question with "all those in the market offering similar traits." But such markets are usually a fiction--individuals obtaining positions are chosen from a restricted set of individuals. It is in those restrictions that crucial sociological factors enter in. Few jobs are filled in an open spot market comprised of bidding by all the relevant sellers of the skill in question. Rather research shows that informal networks are crucial in determining who fills open positions (Granovetter 1995). Networks in turn often form around categorical differences and inequalities--among ethnic, gender, and racial groups. So moving down from the abstract levels of functionalist theory to look at actual matching processes thus shows another way social structure and stratification must be incorporated. Social structure is lurking not only in the overall ranking of positions but also in the way individuals find their way to those positions. In other words, social structure is involved not just in determining rewards to positions but in the matching process itself.

Answering the second question--best by what criteria?--leads to a similar conclusion. The functionalist view cannot be that the best individual gets the job but rather the best individual relative to the cost of getting him or her to perform the job. But what it takes to induce individuals to perform a given job does not fall from the sky or from human nature alone. Those with fewer preexisting resources are in a worse bargaining position and likely will be forced to take less than their better off competitors. However, the resources individuals come with again brings in social structure and stratification. Differences in wealth are obviously one relevant form of stratification. Intersecting with that divide are differences in gender, race, ethnic group, union status, and other informal networks. In other words, social and cultural capital matter too. Again social structure and stratification are not just involved in determining the rungs of the ladder, they are intimately involved in determining who stands on those rungs.

SECTION IV: BRINGING STRUCTURE IN

Blau and Duncan attempt to relate individual behavior to facts about social stratification. But in the end they have no account of social stratification. In this section I look at several recent attempts to give social structure a real place.

Fisher et. al (1996) provide a recent critique of the Bell Curve variant of the status attainment tradition. They do a seemingly powerful job of criticizing Herrnstein and Murray. Moreover, they note the need for a structural alternative to the individual-level story that Hernstein and Murray tell: much inequality "can only be understood by leaving the individual level of analysis and looking at the social structure of inequality" (p. 99).

Here is what Fisher et. al give us: "the answer to why societies vary in their structure of rewards is more political. In significant measure, societies choose the height and breadth of their "ladders"...intentional policies have significantly constructed the inequalities we have." (p. 8-9). It is government decisions to promote jobs, provide education, and the like that determine the structure of inequality, not the traits of individuals.

No doubt government policies matter. Yet pointing to the role of government is not a sufficient account of social stratification--it does not get at the basic social processes at work. Significant stratification exists across very different political regimes and policies. Why does this inequality persist regardless? What processes beyond individual-level sorting are at work? Government policies may explain some of the variation in stratification, but they do not explain stratification itself.

Another influential approach to adding structure goes by the heading of "the new structuralism" (Sorenson and Kahlberg 1981). The new structuralism was a reaction to the status attainment tradition and to its related cousin in economics, human capital theory. The new structuralism objected to the claims of those groups that efficient processes match individual traits to occupations. Social processes, they claimed, play an important role.

The new structuralists claimed that the relevant social processes were best described by identifying two fundamental sectors of occupations or jobs: the primary or core sector and the secondary or periphery sector. Different processes operated in the two sectors, with high paying, stable jobs being found in the core and low paying, low tenure jobs dominating in the periphery. Various traits were identified as crucial to the differences: for example, large firm size, internal labor markets, unionization in the core sector and not in the periphery.

The evidence for the new structuralist accounts came from regressing sector variables along with individual variables and asking whether the former made any difference. Statistical significance and explained variance are once again key criteria for success.

The new structuralism nonetheless does not solve the problems of the occupational attainment paradigm. Critics have focused above all on its apparent circularity. Low wage and job instability is the measure for sectors and the sectors explain low wages and instability. But the bigger problem for my purposes is that the new structuralism really does a poor job of bringing structure in. It does not add the kind of virtues outlined in the opening section in least the following interrelated ways:

> 1.) Sectors are delineated and invoked in a very atheoretical way. Why there should be just two sectors, why different processes should operate in each, and why there should be a division sharp enough to qualify as qualitatively different sector is not well motivated. Traits characteristic of the sectors were identified in an ad hoc manner, often by statistical hunting.

> 2.) It is not clear that the occupational attainment tradition in some form cannot explain the phenomena identified. Differences in employee traits such as education, skill, past training, etc. may equally explain the differences without the need to invoke sectors. Internal labor markets for example may be more efficient at identifying relevant employee traits

than outside hiring in the case of highly skilled jobs. In short, the new structuralism does not show why structure is necessary.

3.) Industrial sectors are not homogeneous in terms of the kinds of jobs, processes, etc. that are found. Internal labor markets and outside hiring can be combined in the same firm. In effect, industrial sectors are not "real entities," firms and governments are. Sectors are constructs that are orthogonal to the actual institutions that matter.

4.) The new structuralism does not provide convincing mechanisms or processes that bring about structural difference--that realize or ground categorical distinctions between occupations.

The overriding moral is that the new structuralism does not really explain stratification. What prevents it from doing so is its implicit abstract empiricism in Mills' terminology--its inability to move successfully up and down the ladder of abstraction. Social structure is treated as another "variable" to be added to the equations, a variable specified in an ad hoc, atheoretical way.

I want to turn now to another attempt to bring structure in that fares considerably better, namely, that of Charles Tilly in *Durable Inequality* (1988). Tilly's work is an improvement in that it both avoids the individualism of the occupational attainment literature and in that it provides a much more theoretically motivated account.

Tilly argues that inequality cannot be explained simply as a function of the traits of individuals. Crucial is "categorical inequality": the social grouping of individuals into types which is part and parcel of producing systematic differences. The differences are systematic in that mechanisms exist reinforcing the differences; categorical inequalities do not depend solely or primarily on conscious discrimination.

Tilly's mechanisms are four: exploitation, opportunity hording, emulation, and adaptation. Categorical inequality exists because it allows individuals with control over resources to exclude others. Exploitation occurs when those controlling a resource use a categorical difference to prevent individuals from receiving the full value of their contribution from a joint activity. Opportunity hoarding results when a resource is confined to one category of individuals. Emulation is the process of starting new organizations by drawing on existing categories. Adaptation involves developing more effective ways of interacting that draw upon existing social categories. These processes gain strength when categorical differences are paired (whites are supervisors and blacks production workers), when many organizations adopt the relevant categories, and when the categorical differences lead to systematically different experiences for the corresponding individuals.

The virtues of this account over those considered previously are many. It is not just the traits of individuals--either skills of those placed or the attitudes of those doing the placing--that explains. Individuals promote their own well being by producing and reproducing existing social categories. The categorical differences are tied to individual behavior by a set of mechanisms that provide a general theory of why and how differences are sustained. Social structure is explained rather than simply invoked as it was in the new structuralist approach.

Tilly's account goes far beyond the occupational attainment literature, the new structuralism view, or the political explanations of Herrnstein and Murray's critics. It gives social stratification a real place and does so without simply treating it as a piecemeal variable along the lines of abstract empiricism. In that regard it shows how moving up and down the ladder of abstraction can greatly contribute to our understanding. Yet it does not go as far as we would like in that direction. If we take the web of theory and ladder of abstraction ideas seriously, we can note distinct ways that Tilly's story can be deepened and improved.

One sign that Tilly has not fully balanced detail and abstraction is the functionalism implicit in his account of structure. On Tilly's view, categorical inequality : "categorical inequality persists [because it]facilitates exploitation and opportunity hoarding...lowers transaction costs....solves organizational problems." In short, categorical inequality exists because it serves certain purposes.

I do not think that functional explanations are inherently suspect (see Kincaid 1996, Chpt. 4). But they are suspect when they do not move up and down the ladder of abstraction. Attributing functions and needs at the societal level without further detail is grand theory of the sort we want to avoid. Tilly (2000) explicitly denies that he makes such attributions, arguing that his functionalism is only a "weak" variant, one that only claims that practices exist because they serve particular actors.

Such "weak" functionalism is not so innocuous, however. We can claim to eliminate societal functions in favor of individual purposes, but then we have to ask whether our picture of individual motivation is plausible. And it is here that Tilly's story runs aground. Tilly has implicitly relied on a rational actor model and the poverty of individual motivation that it promotes.

For Tilly categorical equality persists because it promotes individual self interest, given the social structure already in place. This is doubtful on two counts: it is not at all clear that categorical inequality is as productive as Tilly makes it out to be and it is very clear that Tilly gives us a very truncated picture of individual motivation. The first problem arises because we get no detailed story why emulating and adapting to existing categories is most efficient. After all, categorical inequalities have their costs as well--individuals rebel against discrimination, for example. Why think that those costs are always outweighed by the relevant gains? Short of some strong functionalist assumption, there is no a priori reason that reproducing discrimination, sexism, etc. is inevitably the most efficient way of proceeding.

Tilly's account makes important contributions to tying individual processes to larger social structure and in that sense illustrates moving up and down the ladder of abstraction. However the web approach to inquiry suggests much more can be done and that doing so will help remove his functionalist accesses in the process. There are psychological and social psychological processes that undergird categorical discrimination and that more fully explain its persistence than does the simple self interest model of Tilly. There are other social process not mentioned by Tilly that also contribute to the persistence of inequality. Bringing these different phenomena into the story would strengthen Tilly's mechanism and increase the empirical warrant for his account by relating it to other well developed work.

I want to sketch briefly how these bridges might be built. Let's start with the psychological underpinnings. There is a significant body of work describing psychological mechanisms that promote categorical inequality. Among them are:

The fundamental attribution error (Ross 1977): A substantial body of experimental research shows that individuals naturally tend to make environmental causes into traits of individuals. Whether this is a fundamental feature of human cognitive architecture or has some more contingent, social roots is beside the point. Apparently there are deep-rooted psychological processes that lead individuals to ignore the social construction of categories and to treat them as inherent features of individuals. These processes can help explain the persistence of categorical inequality independently of its usefulness.

Blaming the victim: A clearly related process is that individuals, when confronted with innocent victims in experimental situations easily concoct stories that eliminate the injustice and attribute the responsibility to the victim (Lerner and Miller 1978).

The nature of human categories: A substantial literature shows that humans reason with the use of prototypes--paradigm exemplars (Rosch 1978). In the social realm this translates into using social stereotypes (Bar-Tal, et.al 1989) that accentuate group differences and influence how information about groups is processed. Again regardless of the social or inherent roots of this practice, it can contribute to reproducing social categories and thus categorical inequality.

Ingroup bias: Experimental small group research shows that when individuals are divided into groups, they exhibit biased judgments towards that group no matter how arbitrary the group is in terms of individual traits (Tajfel and Turner 1979). Once again we have a psychological mechanism that would help explain the persistence of categorical distinctions and thus categorical inequality.

Intrapunitive response patterns (Milner 1983): members of oppressed groups across a wide range of circumstances show a tendency to attribute responsibility for their position to their own individual traits. Such a response would contribute to categorical inequality.

The work cited above is largely done from a tradition that treats the psychological separate from the social. That does not prevent it from nonetheless helping us to move down the ladder of abstraction to get some better idea of how categorical inequality is brought about by individual behavior. However, a better account yet would connect individual level process more intimately with their social context. On the view defended in this volume it is an error to treat the psychological as somehow separate from the social--as just another independent variable as it were. The need for this connection is lurking in the work described above. "Intropunitive response patterns," for example, hints at the emotional responses resulting from and feeding into inequality, but does so in a lame way.

A more thorough going psychological and social account might connect categorical inequality to work on shame and its social origins. "Intrapunative responses" are indications of shame. Shame is a social emotion by definition, and a plausible account of its origin is that shame arises from threats to the social bond (Scheff 1988, 2000). Categorical inequality is one such threat--it excludes and precludes social ties. The work of Van Ausdale and Feagin discussed below shows that categorical inequality begins breaking social ties at a very young age indeed--as early as three years of age. Breaking those bonds leads to shame; shame in turn leads to actions that reinforces categorical inequality. Howard (1995) for example notes how gender inequality promotes self mutilation. Self mutilation is an adaptation to categorical inequality that allows it to persist. This is no doubt the rudiments of a theory, but it shows again how both Tilly's account can be further tied to other work as we move down the ladder of abstraction and psychological accounts of difference might be improved by moving up the ladder of abstraction to bring in more general social categories.

So we can replace Tilly's functionalism with plausible processes at the individual level described in their social context. Moreover, there are further social processes that can be used to extend those already identified by Tilly. The most obvious is socialization. Van Ausdale and Feagin (2001), for example, have observed young children at play in a natural environment (rather than being questioned by adults) and have shown that children make racial distinctions very early on. Moreover, those distinctions are used by children in a systematic way in their interaction with each other--they not only have the concept of race but employ it in learning and defining authority and status relationships outside the home. Categorical inequalities are not just used by adults to "solve problems"; they are built into ways of relating as children develop.

Other social processes worth mentioning include the cultural values that penetrate media of all kinds and direct violence by those on the more powerful side of a categorical inequality. In US society violence enforcing racial categories may be much diminished from past decades (though not eliminated). That is not the case with violence against women which remains rampant and certainly helps reinforce categorical divisions of gender. Media take up and amplify the categories behind categorical inequality--many of the children discussed above who used racial categories had parent who strongly denied ever using such categories at home.

CONCLUSION

A central idea of this volume is that progress in social science requires acknowledging the web of theory, the process of moving up and down the ladder of abstraction, and the social processes influencing social research itself. The problems with traditional attainment models of social structure flow in large from missing these morals, both in interpreting evidence and in the kinds of explanations given. Attempts to go beyond the attainment tradition make important steps towards removing these difficulties. But a firm emphasis on the web of theory and ladder of abstraction notions suggest that more can be done. I have sketched how diverse other literatures might be brought in to deepen, further support, and correct work like that of Tilly, which in itself is an important advance of the attainment approach to inequality.

REFERENCES

Bar-Tal, D., Graumann, C., Kruglanski, A., and Stroebe, W. 1989. *Stereotyping and Prejudice: Changing Conceptions*. Berlin: Springer.
Becker, G. 1975. *Human Capital*. New York: National Bureau of Economic Research.

Blau, Peter M. and Duncan, Otis. 1967. *The American Occupational Structure*. New York: Free Press.

Fisher, C., Hout, M., Jankowski, M., Lucas, S., Swidler, A, and Voss, K. 1996. *Inequality By Design*. Princeton: Princeton University Press.

Gigerenzer, G., Swijtink, Z., Porter, T., Daston, L., Beatty, J., and Krueger, L. 1989. *The Empire of Chance*. Cambridge: Cambridge Unversity Press.

Granovetter, Mark. 1995. *Getting A Job*. Chicago: University of Chicago Press.

Jencks, C., Smith, M., Acland, H., Bane, M., Cohen, D., Gintis, H., Heyns, B., and Michelson, S. 1972. *Inequality: A Reassessment of the Effect of Family and Schooling in America*. New York: Basic Books.

Howard, Rhonda E. 1995. *Human Rights and the Search for Community*. Boulder: Westview Press.

Kincaid, Harold. 1996. *Philosophical Foundations of the Social Sciences: Analyzing Controversies in Social Research*. Cambridge: Cambridge University Press.

Lerner, M.J. and Miller, D.T. 1978. "Just world research and the attribution process." *Psychological Bulletin* 85: 1030-1051.

McCloskey, D. N. 1985. "The Loss Function Has Been Mislaid: The Rhetoric of Significance Tests." *American Economic Review* 75: 2011-205.

Milner, D. 1983. *Children and Race: Ten Years On*. London: Ward Lock Educational.

Rosch, E. 1978. "Principles of Categorization." In E. Rosch and B. Llloyds, *Cognition and Categorization*. Hillsdale, N.J.: Erlbaum.

Scheff, Thomas. 1988. "Emotion and False Consciousness." *Theory, Culture, and Society* 5: 57-80.

Scheff, Thomas. 2000. "Shame and the Social Bond: A Sociological Theory." *Sociological Theory* 18: 84-96.

Sorensen, Aage and Kalleberg, Arne. 1981. "An Outline of a Theory of the Matching of Persons to Jobs." In *Sociological Perspectives on Labor Markets*. Ed. Ivar Berg. New York: Academic Press.

Tajfel, H. and Turner, J. 1979. "An Integrative Theory of Intergroup Conflict." In W. Austin and S. Worchel, *The Social Psychology of Intergroup Relations*. Monterey, CA: Brooks/Cole.

Tilly, Charles. 1998. *Durable Inequality*. Berkeley: University of California Press.

Tilly, Charles. 2000. "Relational Studies of Inequality." *Contemporary Sociology* 29:782-785.

van Ausdale, Debra and Feagin, Joe. 2001. *The First R: How Children Learn Race and Racism*. Lanham: Rowman and Littlefield.

Introduction to Chapter 6

Granting Weber's contributions to the development of a discipline that yields insights into all social phenomena, his *The Protestant Ethic and the Spirit of Capitalism* is simplistic in its analysis of the early development of capitalism. Weber can best be honored not by an uncritical assessment of his thesis but rather by acknowledging the complexity of the phenomena he examined and bringing to bear our current broad understanding of that empirical reality. Lachmann does not limit himself to looking at the broad sweep of history. Much as historians generally do, he developed a detailed focus on specific historical situations which yielded a transformation from feudalism to capitalism in his earlier work, *Capitalists in Spite of Themselves*: *Elite Conflict and Economic Transitions in Early Modern Europe*. Using that work as a starting point, he employs a web approach to the scientific method to develop broad generalizations and link literatures to one another. In this way he is able to move from his earlier findings about how elites have operated at specific times and places to how social behavior is generally constructed and understood. In this way he builds on his earlier research on conflicts among elites operating within certain historical contexts by linking that understanding to long-term and very general processes that include large-scale social structures along with the structures of the individual. We can understand this breadth from Table 1-1, with its inclusion of social structures, the situation, and individual structures. Lachmann succeeds in providing a vital historical illustration of this incredible complexity, teaching us that it is indeed possible to understand the forces involved.

Chapter 6

A Critique of Pure Structure: The Limits of Rationality and Culture in the Transition from Feudalism to Capitalism

Richard Lachmann

Marx, Weber, and Durkheim were of two minds about the social science each thought he was founding. They each believed that the world had undergone a historically unique social transformation, beginning several centuries before their births. All three saw the need for a discipline that could describe that transformation, explain its origins, predict its future course, and determine the opportunities for altering, harnessing or ameliorating its effects. Thus, all three at times presented their intellectual project as a science of the specific origins and dynamics of modern society.

One way of explaining what was new and different about modern society is through comparison with the universe of social forms. Thus, Marx, Weber, and Durkheim moved in their writings between the specific and the general, from descriptions of one social transformation to the formulation of general typologies and methodologies that they saw as applicable to all societies. In so doing, Marx, Weber, and Durkheim became founders of a general "science of society," and that is how they have become established within the field of sociology, especially in the United States.

Few sociologists today see themselves as part of a discipline that is concerned with the study of a single transformation. As a result, empirical challenges (from historians, mainly) to Marx and Weber's writings on specific historical transitions have had little effect on the reception (by sociologists) of their general theories. At the same time, sociologists have been prevented by their uncritical presentation of the Protestant Ethic thesis from responding to the decades-long assault by historians upon Weber's theoretical claims. Many sociologists are unaware of how some of the classics of our field are regarded from beyond the discipline[1], and therefore have not troubled themselves to reinvigorate Marx's and Weber's empirical studies with new research and fresh analysis. Sociologists (with the notable exception of world systems theorists) have abdicated the study of early capitalist development to scholars in other disciplines.

Historians, in the face of the current sociological absence from debates on the origins of capitalism (and on the origins and consequences of the Protestant Reformation), use their refutations of specific empirical findings by Marx and Weber to reject Marxist and Weberian and indeed all sociological theory. We can preserve Weber's important justification for a cultural turn without having to pretend that his Protestant Ethic thesis still provides the best interpretation of the consequences of the Reformation. Indeed, we can best honor Weber's contribution by developing models that acknowledge our current, broader understanding of the empirical reality of religious practices during the Reformation.

Marx's and Weber's original projects did inspire avenues of research in various corners of sociology and related disciplines. One such corner was the (mainly Marxist, and mainly historians' and economists') study of the "transition from feudalism to capitalism." Another niche is the Weberian-inspired study of rationalization and modernization, which draws inspiration from the Protestant Ethic thesis.[2] My interest in studying the origins of capitalism stemmed from my conviction that existing work in both these areas was inadequate. The Marxist transition debate has never yielded an explanation for the temporal and spatial differences in the forms of capitalist development. Modernization theory has been rejected just as thoroughly (and with even more justification) as Weber's original Protestant Ethic thesis.

Marx, while vague on the historical details of the process, presented class conflict as the dynamic within feudalism that gave rise to a bourgeoisie and to capitalism. The perceived inability of Marx and his successors to draw a clear causal connection between feudal class conflict and capitalism has led most subsequent scholars, Marxist and non-

Marxist alike, to assert that there was no dynamic within feudalism that could yield capitalism, and therefore an external dynamic set in train the transition from feudalism. The external dynamics are variously urban markets, a world system, demographic crisis or expansion, the Protestant Ethic, or intellectual and technological innovation. The difficulty with this position is that the favored external force had such widely varying effects across time and space. The urban centers of medieval Europe did not become the loci of subsequent economic development, despite their advantages of greater capital accumulation and control over then existing trade networks. Similarly, not all the original Protestant regions of Europe became early centers of capitalist enterprise. Technological innovations often took centuries to be adopted, and the original utilizers of a new technology often failed to achieve market dominance, or lost their advantage selling their know-how to rivals.[3]

The Black Death of 1348 is seen by most historians as the great divide in the history of feudal agrarian economies. Thereafter, the peasants of most of Eastern Europe were reenserfed while most English and French tenants won greater degrees of autonomy from their manor lords. Authors who see the Black Death as the external force that undermined feudalism have been unable to explain the divergent results of the common European demographic decline (Brenner, 1976, 1982).

Maurice Dobb (1946) initiated modern Marxist scholarship on this point by noting that serfdom, like all other systems of forced labor, required extensive supervision to ensure that laborers worked hard enough to produce a surplus in addition to their own subsistence needs. The low level of agricultural productivity in feudal times made it unprofitable in many places for lords to invest in the military and administrative forces necessary to detain and supervise peasant laborers. Dobb argues that serfdom was financially feasible only in those areas where there was a high land to population ratio and where greater inputs of labor would not raise the productivity of land (1946: 50-60). The former condition allowed lords to grant farms to serfs (thereby leaving to peasants the problem of their subsistence) while still retaining vast demesnes to produce grain which the lords could use or sell for their own needs. The latter condition obviated the need for much supervision: If land was only minimally productive regardless of the level of labor input, then highly motivated or intensively supervised labor would get no more out of poor quality land than would unmotivated and poorly supervised serfs. Both conditions were met only in Eastern Europe; thus peasants were reenserfed only in those areas.

Implicit in his logic, for Dobb does not analyze the dynamics of agrarian class relations under feudalism, is the conclusion that landlords in Western Europe did not impose serfdom because they could not make it pay. Instead, they commuted labor dues and rented out the demesne, thereby reducing administrative costs and ensuring rising rents when population began to recover in the latter half of the fifteenth century (1946: 60-70). Producers' abilities to accumulate capital and to transform the post-plague "petty mode of production" into genuine capitalism were limited by unfair competition from guilds and mercantile monopolies and from lords who continued to collect rent under the protection of the feudal state. Thus, the failure by Western European lords to reenserf peasants, which gave rise to the petty mode of production, was a necessary but by no means sufficient condition for the development of capitalism. Opportunities for producers to profit from exploiting a growing proletariat (as opposed to guilds profiting from market monopolies or petty producers profiting from self-exploitation) awaited the destruction of guild and aristocratic power in the 1640 English Revolution, which allowed "England...to accelerate enormously the growth of industrial capital in the next half-century-- a growth surpassing that of other countries which as yet lacked any similar political upheaval" (1946: 176).

Dobb's analysis of the transition from feudalism to capitalism suffers from a major flaw: He is unable to explain why there was a two-century lag from the abolition of servile labor after the Black Death to the development of private property in land and the proletarianization of a plurality of peasants in the century following the Henrician Reformation (Lachmann, 1987: 17). Nor is Dobb able to explain why similar petty modes of production, and similar late-feudal political systems produced a bourgeois revolution in England a century and a half earlier than in France.

DEVELOPING A SOLUTION TO A SOCIOLOGICAL PROBLEM: STUDYING ENGLAND FIRST

I saw that much work on this question went wrong because it adopted an essentialist approach, seeing a necessary unfolding of capitalism and/or modernity from within feudal or traditional society. New social forms can be created only by social beings acting within existing societies. Capitalism could only be a product of feudal actors in feudal societies. Thus, I began my study of capitalism with an investigation of the dynamics of feudalism.

I felt a need to slow down the examination of historical change. I turned away, for a start, from the broad sweep of transformation and sought instead to trace each change in social relations. My first goal was to specify the sequences of structural change, to try to specify when and where feudal social relations were transformed. I chose England as a first case study for two reasons. One was that capitalism developed in England first. Thus, by focusing on England I could avoid issues of borrowing. An explanation for English capitalism would have to be found within England itself. The other advantage of studying England was that the transition happened more quickly there than in any other early modern society. In 1500, more than 90% of English families were tenants on manors, enmeshed in the same social relations as their ancestors had been in the previous centuries of feudal society. By the time of the 1640 Revolution at least 40% of English families were landless, dependent upon wage labor for their subsistence. A majority of English families were landless wage laborers by the time of the 1688 Glorious Revolution (Lachmann, 1987: 17).

What happened in sixteenth century England? I found that the Reformation disrupted the balance of power among medieval elites and classes, although not in the way Weber imagined. Feudal societies were characterized by multiple elites, each of which maintained its own organizational basis for regulating agrarian production in order to sustain its capacity to independently extract resources from peasants.

My effort to diagram the flows of resources among English peasants and their exploiters allowed me to identify three distinct elites: the monarch, lay landlords, and the clergy. All three were part of what Marxists would view as a feudal ruling class in that they all extracted a surplus from peasants. However, they also constituted distinct elites in that they each had an interest in guarding their independent access to peasant resources from challenges by rival elites.

The organization of English manors reflected the ways in which each elite succeeded in institutionalizing its interests against rival elites as well as against peasants. The crown, clergy, and lay landlords manned separate judicial systems that regulated agrarian production so as to protect their income bases within manors. The system of land tenure and the structure of the peasantry as a class were shaped by this triple regulation.

The Reformation transformed the terrain of elite conflict. The crown was able to eliminate the clergy as an independent elite in one blow. Yet the crown was unable to realize most of the benefits of its appropriation of clerical powers and properties. Lacking the personnel to manage clerical institutions (the English crown had only a few dozen officials in the early sixteenth century), the crown surrendered most clerical lands and control over peasant land tenure to lay landlords (the gentry). The gentry were able to extract resources and regulate agrarian production as a single elite, no longer encumbered by the rival claims and demands of other elites.

The crown and clergy both, and usually in alliance, sought to reassert claims to agrarian production in the seventeenth century. Such efforts were understandable since each elite's survival and attainments were grounded ultimately in its control of resources, with land and agrarian labor being the preeminent sources of wealth in England and in the rest of Europe until the Industrial Revolution. The gentry responded to royal and clerical assertions by obliterating the manorial institutions that provided the juridical bases for the claims of those elites to agrarian resources. Landlords adopted an array of strategies (most famously enclosure) designed to eliminate the institutional bases for determining ancient crown and clerical claims upon manorial resources as well as to undermine tenant rights. Once enclosure was complete, with each landowner's holding marked by fences or hedges, the very ground upon which feudal elites or peasants could challenge the gentry's land rights had been scoured of the farming strips, the commons, and often the very villages that embodied feudal elite and class relations. The clean lines of private property and the new common law of land ownership ensured that kings, magnates, clerics, and peasants never would be able to reassert their medieval rights to land or its products.

FROM CASE STUDY TO COMPARISONS AND GENERALIZATIONS

The concept of elites I developed to explain the origins of English capitalism draws from Mills (1956). Like Mills, I see elites as defined by the institutions within which they are embedded. I also follow Mills in his realization that there can be multiple elites, as opposed to Mosca and Pareto who allowed for only a single dominant elite. I depart from Mills in that I see relations between elites as characterized by conflict much more than by cooperation.

I drew upon empirical investigations, carried out by historians and others, to understand the nature of elite and class relations in early modern England. In so doing, I hoped to identify the causal processes that resulted in the transition from feudalism to capitalism in a particu-

lar time and place. However, my interest was not confined to just constructing a better explanation of the origins of English capitalism. At
the same time, I was concerned with constructing a theoretical model
that could identify the salient differences across epochs of English history and that could allow me to make comparisons between England
and other cases. *From Manor to Market* was written to answer questions Marx and Weber posed in their work about historical change. My
answer, which departs significantly from Marx's and Weber's own arguments, generated theory that (I hope) offers a way to synthesize
Marxian and Weberian insights into a general model of historical
change that is applicable to different epochs and to various types of
social transformations.

From Manor to Market, in moving between empirical analysis and
theory formation, is an example of the process of tying the abstract to
the concrete. Scheff, in Chapter 10 in this volume, describes that as
tying together parts (specific moments of conflict and structural change
in my work) and wholes. The whole I attempt to realize is an understanding of the causal progression from elite to class conflict.

When I expanded my analysis to compare elite and class relations
across Western Europe, I found variations in the number of elites and
in the institutional bases for their autonomy and powers. Differences in
the structures of elite relations shaped the particular relations of production within each country or region. (This mode of comparison
makes clear that the significant unit of comparison often is the province or county rather than kingdom.) Elite relations, thus, determined
the varying outcomes of landlord-peasant conflicts and of the new systems of production which emerged across Europe after the Black Death
and then again in Western Europe in the centuries following the Reformation. I explain the differing and partial developments of capitalism, and of nation states, in Europe in the sixteenth through eighteenth
centuries by tracing the dual and interacting dynamics of elite and class
conflicts.

I want to illustrate the ways in which my approach addresses central Marxist and Weberian questions with an example from *Capitalists
in Spite of Themselves*.[4] Weber was concerned with rationalization and
Marxists (if not Marx himself) with the growing capacity of the ruling
class to regulate and mold peasant and working class ideologies. One
key instance of those processes was the decline of belief in witchcraft
and magic in England and France in the sixteenth and seventeenth centuries.

Historians' discoveries of how lightly Europeans bore the 'iron
cage' of rationality in the sixteenth through eighteenth centuries and
even beyond poses a theoretical as well as historical challenge to We-

ber's thesis. A difficulty with broad theories of rationalization, and with Marxist analyses of witch trials as a form of class war, is that they lack the specificity to account for the relatively few and localized episodes of witch trials in England and France or for differences in the timing of campaigns against witches across Europe. Elite efforts to control magic and to suppress witchcraft were episodic and localized; in neither England nor France did elites display a generalized impulse to uphold norms of rationality. Most French witch trials were between 1500 and 1670, and they were concentrated in particular villages and towns. In England, witchcraft was a crime only in the years 1542-47 and 1563-1735, with almost all prosecutions between 1580 and 1647. Most English witch trials were in Essex and a few other counties.

The numbers of trials and executions in England and France were slight compared with the far greater blood baths in the witch panics and inquisitions in Switzerland, Germany and Austria from 1561 to 1670. At the height of witch accusations and executions only 15 percent of English defendants in witchcraft trials were executed, compared with 49 percent in France, and over 90 percent in the German-speaking regions of Europe.

Elite attitudes toward magic were bound up in the wider web of interests surrounding religious offices and properties. This is not to claim that elites determined their views of magic after calculating their political interests. In any case such calculations often were confounded by the ideological confusion of the age: the proliferation of religious sects, competition among magical practitioners, and growing skepticism about man's capacity to mobilize supernatural forces in this world combined with optimism about the possibility of discovering and manipulating the forces of nature. People attempted to make order out of confusion by evaluating the character of magical claimants along with the content of their assertions. In other words, people of the Renaissance decided what to believe in part by settling upon whom to believe.

Spiritual allegiance to priests, ministers, and magicians had political and economic, as well as spiritual, consequences. As a result, lay people tended to trust magical practitioners whom they were able to control (or who were subordinated to the same authority as they were) and to fear magicians who were immune from their power. People who found all claimants of magical power were beyond their influence, or were allied with their enemies, tended to become skeptical of the very possibility of mobilizing supernatural forces in this world through the use of magic.

The stances of the official churches of the two nations toward magic varied in two significant ways.   First, the French Catholic

Church took the lead, in the seventeenth century, in educating laymen to its realization that most unofficial magicians were frauds rather than genuine instruments of the devil, while in England Anglican ministers were the last elite to doubt the ubiquity of white and black magic in this world. Second, French clerics enjoyed strong support from the crown and lay elites in their antimagic campaigns, while in England the gentry successfully attempted to undermine Anglican prosecutions of witches in almost all instances, and only rarely instigated its own trials of witches in secular courts. These differences in the sources of intellectual leadership for skepticism toward magic (clerical in France, lay in England) and in lay support for clerical attacks on magic (strong in France, negative in England), affected the differences in the post-Reformation practice of magic. French Catholic priests were the prime purveyors of magical solutions to quotidian problems, while in England commercial wizards filled most of the demand for such services. In England, the political uses of magic were successfully suppressed by the end of the Civil War even as commercial wizards continued to be left alone by state and church, while in France state and church battled with limited success against both political and commercial uses of magic through the end of the *ancien* regime.

The bishops and ministers of the Church of England, joined at the end of the sixteenth century by their royal sponsors, sought to restore a unified hierarchy of religious authority in the nation. From their perspective, rival ministers and practitioners of magic were at best misguided but more probably were instruments of the devil. The Anglican dream of reestablishing a monopoly of religious and magical power required challenging the spiritual as well as the institutional legitimacy of their rivals and proving the unique correctness of their own divine authority.

The Anglican hierarchy was the only English elite with a clear and unchanging opposition to popular magic during the entire period from the Henrician Reformation through the Civil War. Anglican efforts to act on their opposition to magic were stymied, until the end of the sixteenth century, because the crown supported gentry claims to authority over clerical offices and properties and tolerated religious dissent, including magic, as a way of weakening clerical autonomy.

The fusion of crown and clerical interests in opposition to dissent at the end of the sixteenth century affected gentry attitudes toward popular religion and magic. Before that moment, the gentry could oppose popular magic and radical sects without having to fear crown support for an attack by the Church of England on their religious autonomy. Once Elizabeth I shifted her policy to ally with the episcopacy, the gentry's prime religious interest became the protection of their dissent, even if that meant tolerance for lower-class magic and religion. The gentry became confident in their tolerance as they consolidated political control over county government and Parliament in the first decades of the seventeenth century.

The Anglican episcopate and the surviving Catholic priesthood made strong though conflicting claims to magical power; this predisposed gentry and other dissenters, who already distrusted both groups, to skepticism toward all magical claims. Many dissenters went further and denied Anglican and crown assertions to any form of magical power. Such "rationalism" among elite dissenters was reinforced in turn by fear of the consequences that would follow from a successful Anglican assertion of a monopoly on the legitimate use of magic.

The dissenters' rejection of magic *in toto* did not lead them, for the most part, to replace the Church of England's campaigns against popular magic with their own efforts to suppress witches and magicians. The institutional pluralism that dissenting ministers and their sponsors demanded to secure their own positions was linked of necessity to tolerance for the dissenting beliefs of other ministers and of common preachers and wizards. The institutional location of dissenting ministers and their lay sponsors predisposed them to oppose Anglican efforts to enforce orthodoxy against any targets.

How, then, can we explain the two waves of prosecutions of witches in England, which were mounted by laymen and heard in courts dominated by the gentry? Those prosecutions were concentrated in two periods, the 1580s and 1590s and 1645-47. Most trials were in Essex and Kent in the early period, and Essex, Norfolk and Suffolk in the 1640s. Trials were rare in the sixteenth century because while the crown and gentry lacked the capacities to enforce their faiths, they did have the institutional means to veto efforts by rivals to enforce orthodoxies of which they disapproved. Essex and Kent stand out as counties in which the gentry consolidated power unusually early, while they still had an interest in combating popular magic, because the crown had not yet attempted to enforce orthodoxy at their expense.

The second wave of witch trials, in 1645-47, followed Charles I's decisive defeat in the Civil War. Once the gentry had removed the threat to their interests from above, they turned on their former anti-royalist allies among the lower classes, purging radical elements in the New Model Army and sponsoring witch trials to counter popular assertions of access to magico-religious power.

The conjuncture, in 1645-47, of the royalists' imminent defeat and the heightened radical threat created a renewed gentry interest in limiting pluralism to attack popular magic. Only in Essex, Suffolk, and Norfolk did the gentry recreate unified county governments with the capacity to mount witch trials in time to meet the gentry's momentary political interest. After the decisive gentry victory over both royalist and radical forces, popular magic no longer represented a political threat. Apolitical wizards were tolerated because the absence of viable radical political movements emptied magic of its millennial content, reducing it to a quotidian service for the superstitious. The gentry no longer had an interest in pursing witches.

Catholic skepticism toward magic was first enunciated at the Council of Trent in 1564 when impostor sorcerers were distinguished from true practitioners. In the early seventeenth century, lay French judges began to punish impostor sorcerers as a category of criminal separate from, if as dangerous and as deserving of execution as, real witches. Despite those conceptual advances, neither lay nor clerical judges possessed the institutional capacities to pursue many witches or to educate the populace to the differences between witches who actually made pacts with the devil and the more common fraudulent witches. Catholic clerics' institutional and spiritual powers were under challenge from the crown, aristocrats, and corporate bodies throughout the sixteenth century. No French elite was willing to allow another the authority to regulate magical power, since each elite continued to exert control over spiritual forces and clerical offices.

As clerics were incorporated within the absolutist state, the French Catholic Church gained the institutional resources and cooperation from lay elites and judicial officers to carry out the post-Tridentine attack upon real and false witches and a reform of popular practices. The causal primacy of institutional over ideological factors in the initiation of antimagic campaigns is demonstrated by the geographic location as well as the timing (beginning more than a century after the Council of Trent) of reform efforts by the Catholic hierarchy. Tridentine reforms were most successfully carried out in those provinces where bishops were appointed by royal governors who exercised control over lesser nobles and over lay courts, and enjoyed the support of the crown.

Once French elites, Protestant and Catholic, were incorporated within the absolutist state, the exercise of magical power no longer was a criterion for, or a reflection of, the distribution of clerical assets. Magic ceased to be a basis for elite competition. Lay elites abandoned their claims to magical powers in the late sixteenth and seventeenth centuries and acquiesced in the suppression of such practices in areas under their control.

The final defeat in 1653 of aristocratic Frondes against the crown ushered in more than a century of relative peace among French elites. Elite magic neither advantaged its practitioners in efforts to control clerical assets nor threatened the positions of other elites. Elites perceived magic as a danger only when popular magicians who inspired or directed peasant rebellions invoked it. Magic, then, remained a source of danger to the French ruling class without providing a source of power to any elite in that class against another. Under such conditions, lay elites and parish clergy became more receptive to the longstanding position of Catholic intellectuals that most magicians were frauds rather than true witches in a pact with the devil.

Elite skepticism became so strong during the eighteenth century that prosecutions of witches was largely abandoned in favor of efforts to stamp out popular religious practices through education and clerical supervision. Prosecutions were employed only during times of peasant rebellions, and then radical witches were usually tried for crimes of sedition rather than for sorcery. Trials of witches, thus, fell off abruptly at the end of the seventeenth century.

Elites and to some extent others in England and France became more skeptical toward magicians and their claims in the Renaissance era. My historical analysis indicates that elites lost an interest in manipulating supernatural forces themselves as the possibilities of increasing their control over clerical institutions was lost. The timing and manner in which specific elites lost the opportunity to compete for clerical assets varied in the two countries and, as a result, the sequence in which English and French elites rejected magic differed as well. Further, the degree to which lay and clerical elites attempted to enforce conformity to their views depended upon their perceptions of threats to their interests from magicians and their followers.

My comparison of antimagic campaigns in England and France suggests that elites weighed that threat primarily in terms of their control over clerical properties and powers. Such control, in turn, was determined primarily by the structures of relations among elites. Those structures determined who had the capacity to persecute witches and thereby selected the timing, the geographical and social locations, the targets (black witches or charlatans), and the strategies (countermagic, witch trials, or education) employed by elites to eliminate the dangers that uncontrolled magic appeared to pose to their social worlds.

Early modern Europeans were rational about their this- and otherworldly spiritual interests in the same way they were rational about their economic and political interests. Elites and others were able to determine their immediate and local interests and were capable of identifying which allies-- temporal and spiritual--and which magical or "rational" modes of action would help them to sustain their positions against their enemies. Europeans approached the Weberian ideal type of rationality only when, and to the extent to which, their social situations created opportunities for and interests in such thoughts and actions. Such rational ideologies and strategies developed in response to the unanticipated structural changes that were engendered by elite and class conflicts.

Elite conflicts consolidated states and classes and narrowed local variations in elite interests and capacities. Elites came to share similar "rational" orientations to the extent that they merged into unified classes, inhabiting nation-states within a consolidating transnational capitalist economy. Elite conflicts propelled structural change that in turn altered the contexts within which all social actors understood and pursued their material and spiritual interests.

From Historical Answers to Appropriate Theoretical Generalizations: A Secondary Analysis of *Capitalists In Spite of Themselves* in Terms of the Web Approach

How does the elite conflict model developed in *Capitalists In Spite of Themselves* contribute to the development of sociological theory? I see two benefits stemming from this comparative historical analysis. First, *Capitalists in Spite of Themselves* offers new answers to the historically specific questions posed by Marx and Weber, questions which they and their successors have not been able to fully answer. My identification and specification of elite conflict as the primary dynamic of change in medieval and early modern Europe provides a way of explaining the two-century lag between the Black Death and the first development of capitalism, and of accounting for divergences in the timing and forms of development across Europe. In so doing, I am able to address Weber's accurate observation that capitalism began to emerge after the Reformation, without having to resort to his historically discredited argument in *The Protestant Ethic*. I even am able to explain the scope and timing of religious rationalization and the decline of magic, issues central to Weber's work, as outcomes mediated through elite conflict.

Second and more broadly, my model provides a new way of thinking about human agency. I sought to explain when and how social actors decide to change their usual behaviors, and how social actors understand the choices, of both actions and allies, open to them in moments of unusual flux.

I began to address those issues by highlighting my findings on the whens and wheres of structural change. Significant structural change, I found in my study of Western Europe over five centuries, was rare. Non-elites were doubly constrained in their opportunities for effective agency. First, as Marx indicates, by the slow change in the forces of production and the resulting balance of class forces; second, by the capacities of multiple elites to embed their autonomy in organizational means for extracting resources from the productive classes. Non-elites were divided and their interests shaped by the ways in which groups of producers and facets of production were incorporated within different elite organizations of appropriation. Opportunities for agency by subordinate classes were created primarily by changes in the structure of elite relations. Elite conflicts, by disrupting ties between elites and fractions of the producing classes, increase opportunities for class agency by allowing producers to merge interests and capacities previously lodged in separate elite-imposed organizations of production.

Capitalists in Spite of Themselves was written to address a single, albeit seminal, social transformation. The book concludes with a brief chapter that identifies some general theoretical implications of my specific comparative historical findings. The conclusion addresses literatures on world systems, revolutions, geopolitics, ideology, networks, and rational choice. The conclusion does not attempt to draw a map that relates those literatures to one another, or to locate my work's place within a holistic vision of sociology as a discipline. I take up *that task now with a secondary analysis of Capitalists in Spite of Themselves* through the prism of the web approach to the scientific method, as presented in the Chapter 1 of this volume and embodied in Table 1-1, "Elements of Behavior and Structuring of Behavior."

The web approach to the scientific method in parallel with my structural analysis is concerned with the ways in which social actors proceed from understanding and reproducing their existing social situations to attempting the rare and difficult task of transforming their social world. While writing my book, I was concerned with explaining how social actors engage in that process in certain historical moments. My concern with general sociological theory was confined, for the most part, to refuting what I saw as false propositions from various perspectives.

The web approach is most helpful, for me, in identifying a way to build my specific findings about how elites embed their interests in institutions into a general model of how social behavior is constructed and understood. That process has been described by Wallerstein as a "war on two fronts" (1991: 8). Wallerstein explains that the *Annales* movement found a way to escape "the epistemological squeeze between the concentration on the infinitely small in space and time by idiographic historians and the concentration on the infinitely small in scope and eternal in time of nomothetic social scientists." They did so by "using the double temporality of persisting structures slow to change and cyclical conjonctures within these structures (12).

The *Annales* solution was one way; there are others, including Wallerstein's own world system analysis. The web approach is a third, and it is one that I am able to use to explain (in a way I did not accomplish directly in *Capitalists in Spite of Themselves*) how my elite conflict analysis engages in the war on two fronts.

My two books identify and analyze the material of idiographic historians, the specific sites and moments when structural change occurred. However, those moments are not studied to compile a chronological narrative. Nor do I use moments of historical transformation as a nomothetic social scientist would, as cases to test a universal social science model. Instead, I am concerned with using historical change to explore the dynamics of social action within feudal and capitalist societies. I conclude that transformative social change begins with conflict among elites in both types of social formations.

The web approach to the scientific method provides another way of engaging in the war on two fronts. My elite conflict model can be reanalyzed, through the web approach, as an explanation of the process through which social actors come to perceive their social situation, move to take action, and then come to reassess themselves and their social situation on the basis of their actions. That process can be viewed as a progression through the cells of Table 1-1, with my elite conflict model providing an explanation of the mechanism by which actors move from cell to cell in their consciousness and behavior.

The web approach begins with human perceptions of the social and of how social actors embed their understandings of their identities and interest in institutions. Cells 1 and 2 identify the mutually reinforcing, and therefore powerful in ordering human behavior, norms derived from social structures (specifically elite and class relations). The very stability of social relations serves to clarify and to reinforce actors' cultural understandings of the privileges and obligations of their social positions. Those cells give insight into the stability of the medieval social order, and indeed of all social structures, at most times. The web approach, by beginning the study of social action with institutions, shows why my historical investigation revealed that elites almost always were reactionary, seeking to preserve their land rights, judicial powers, and offices.

Wars, famines, and demographic crises may have killed elite individuals and families but their positions as rulers, magnates, seigneurs, clerics, or bourgeois endured and were inherited by old members or new entrants into existing elites. The new occupants of old social positions assumed the norms and values (cells 1 and 2) that guided and justified the occupants of those positions. That is why individual and family mobility had virtually no effect upon social structure in medieval Europe. The top row of the Table identifies the constrictions placed upon agency by social structure. "Hand" or agency is constrained within social settings (those of social organization, social stratification, bureaucracy, group, and social relationships in cell 3) which are defined and bounded by larger structures.

The norms and values of cells 1 and 2 are embedded in institutions, and those institutions shape the agency of the "hands" in cell 3. The Web approach differentiates action within existing structures (reproduction) from transformative modes of action. The Table presents "Scenes" (cells 4 through 6) as a distinct level, a site of social action different from both social structures on the one hand and personality structures on the other.

My book analyzes historically specific scenes (with the Reformation being the most significant). The web approach offers a way to understand how and why actors were able to produce dramatic transformations in such situations. Ruptures in existing social structures, and in the reproduction of personality structures, allowed actors to examine their social roles and selves with fresh eyes. The Reformation was so powerful in spurring radical action because it combined actual situations of conflict and competition along with opportunities to reconsider norms and values. This is the point at which situations are (re)defined and (re)imaged (cell 4).

The web approach to the scientific method allows me to specify and to generalize the consequences of the structural disruptions wrought by heightened elite conflict. Actors experienced the new challenges to their existing roles and social relations with fear (relative deprivation) more than they did with opportunism (reinforcement, as described in cell 5). The strategies successful elites adopted to fend off immediate threats from rival elites and from nonelites determined the long-term consequences that conflict had upon relations of production. Thus, capitalist development (or other forms of economic change and state formation) are the unintended end-products of chains of contingent action which began with the post-Reformation opening of new opportunities for elite and then class conflict.

Elites were fearful, defensive and reactionary in their agency for three main reasons. First, no one could anticipate or control the ultimate effects of their actions, if only because the chains of conflict and structural change were so long in their duration. The English (and

Dutch) transitions were (as I noted above) the fastest, taking under two centuries to go from a manorial to a capitalist system of agrarian production. The transformations sparked by the Reformation lasted over three centuries in France and Spain and even longer elsewhere.

Second, decisions needed to be made quickly because opportunities for effective action arose suddenly and unpredictably as well as infrequently. The chance to take effective action or to mount a sufficient defense would have been lost before any actor could determine the material interests of each potential ally. Since the ultimate outcome of transformative conflicts were unpredictable, each actor could not know if what seemed to be common interests at that moment would diverge in the whole course of conflict, leading an early ally to defect from the coalition as circumstances changed.

Finally, as the scale of social action expanded beyond small locales, elites were forced to rely upon the allies of allies of allies. Not only did actors have to fear being betrayed in the future; they had to try to find ways of ensuring that the strangers offering an alliance were acting in good faith today.

How can social actors overcome these barriers to effective action? How can they move beyond defense and reaction to take innovative actions that transform social circumstances? Solutions to problems of predictability, speed, and reliability find expressions specific to each time and place. Historical specificity derives in part from social actors' capacities to learn from the failures of previous solutions. My comparisons of various European societies over five centuries allow me to develop theoretical models that fit a limited range of cases.

My main finding is that social actors settled on allies more than they agreed on programs that would fulfill their particular interests. Alliances were built upon intermarriage, business alliances, or mutual support for candidates to offices or religious ministries. Decisions to extend political support, to appoint ministers, to invest money, to profess a faith, or to oppose a king or local political machines were momentous. They were made to protect and hopefully to further one's life chances and those of one's family and descendents. Fateful decisions were made more confidently in concert with other like-situated and therefore like-minded individuals.

Elites and nonelites took steps to deepen the ties that made for mutalities of interests. That is why familial, religious, geographic, political and financial ties strengthened rather than shattered during periods of economic change, religious conflict, civil war, revolution, and international wars. Choices became more dangerous and less likely to satisfy during those moments of heightened conflict as the terrain of meaning and interest shifted rapidly. Social actors were able to go forward with confidence when their immediate allies were partners of long-standing, and knowing that those allies would jeopardize their social and economic standing (and perhaps their likelihood of going to heaven) if they abandoned existing loyalties.

How did social actors come to those conclusions? How did they make sense and develop strategies in the flux of unprecedented social change? Those questions receive historical answers in my book, answers that I presented in a generalized form in the preceding paragraphs.

The web approach offers another way to answer to those questions, one which places my historical conclusions in the context of the broad web of relationships between social and personality structures as mediated by situational action. The behaviors which generated solutions to the problems of uncertainty, unpredictability, and unreliability are found in the middle level (cells 4-6) of Table 1-1. That middle level identifies the bridges between the structures of large-scale social organization and the actual constitution of social actors in their personality structures. My historical investigation finds support in the Table's presentation of scenes as a mediator between macro social and micro personality structures. The one level of the table not labeled as structural is the site where strategies of action (albeit defensive and fearful reactions to social structural disruption) are most likely to be formulated. Those strategies reconstitute social structures. Strategies of action also evoke new worldviews and self-definitions on the most conscious and rational end of personality formation (cell 7, the "head" of the level of personality structures).

TOWARD A NEW SOCIOLOGICAL UNDERSTANDING OF MEANING AND ACTION

My book, in its concern with a specific social change, necessarily can't encompass the whole of human social experience. The web approach to the scientific method is useful as well for specifying what is not discussed in my work. I examine personality in its most rational form. I present individuals as self-conscious and self-defining in terms of their social ties, interests and obligations. Largely missing are the more subjective, expressive and self-actualizing aspects of personality, expressed in the web approach as the "Heart" and "Hands" of personality (cells 8 and 9 in Table 1-1).

The web approach shows what is missing (and what perhaps could be added) to my analysis. An effort to integrate those aspects to my analysis, and thereby produce a fuller conception of culture, is beyond the scope of this chapter. Instead, I conclude by considering whether the analysis of the changes I seek to explain is harmed by the exclusion of a fuller discussion of personality. I expand on my notion of culture, and address a line of criticism of that conception, in this section.

My understanding of the ways in which early modern Europeans built alliances to protect their interests leads me to redefine the ways in which social actors find meaning in their lives. Culture and ideology did not substitute for, nor did they merely reflect, interests. They were programs for building common interests strong enough to prevent allies from betraying one another and strong enough to compel allies to invest their human and materials assets in their combined cause.

My historical analysis draws upon and addresses the first two rows of the Table. I address the process of socialization only in the "Head" column, and only in so far as it helps explain the ways in which social actors understand their obligations toward and interests in social groups.

My notion of culture as both a means for creating meaning and for building concrete social alliances provides a way of addressing the most salient objections leveled against the sort of structural analysis I conduct in *Capitalists in Spite of Themselves*. Emirbayer and Goodwin's (1994) critique of what they call "structuralist instrumentalism" in the work of Roger Gould on the Paris Commune could be applied to my book as well. They write: "The difficulty here is not that Gould neglects 'culture' per se, but rather that the underlying logic of his argument--its theoretical logic--fails to accord normative commitments any independent explanatory significanceî (1430). Emirbayer and Goodwin attack network analysis for "its tendency to devote almost all of its analytical attention to uncovering the 'structural preconditions' for this elective affinity, rather than to also exploring the independent causal significance of these discursive frameworks themselves" (1431).

Emirbayer and Goodwin argue that we must pay attention to culture because "cultural formations. . .both constrain and enable historical actors" (1440). Culture, in their view, forecloses some possible strategies that might be materially advantageous, but would violate culturally constructed norms. Such cultural foreclosing also reduces complexity and in that way enables action by focusing it at certain sites and along particular pathways. "Under such circumstances, certain identities, interests, and courses of action come to be more valued than others, to the point where individuals and groups often prefer to sacrifice their own material interests out of a deep-seated commitment toward them, as in the cases not only of the Medici's ascension to power, but also of the English Civil War, the Paris Commune, and the civil rights struggle in the United States" (1441).

Capitalists in Spite of Themselves examines the first two cases identified by Emirbayer and Goodwin and comes to a different understanding of the interplay of ideals and interests in the rise of the Medici and the English Civil War. What is remarkable about both events was the ways in which actors on all sides in those conflicts sought to reconcile social reality with their "normative commitments." Sometimes that meant altering behaviors and switching allegiances to bring social relations into accord with one's ideological beliefs. More often, actors developed ways of giving meaning to the pursuit of their common interests. As Emirbayer and Goodwin allow, "Cultural structures. . .are also. . .multiple and interpenetrating. . .There has probably never been but one overarching cultural idiom, narrative, or discourse operative in any given historical context" (1441).

Cultural idioms in Renaissance Florence and seventeenth century England (and perhaps in many other times and places) were lived as well as believed. Ideological allegiances were expressed by working together with co-religionists. Living in the midst of competing political and religious orthodoxies, Florentines and English attempted to make order out of confusion by evaluating the character of official and clerical claimants along with the content of their assertion. That is why people decided what to believe in part by settling upon whom to believe.

Allegiance to political factions and religious denominations had material as well as spiritual or cultural consequences. As a result, people tended to trust priests, ministers and magicians as well as officeholders they could control (or who were subordinated to the same authority as they were), and to fear ideological claimants who were immune to their power or entreaties. I am not saying that people pick and choose among ideologies for the ones that further their material interests. Rather, people often become uncertain when new discourses and practices challenge old cultural norms and ideological certainties. Florentines evaluated rival claimants to power, and seventeenth century English weighed competing religious and political assertions on the basis of their proponents' past records. Had they been reliable allies? Could their religious and political visions for the future be reconciled with existing cultural commitments embodied in decisions to intermarry, attend church together, and endorse one another's candidates for religious and political office?

Florentines and English became confident of their decisions to pick sides in moments of revolution and civil war when they could observe that their ideological positions were shared by allies who also visibly committed their families, fortunes, lives and afterlives to the cause. In other words, certain ideologies came to be seen as true and correct because they appeared to elicit appropriately loyal behavior in others who shared the same beliefs. People acted out of deeply held convictions, but those convictions came to be deeply held because they could be observed working for allies engaged in similar struggles to defend their positions against challenges from enemies.

This sense of culture, as presented in the historical analysis of *Capitalists in Spite of Themselves*, can be understood through the web approach as a scene designer. Culture offers individuals an understanding of their social world. It also presents a path to construct and express personality that can find meaning in the social structures which individuals inhabit and (at times) seek to transform.

My approach focused on the interactions between scenes and social structures. Emirbayer and Goodwin criticize network analysts' blindness toward personality structures. The web approach makes clear that personality can be incorporated into the study of structure and culture, and that to do so is not inconsistent with the mode and goals of my analysis.

Let me end where I began, with Marx and Weber. Marx wrote that "Men make their own history but they do not make it just as they please; they do not make it under circumstances chosen by themselves, but under circumstances directly encountered, given and transmitted from the past" ([1852] 1963: 15). Weber teaches us that "Not ideas, but material and ideal interests, directly govern men's conduct. Yet very frequently the 'world images' that have been created by 'ideas' have, like switchmen, determined the tracks along which action has been pushed by the dynamic of interest" (in Gerth and Mills, [1922] 1946: 280).

Marx and Weber are saying, in their own ways, that when humans act they do so while doubly constrained: by the social structures that were created by other people in the historical past and by conceptions of the self that are a learned cultural heritage. The web approach to the scientific method shows how those insights can be melded into a methodology for explaining social action that avoids the limits of both idiographic particularism and nomothetic universalism. That method shows how the elements of behavior are constituted, and how humans in the process of constructing themselves and their social world employ them.

NOTES

1. See Braudel (1977, 65-66) for a classic put-down of Weber. Braudel and other historians demonstrate that Weber's thesis is based upon dubious empirical evidence and shows a real misunderstanding of the range of ways in which Protestants and Catholics used the tenets and practices of their faiths to guide their secular lives.

2. Eisenstadt (1968) is an exemplar of this approach, as well as having set the agenda for many of the scholars working in this tradition. Such works ignore Weber's own argument that Protestantism is necessary only to explain the first expressions of rational action. Once a few Protestants, acting from religious motivations, engage in such behavior they create an iron cage of institutional practices and competitive pressures. It is that iron cage, and not any functional equivalent of the Protestant Ethic, that accounts in Weber's model for rational action on the part of non-Protestants and later adherents of milder variants of Protestantism everywhere and forever after throughout the world.

3. I am concerned here with understanding the internal dynamics of feudalism and therefore I do not offer a detailed critique of "external forces" arguments here. See Lachmann (2000, 17-38 and passim.) for a detailed critique of those theories.

4. Readers interested in seeing my full treatment of this issue, as well as the sources of my historical evidence, should consult *Capitalists in Spite of Themselves,* Chapter 7 and passim. My goal in presenting only a brief summary of this comparison is to present the logic of my argument and to highlight the sorts of factors emphasized in my analysis.

REFERENCES

Braudel, Fernand. 1977. *Afterthoughts on Material Civilization and Capitalism*. Baltimore: Johns Hopkins University Press.

Brenner, Robert. 1976. "Agrarian Class Structure and Economic Development in Pre-Industrial Europe." *Past and Present* 70:30-75.

Brenner, Robert. 1982. "The Agrarian Roots on European Capitalism." *Past and Present* 97:16-113.

Dobb, Maurice. 1947. *Studies in the Development of Capitalism*. New York: International Publishers.

Eisenstadt, S. N. 1968. "Introduction." Pp. ix-lvi in *Max Weber on Charisma and Institution Building*. Chicago: University of Chicago Press.

Emirbayer, Mustafa, and Jeff Goodwin. 1994. "Network Analysis, Culture, and the Problem of Agency." *American Journal of Sociology* 99 (#6):1411-54.

Gerth, Hans H. and C. Wright Mills. [1922] 1946. *From Max Weber: Essays in Sociology*. New York: Oxford University Press.

Lachmann, Richard. 1987. *From Manor to Market: Structural Change in England, 1536-1640*. Madison: University of Wisconsin Press.

Lachmann, Richard. 2000. *Capitalists in Spite of Themselves: Elite Conflict and Economic Transitions in Early Modern Europe.* New York: Oxford University Press.

Mark, Karl. ([1852] 1963. *The Eighteenth Brumaire of Louis Bonaparte.* New York: International Publishers.

Mills, C. Wright. 1956. *The Power Elite*. New York: Oxford University Press.

Wallerstein, Immanuel. 1991. "Beyond Annales?" *Radical History Review* 49: 7-15.

Introduction to Chapter 7

Maines and Britt reject the separation of science and the humanities, just as C. P. Snow resisted the separation between those "two cultures," pointing us toward an approach to knowledge which includes both. In other words, an approach which draws on both models and narratives can prove to be fruitful in yielding understanding of human phenomena. Looking to Table 1-1, we might see models as having the capacity to emphasize social and individual structures. And we might see narratives as digging deeply into the concrete nature of a particular situation. Maines and Britt refer to Phillips' *Beyond Sociology's Tower of Babel: Reconstructing the Scientific Method* (2001) as emphasizing this same movement from abstract concepts to concrete description. And that movement is also emphasized throughout this volume. They find that the danger within a one-sided emphasis on models is a loss in understanding the specific nature of a given situation. And the danger within a one-sided emphasis on narrative is a loss in achieving a broad understanding of a given situation's relationships with other situations. . The authors apply this broad approach to research on the impact of a home-based preschool program. They do a secondary analysis of earlier modeling work by Britt, finding it deficient relative to the strengths of an orientation to narratives. As a result, they provide us with an illustration of how to employ the breadth of a web approach to the scientific method by combining a modeling with a narrative approach. In this way we can come to understand more fully how to achieve a successful preschool program. Whereas models by themselves are relatively barren with reference to the range of possibilities, narratives are highly suggestive. Yet models help us to come up with conclusions based on a large number of narratives, and models like the causal loop diagram in Chapter 3 address some of the criticisms leveled at them.

Chapter 7

Parallels and Tensions Between Models and Narratives

David R. Maines and David W. Britt

ABSTRACT

Narrative analysis and conceptual modeling are alternative disciplines for describing and understanding how action in context evolves. There is an irreducible and fundamental tension between the two approaches. Conceptual modeling is strong at disciplining the continual rethinking of the nature of concepts, relationships among concepts, and what should and should not be included in the analysis. Following Britt (1997), we call these concept, relationship and model specification, respectively. But conceptual modeling is dependent upon simplified relationships among concepts to depict process. Narrative analysis, on the other hand, is strong at describing process (Maines, 2001), but has difficulty describing the commonalities among stories that are central to the development of action. We argue that the tension between these alternative disciplines makes their use in tandem productive of richer dialogue and deeper understanding of the phenomena being studied.

PARALLELS IN THE NATURE OF MEANING

Stephen Jay Gould, in his influential *The Mismeasure of Man,* implies that in some fundamental ways scientists may be rather unaware of what they are doing. He puts it this way:

> Science, since people must do it, is a socially embedded activity. It progresses by hunch, vision, and intuition. Much of its change through time does not record a closer approach to absolute truth, but the alteration of cultural contexts that influence it so strongly. Facts are not pure and unsullied bits of information; culture also influences what we see and how we see it. Theories, moreover, are not inexorable inductions from facts. The most creative theories are often imaginative visions imposed upon facts; the source of imagination is also strongly cultural (1981: 21-22).

Science, Gould goes on to write, "must give up the twin myths of objectivity and inexorable march toward truth" (p. 23), which are myths, we would add, that were born of the 17th century Enlightenment. Gould correctly notes that these myths were developed through the configuration of two elements, each of which he regards as fallacies. The first is *reification*, or the tendency to regard abstract conceptualizations as real things. The second is *ranking*, or "ordering complex variation as a gradual ascending scale" (p. 24), with quantitative measurement emerging as a dominant criterion through which rankings can be represented.

Gould, of course, is correct in identifying these elements as consequential constructions in the Enlightenment era development of science. As consequential, however, was the distancing of science from non-science, and that distancing is best seen in the historical separation of science from the humanities.

As Richardson (2000: 925-926) argues, theories of the nature and function of language were crucial for the creation of the categories of "science" and "humanities." Literature, for example, came to be associated with evocative writing—fiction, rhetoric, interpretation, narrative. It was regarded as a kind of false writing insofar as it "invented" reality through literary devices and representation, with David Hume going as far as declaring that poets were professional liars. Science, on the other hand, was associated with facts and objectivity, and as such, scientific writing used plain and unevocative writing that merely "reported" reality in a straightforward and unambiguous way.

As many have described it (e.g., Bannister, 1987), the language of science became incorporated into the social sciences as a kind of preferred form. Intrinsic to that form is the language of measurement and precision, which is the language that has dominated modeling in sociology. We see this language expressed in different although typically explicit ways. In discussing multiple indicator models, for instance, Kercher (1992: 1319) writes that "researchers are subject to making "measurement errors.' Such errors will produce biased estimates of the true causal relationship between concepts." In this case, the language of "errors" and "true relationships" rests in the same assumptions the Marquis de Condorcet made in coining the phrase "social science," namely, that truth can be attained by eliminating errors (Levine, 1985: 4-6). The companion assumption regarding relationships and explanation is that truth may be found by making them explicit and eliminating alternative interpretations (Britt, 1997).

In this chapter, along with Gould, Bannister, Richardson, and others, we recognize the historical and rhetorical construction of science. While we reject its scientist pretension, however, we accept the usefulness of modeling as a heuristic necessary to all social scientific endeavor. In accepting that heuristic, though, we also reject the separation of science and the humanities as a finality. Indeed, as many scholars have observed (see Gusfield, 1976; McCloskey, 1990; Polkinghorne, 1988), the two have much in common. Drawing from the impulse to see scholarship and knowledge as inclusive, we devote ourselves to an inspection of two areas of seeming dissimilarity-- modeling and narrative. We recognize that these two areas conventionally have belonged, respectively, to the language of science and to the humanities. It is our task to identify their similarities and differences and assess the potential of these similarities and differences for furthering our understanding of human group life.

The task we have set for ourselves is compatible in many ways with the web approach described by Phillips (2001) and in Chapter 1 of this volume. This approach addresses the problem of specialized languages in social science that militate against knowledge production and absorption into common vocabularies of description and explanation. While the web approach seems to stress conceptual density of linked levels of abstraction, we key on his observation that there is intellectual virtue in both specialized and generic analysis. Thus, while we search for similarities in two seemingly disparate areas of social analysis, we are well aware of the tensions between them, which may well be driven by their respective strengths instead of their weaknesses.

PARTS AND WHOLES VERSUS
INDICATORS AND CONCEPTS

One of the ways of appreciating that narratives and models struggle with similar phenomena is to examine parallels in the nature of meaning between the two modes of thinking. Several scholars have suggested that narrative meaning is achieved in two different ways: by showing that something is part of something else, or that something is a cause of something else (Polkinghorne, 1988: 7; Richardson, 1995: 200). The same distinction is reflected in conceptual modeling as the continuing assessment of conceptual specification and relationship specification.

In conceptual specification, the part/whole problem is spoken of in concrete/abstract terms. A simplified way of talking about emergent meaning in such pairs is that more concrete indicators "make sense" only with reference to a more abstract concept. Such a way of summarizing the relationship between concrete indicators and abstract concepts, however, masks the extent to which this is actually a continuing, two-way dialogue. Sets of indicators give meaning to concepts by grounding them. They receive meaning from concepts as the latter show the larger, more general implications.

The meaning that emerges from this dialogue between indicators and concepts does not go unchallenged. In narrative analysis, a fundamental criterion of the adequacy of the emergent meaning would be the extent to which the emergent concepts are "recognizable as adequate representations" by "members" of the group in question (Riessman, 1990: 66).

To be persuasive in this regard, it is helpful to embed the indicators in the particulars of the stories of social entities living in the situations being studied (Maines, 1999, 2001). It is one thing to talk about the level of risk of families in a preschool program, for example, but it is quite another to exemplify the concept of risk through a presentation of the stories of individual families as they cope with bullet holes in the walls, recurrent illnesses and serious drug use by family members. Such stories bring to life and give meaning to what may be a relatively cold presentation of types of risk or, in the extreme, a number that claims to represent the level of risk of a particular family or set of families.

Cross-case analysis of concept/indicator models may be conducted more persuasively by showing individual stories of risk insinuating itself into the ongoing lives of family members and their interaction in context. Where risk stories can be bundled together in plausible ways, the nature of the common and divergent elements of risk are made more compelling. At the same time, the concept specification process acts as a touchstone for summarizing the elements of individual stories that might be relevant to an understanding of risk. The rhetoric of concept specification and the rhetoric of story construction thus complement one another in the construction of a more meaningful dialogue between individual and collective stories of risk and between indicators and concepts.

The Nature of Causation

The construction of narrative causal meaning focuses on how events unfold in some plausible way, with some events preceding others (Maines, 1993). Perhaps the most difficult task facing researchers in presenting their data in modeled form is conveying a sense of how certain situations have unfolded to yield a variety of consequences. The idea of scenarios is useful here, though "scenarios" have been more frequently used for talking about situations in which contingencies are involved. In this latter case, a scenario is a pairing of a set of conditions with a particular outcome, where scenario is used as a somewhat less jargonistic way of referring to conjunctural causation (Ragin, 1987; Britt, 1997). Yet there is also another meaning of scenario, one that focuses more on process, on the more or less plausible mechanisms by which things unfold, which is an issue for both additive and non-additive models. This latter use of scenario is compatible with narrative analysis. The former use is more "explanatory." Yet the two together constrain and inform one another in much the same way that McCloskey (1990: 83-96) uses the different elements of the rhetorical tetrad (story, metaphor, fact and logic) to constrain and inform or criticize one another

An example might help clarify the extent to which we feel these different uses of scenario permit the presentation of causal arguments in a less dry and more compelling fashion than might otherwise be possible. The example comes from research recently conducted by Britt on the conditions under which certain outcomes occur, which, if not counterintuitive, are at least more interesting and take our understanding of the respective situations to a deeper level than might otherwise be possible.

Britt (1998) was interested in the conditions under which a home-based preschool program could work. Such programs tend to work better when the families in them are less profoundly challenged by the exigencies of daily life. As a result, if one examines who stays in such programs, one usually gets the pedestrian result that less at-risk families are much more likely to stay in such programs than more at-risk families. The dilemma, of course, is that such programs are designed for higher-risk families. So then the question becomes, how can such programs work for high-risk families? The answer is relatively simple: only if such programs are able to reach out to the more at-risk families in ways that facilitate their coping with the problems of living they are facing can higher-risk families stay in the program.

These are the patterns of "facts," in McCloskey's (1993) sense of the word, that stand out. Bringing them to life in a way that can be appreciated not only by other researchers and policy analysts but also by program personnel and the families themselves requires getting much closer to the stories of particular families and the program personnel with whom they interact. Neither the nature of higher risk nor the nature of "reaching out" (Britt, 1997) can be appreciated and grasped in a meaningful way without grounding the factual patterns in representative stories that give life to and stretch the boundaries of both concepts and relationships.

Figure 7-1 represents the alternate scenarios that lead to program

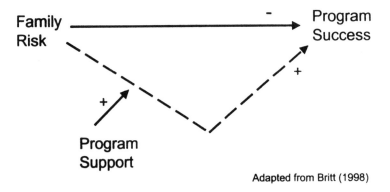

Adapted from Britt (1998)

Figure 7.1. Alternative scenarios for success in a preschool program.

involvement by parents in the HIPPY preschool program that Britt (1998) was studying. The more mundane scenario simply reflects the fact that less at-risk families are more likely to stay in the program. The second scenario reflects the contingent and subtle mechanisms involved in keeping high-risk families in the program.

Each of these scenarios is a collective story, a story that becomes more meaningful as the tension between individual and collective stories of how parents stay in and drop out of the program are explored. The second scenario represents a more complex and contingent collective story involving collaborative effort between family members and program staff. Approached as alternate scenarios in a model, what stands out is the structure of the logic. Approached as alternate stories, what stands out is substance, richness of detail and a sense of mechanism and process that can only be spoken of relatively abstractly as a model.

Hirsch et al (1987) make a case for there being a trade-off between realism and elegance. One aspect of realism, however, is theoretical. Narrative analysis is not particularly parsimonious and elegant (but see Abbott, 1992, and Griffin & Ragin, 1994). There is little emphasis on finding the smallest number of assumptions and concepts that can describe a phenomenon. Rather, there is much emphasis on the achievement of a detailed understanding regarding how things unfold.

Causal mechanisms require a certain density to be plausible and credible (Blumer, 1990; Soulliere et al, 2001). As Britt (1997) points out, in attempting to resolve the tension between simplification and elaboration there often is the temptation to arrive at solutions that make models too oversimplified. Combining narrative and modeling, however, helps inject a bit of common sense into this process: narrative analysis may provide an indispensable understanding of context that dampens the risk of oversimplification.

Evans (2000) found, for example, that one could represent differences in the receptivity of urban prenatal clinics with the following simple model:

$$R = D$$

where R = the level of receptivity in a clinic,
and D = the intensity of the ideological commitment of the
clinic's dominant coalition to serving patients.

This model argues, in effect, that it makes no difference how effective the leader is in shaping the ideological tone of the clinic and molding a dominant coalition who felt the same way. As long as the dominant coalition was ideologically committed, that was enough. Such a model does "account" for the variations in the data using the dictates of comparative analysis (Ragin, 1987), and it is the most parsimonious accounting of the data. However, it is oversimplified in important theoretical and practical ways. The unreduced equation for this combinatorial argument was the following:

$$R = DL + Dl$$

In this model there are two alternative scenarios that lead to clinic receptivity. The first is the combination of an ideologically committed dominant coalition (D) and an effective leader (L). Each of these successful clinics had a somewhat different story in terms of how the level of receptivity that characterized them was produced. What they had *in common*, however, was the shared story of a leader's being instrumental in helping to shape the dominant coalition and its ideological commitment across time, making use of different opportunities and using somewhat different strategies.

The second scenario, where there was an ideologically committed dominant coalition (D) and an ineffective leader (l), tells the very different story of one in which the ineffectiveness of the leader was created by a higher administration that wanted to close the clinic. This created a "John Brown" effect (Cook & Campbell, 1979) among the dominant coalition. They became committed to keeping the clinic open and serving the patients in spite of the dictates of the higher administration.

Theoretically, it is useful to know that the ideological commitment of the dominant coalition is important as a proximate cause of clinic receptivity. And this is certainly parsimonious, requiring only one concept to explain why some clinics are more receptive than others. Without knowing *how* leadership--or the lack thereof---is part of the relevant context, however, the resulting parsimonious model is also both theoretically misleading and practically useless. Where the stories of the two sets of clinics are told, the risk of oversimplifying would be much less. There would be a greater awareness of how relevant changes were unfolding in the clinics characterized by good and bad leaders.

What does the individual/collective-story dilemma have to contribute to an understanding of conceptual modeling? One of the complex dilemmas faced by narrative researchers is whether to focus on individual narratives or collective narratives. Describing and reflecting on her own approach to this dilemma in the analysis of working-class American women's life stories, Luttrell (2000) writes:

> At that point I made a decision to focus on patterns, not indi-
> viduals, and as a result something was lost and something else
> gained. I lost the capacity to see each woman primarily as an
> individual with her own story to tell, but I gained clarity on what
> I came to understand as links between the social and the psycho-
> logical in the women's narratives. I think the alternative ap-
> proach (developing more complete and holistic case studies of
> individual women) would have had certain benefits...The trade-
> off, as I saw it, was that insofar as the women's individuality
> (the personal context of their stories) would be lost, building a
> theory about how school structure and culture shapes identities
> and self-understandings would be gained. (Luttrell, 2000: 508)."

Models, almost by definition, concern themselves with cross-case analysis, and cross-case analysis requires a continual rethinking of the nature of concepts and their relationships. Staying close to narrative detail contributes in important ways to both of these specification problems. As the number of cases increase, it becomes more difficult to keep coding decisions regarding the grounding of concepts from becoming anything but a mechanical exercise for either qualitative or quantitative analysis. Staying sensitive to personal and collective narratives would increase the sensitivity and realism of such decisions. There is a connection between "the personal context of women's stories" and the contextual differences that subtly change the meaning of indicators. Casting off these subtleties as irrelevant contextual varia-tion--which is what is being done when contextual information is not melded into the coding process--should not be mechanical and easy. Rather, it should be thoughtful and challenging, and incorporating narrative would nudge these decisions toward such thoughtfulness and challenge.

Similar advantages apply to the consideration of relationships. The analysis of relationships increases in credibility when it is embedded in a mechanism that is theoretically informed (Little, 1991). As several have noted (Polkinghorne, 1988, Abbott, 1992, Maines, 1993), this is one of the special strengths of narrative analysis.

People do not live in a world of concepts. They may live in a world of real or imagined individuals who embody the essence of con-cepts and/or their relationships. We believe that narratives have the capacity to breathe life into the conceptual specification process. Con-sider the following use of E. P. Thompson's earlier work on class con-sciousness in Luttrell's (2000: 512) attempts to get close to how the working women she was studying conceptualized class and race con-sciousness.

These women are not using etic abstractions to talk about why they feel comfortable in some contexts and not in others. They are using real people to embody and give life to what they were experiencing. The capacity of narrative to bring to life and serve as a check for more abstract concepts and patterns of relationships, then, seems really promising.

Context in Narrative Analysis and Conceptual Modeling

Narratives focus on sequences of meaningful events in context. Conceptual models focus on patterns of variation within and across contexts. Context may or may not be constant, but assume for the moment that it is relatively stable. Context is factored into the alternative disciplines of narrative analysis and conceptual modeling in complementary ways. For collective and individual narratives, context becomes something against which individuals may struggle or which they actively incorporate into their understanding and articulation of how particular events have unfolded. In conceptual modeling, contexts frame the unfolding of dynamic processes and may affect either the meaning of particular concepts or the nature of relationships, or both.

How context insinuates itself into the research process is important. We believe that sensitivity to context is often an explicit or implicit framing of what is important in a situation. Consider how Luttrell (2000: 509) speaks of her sample of working women in North Carolina:

> I conducted short interviews with 50 program participants about why they were returning to school. Then I selected fifteen women to observe and interview. These women had all been raised in southern, rural communities, growing up mostly on tenant farms. Their past schooling had been sporadic, in part because of the demands of farm work, and in part because of racial discrimination. All had attended segregated one-room schoolhouses. The women were all employed as housekeepers; most had also worked as domestics; some had been waitresses and factory workers.

Sampling is at its heart an exercise in encouraging diversity (Becker, 1998). We often forget that when we summarize in tabular form the characteristics of individuals (age, education, etc.) in our sample. Means and standard deviations coldly portray commonality and diversity. Such matters are essential to quantitative forms of modeling, but how much closer and knowledgeable about these women and the background or shared context of their lives we feel with Luttrell's narrative description of the diversity and commonality of their collective experience.

EXAMINING TENSIONS

A second way of examining the relationship between stories or narratives and models is to examine the presumed tensions that exist between the two modes of analysis. On the one hand, with stories and narrative, one is interested in understanding "what things are how they got that way" (Becker 1992). There's strong emphasis on process, coherence and emergence across time. On the other hand, with conceptual modeling, one is interested in the continual reexamination of what factors are important for understanding a particular situation, what their nature is, and how they are related to another, or what Britt (1997) has called the three continuing respecification tasks.

Some of the tension that exists between these alternate ways of thinking about dynamics may be traceable to setting up modeling as a straw man. Becker (1992: 210), for example, in contrasting narrative and modeling, argues that with the latter, researchers are reduced to: "... the refinement of measures of association between independent and dependent variables." It is certainly true that some quantitative researchers may overemphasize precision of estimates (both in terms of measurement and in terms of relationships). On the quantitative side, however, Freedman (1991) and Tukey (1962) have both reminded us that such emphasis is misplaced and narrow. In Freedman's case, he suggests an alteration in the imagery that we have used to talk about such matters (with particular reference to regression analysis). Rather than using the imagery of a scalpel--with its implication of precisely cutting situations up and having a very precise understanding of how these slices relate to one another--we should be using the image of a machete. This is a tool much more suited to roughly cutting a path through the forest. The big things should stand out, in other words. This is very similar to Tukey's observation that such an overemphasis on precision diverts attention from the real business of modeling: namely, asking the right questions.

All procedures, whether they are quantitative or qualitative, are subject to being reified and generating too narrow a focus. On a deeper level, however, it is not just precision that is being called into question by Becker. It is also assuming that variables have some predefined existence that does not change over time as new information is brought to bear. While it is true on the quantitative side that researchers are to some extent trapped by the information they are able to squeeze into numerical form, advances in structural equation modeling, for example, have allowed quantitative researchers the luxury of continually rethinking the nature of what variables are while at the same time examining how they are related to one another. And with advances in soft modeling technology, it is not even necessary to have solid, measurable variables for one's analyses.

Thinking about this problem from a conceptual rather than a technical viewpoint, moreover, enables us to suggest that a false emphasis on precision may blind us to the continual rethinking of what things are important, what they are, and how they are related, or the interpenetration of specification criteria (Britt, 1997). Simply put, interpenetration refers to the idea that the nature of concepts, their relationships, and an overall sense of what concepts are important have implications for one another. Hence, as one reassesses what is important to the situation, this may have implications for both the nature of concepts and their relationships. And as relationships turn out to be faulty, it may have important, clarifying implications for the nature of concepts and what is important in the situation. The interpenetration of specification criteria is a relatively subtle idea, but it goes to the heart of considering models as a shorthand vehicle for the continual reassessment of what concepts are important, their nature, and how they are related to one another.

The interpenetration of specification criteria also helps us understand another presumed difference between modeling and narrative, how anomalous cases are treated. Becker states (1992: 212):

> Part of the process of constructing a narrative is a continuous re-definition of what the theory is explaining, of what the dependent variable actually is.

Such a process is not peculiar to narrative analysis, or even qualitative work more generally. And only the most fanatical quantitative model-as-test researchers have not incorporated such processes into their repertoire of techniques. Cook (1993), for example, gives a careful discussion of how the redefinition of the nature of a cause after an initial analysis of the relationship between cause and effect improves their researchers' understanding of what is happening in a situation. And as Ragin (1987) and others have shown, such processes are at the very core of comparative analysis.

Another straw man argument is reflected in the assumption that the only way to evaluate causal models is through the amount of variance that they explain. Becker (1992: 212), for example, contrasts narrative and causal modeling this way:

> We do not search for causes so much as look for stories that explain what it is and how it got that way. When an analyst of causes has done the job well, the result is a large proportion of variance explained. When an analyst of narrative has done the job well, the result is a story that explains why it is inevitable that this process led to this result.

Aside from the fact that looking only at variance explained ignores the patterns that might be present in relationships among variables, looking only at variance explained limits the evaluation of models to a purely *descriptive* mode. There are other ways of evaluating and critiquing models that are more multidimensional. Britt (1997), for example, discusses several alternative ways of examining the validity of models. One may look at their *explanatory validity*, assessing their consistency with alternative theoretical positions and the extent to which they provide insight or new ways of examining a phenomenon. One may look at their *predictive validity*, a useful discipline for both qualitative and quantitative research. And importantly for this discussion, one may also examine a model's *interpretive validity*. Interpretive validity is high when a model captures how the individuals living through a situation understand what is going on. A simple way of understanding this implication is to think of the anthropological distinction between emic and etic concepts and extending it to the evaluation of relationships and an overall sense of what is important.

Another source of tension based on a mischaracterization of modeling argues that in models all agents must be constrained to have the same story. Abbott (1992: 56), for example, correctly points out that for "...any particular *set* [our emphasis] of causal variable relations to hold, all agents (cases) must follow only one story." The misconception comes with a generalization from a set of relationships to an entire model: "...that the causal model is exactly the same for every case." This would be true only for individuals having the same approximate outcomes and where the more exogenous variables are highly intercorrelated with one another. More likely is the possibility that alternative scenarios might exist within the same model. This is easiest to see in models in which contingencies and conditions are present, but the same holds true for more additive models.

Let us look again at Figure 7-1. There are two very different scenarios present here that are differentiated by the extent of risk in the family. It is correct to assume that the model treats all families with the same level of risk the same way and assumes that they have the same story. That by itself is enough of a problem and reason enough to never rely solely on models to present a compelling argument (Mahoney 1999). But it is not true that the causal models are exactly the same for every case. Low-risk families stayed in the program no matter what level of support they received. High-risk families could only stay in the program if they received a high-level of support for their problems of living. Two different kinds of families; two basic scenarios. Oversimplified? Of course. One story for all the agents (cases)? Clearly not. Alternative models may exist within the same situation-- even with the same set of concepts--in much the same way that alternative individual on subgroup stories may exist within the same collective story.

Conclusions

In sum, we have reviewed some of the ways in which modeling and narrative are said to differ from one another that are overdrawn. Models need not be consumed with precision either in "measurement" or in the estimation of coefficients. We have also shown that rather than assuming that relationships, concepts and models having some pre-existing, reifiable existence, it makes more sense to think of them as short-hand ways of representing what we think we know about the dynamics of a situation. As part of this posture, it should be understood that these understandings may change and that the changes have implications for one another. Further, we have shown that models need not be limited to essentially descriptive bases for evaluation. Validity is a multi-dimensional concept involving description, explanation, interpretation and prediction. Finally, we have shown that models contain a variety of stories rather than being limited to one story.

Even with all of these over-drawn assumptions corrected, however, there are still fundamental differences in the way models and narratives simplify situations. Models are useful for examining concepts that are important to a number of the agents in a situation, isolating the concepts that appear to be most critical for most cases, and specifying how these concepts are related to one another. They are useful for conveniently summarizing complications such as contingencies, context and feedback.

One of Becker's (1990) criticisms of quantitative modeling is also relevant here. Referring in particular to the convention in quantitative work of reporting summary diagrams with estimates of coefficients, he says:

> [W]hile [such conventions of representation] make communication of some results easy and efficient, they make communication of other kinds of results difficult or impossible. The arrows that convey the results of causal analyses so well are not very good at communicating the complex interdependencies embodied in stories or in the visual materials (still photographs, film and video) which social scientists are increasingly using….

It is easy to see where this comes from, as when quantitative researchers summarize their results in diagrammatic form they include the measurement-model and causal-model coefficients, suggesting that all that is important about the concepts and relationships is contained in the statistical estimates. In conceptual modeling, however, the richness and multiplicity of relationships is given more respect (Britt, 1997; Soulliere, Britt & Maines, 2000). In principle at least, the use of tests, photographs, film and video to present a case for the nature of relationships is a straightforward extension of the intensive use of field notes. Modeling qualitative conclusions reflects an emphasis on treating modeling simply as a toolbox for summarizing conclusions. If articles were constructed in HTML it would be a simple matter to have links from particular relationships in represented models to film clips, photographs and a host of other artifacts from the research process.

Models *do* have trouble conveying the richness of the human experience of individual stories. Nor can they do more than approximate a sense of process. Yet this does not mean that modelers take such matters lightly. Blalock used to exhort his students in class to imagine themselves as being inside their models, "making decisions and acting accordingly." Having wrestled with this exhortation for a number of years, I (Britt) think he meant that constructing models was a tool that could get you closer to some of the important dynamics of situations. However, without trying to imagine people confronting events and their own biographies, and the context in which they were acting, making decisions and acting accordingly, modeling would be at best an exercise based on simplistic rational-calculus assumptions.

Abbott (1992: 55) gets close to this bottom-line problem when he talks about the role that cases play in quantitative (read "modeled") research. Commenting on a passage drawn from a 1989 article by Halaby and Weakliem in which they propose the hypothesis that excessive supervision violates cultural norms, he argues as follows:

Here the variables are directly personified as agents. '[P]ractices...violate the...norm...and result....' We have moved away from the simple causal language ('becomes,' 'carries over,' 'effects') of hypothesis 1 to a more active vocabulary ('violates'). Again, this is presumably a psychic shorthand, yet there is no case agency even at the psychic level. *The worker doesn't think about these things; the things themselves directly act on his or her psyche. The personality is merely the setting in which the causes act, not itself an agent acting (i.e.., reflecting) on them* [our emphasis].

Without reflection there cannot be a true sense of agency. Variables do not make decisions; people make decisions (Maines, 2001). The interesting tentative conclusion that Abbott makes about this process is that when results confirm initial expectations or hypotheses, a simple, presumptively rational framework is imposed on the results. It is when expectations go awry and hypotheses are not confirmed that researchers try to move from variables to people in an attempt to make sense of their findings.

We can see no reason for this pattern to be so limited. If we think of alternative scenarios in models as bundles of individual stories that attend to the same important concepts, then narrative can serve to bring a much richer understanding of the processes by which certain scenarios may play out than would otherwise be possible. Working in the other direction, models may bring an alternative discipline to the issue of how collective and individual stories interpenetrate one another. Indeed, we join Mahoney (1999) and others in suggesting that alternate logics and alternate disciplines may constitute touchstones for one another and, in so doing, set off research cycles among communities of scholars.

REFERENCES

Abbott, A. 1992. "From Causes to Events: Notes on Narrative Positivism." *Sociological Methods and Research 20*:428-455.

Bannister, Robert. 1987. *Sociology and Scientism: The American Quest for Objectivity, 1880-1940*. Chapel Hill: University of North Carolina Press.

Becker, H. 1990. "Generalizing from Case Studies." In Eisner, E. W., and A. Peshkin (eds.), *Qualitative Inquiry in Education: The Continuing Debate*. New York: Teacher's College Press.

Becker, H. 1998. *Tricks of the Trade*. Chicago: University of Chicago Press.

Blumer, Herbert. 1990. *Industrialization as an Agent of Social Change*. Hawthorne, NY: Aldine de Gruyter.

Britt, D. 1997. *A Conceptual Introduction to Modeling: Qualitative and Quantitative Perspectives*. Mawah, NJ: Lawrence Earlbaum.

Britt, D. 1998a. "Reaching Out and Making a Difference: The Context of Meaning in a Home-based Preschool Program." *Journal of Community Psychology 26*:103-118.

Britt, D. 1998b. "Beyond Elaborating the Obvious: Context-dependent Parent-involvement Scenarios in a Preschool Program." *Applied Behavioral Science Review 6*:179-197.

Cook, T. D. 1993). "A Quasi-sampling Theory of Generalization of Causal Relationships." *New Directions in Program Evaluation* 57:39-82.

Cook, T. D., and D. T. Campbell. 1979. *Quasi-experimentation: Design and Analysis Issues for Field Settings*. Chicago, IL: Rand-McNally.

Evans, W. 2000. "A Comparative Analysis of Levels of Receptivity in Urban Prenatal Clinics." Unpublished doctoral dissertation, Wayne State University, Detroit, MI.

Freedman, D. A.. 1991. "Statistical Models and Shoe Leather." In Marsden, P. V. (ed.), *Sociological Methodology*. Washington, DC: American Sociological Association, pp. 291-313.

Griffin, L., and C. C. Ragin. 1994. 'Some Observations on Formal Methods of Qualitative Analysis." *Sociological Methods and Research* 23:4-21.

Gould, Stephen Jay. 1981. *The Mismeasure of Man*. NY: W. W. Norton.

Gusfield, Joseph. 1976. "The Literary Rhetoric of Science: Comedy and Pathos in Drinking Driver Research." *American Sociological Review* 41: 16-34.

Hirsch, P., S. Michaels, and R. Friedman. 1987. "'Dirty Hands'" and "'Clean models.'" *Theory and Society* 16:317-336.

Kercher, Kyle. 1992. "Multiple Indicator Models." In Edgar Borgatta and Marie Borgatta (eds.), *Encyclopedia of Sociology*. NY: Macmillan.

Levine, Donald. 1985. *Flight From Ambiguity*. Chicago: University of Chicago Press.

Little, D. 1991. *Varieties of Social Explanation: An introduction to the Philosophy of Social Science*. Boulder, CO: Westview Press.

Luttrell, W. 2000. "'Good Enough'" Methods for Ethnographic Research. *Harvard Educational Review* 70:499-523.

Mahoney, J. 1999. "Nominal, Ordinal and Narrative Appraisal in Macrocausal Analysis." *American Journal of Sociology* 104:1154-1196.

Maines, D. 1993. "Narrative's Moment and Sociology's Phenomena: Toward a Narrative Sociology." *The Sociological Quarterly* 34:17-38.

Maines, D. 1999. "Information Pools and Racialized Narrative Structures." *The Sociological Quarterly* 40:317-326.

Maines, D. 2001. *The Faultline of Consciousness: A View of Interactionism in Sociology*. Hawthorne, NY: Aldine de Gruyter.

McCloskey 1990. *If You're So Smart*. Chicago: University of Chicago Press.

Phillips, Bernard. 2001. Beyond Sociology's Tower of Babel: Reconstructing the Scientific Method. Hawthorne, NY: Aldine de Gruyter.

Polkinghorne. 1988. *Narrative Knowing and the Human Sciences*. Albany: SUNY Press.

Ragin, C. 1987. *The Comparative Method: Moving Beyond Qualitative and Quantitative Strategies*. Berkeley: University of California Press.

Richardson, Laurel. 2000. "Writing: A Method of Inquiry." In Denzin, N., and Y. Lincoln (eds.), *Handbook of Qualitative Research, 2nd edition.*. Thousand Oaks, CA: Sage, pp. 923-948.

Riessman, C. K. 1990. *Divorce Talk*. New Brunswick: Rutgers University Press.

Soulliere, Britt and Maines. 2001. "Conceptual Modeling as a Toolbox for Grounded Theorists." *The Sociological Quarterly* 42: 253-269.

Tukey, J. W. 1962. "The Future of Data Analysis." *Annals of Applied Statistics 33*:1-67.

Weik, K. 1995. *Sensemaking in Organizations*. Thousand Oaks, CA: Sage.

Introduction to Chapter 8

Jack Levin's 1968 doctoral dissertation, "The Influence of Social Frame of Reference for Goal Fulfillment on Social Aggression," presents us with a microcosm of the forces producing prejudice and aggression in the macrocosm of modern society. Phillips attempts to understand the broad implications of Levin's dissertation by employing the web approach to the scientific method. By so doing, he discovers that individuals with a bureaucratic worldview--namely, all of us, to slightly varying degrees--increase their levels of prejudice when confronted with relative deprivation. By contrast, those who show the beginnings of an interactive worldview do not do so. When he combines this finding of the escalating gap between aspirations and fulfillment, as discussed in Chapter 1, then he comes to see the pervasiveness of relative deprivation throughout society. The result of this coupling of relative deprivation with a bureaucratic worldview, then, is prejudice and aggression. In other words, Phillips finds that the fundamental structures of modern society--our worldview and patterns of relative deprivation--are largely responsible for the development of prejudice and aggression. Yet this conclusion need not be a pessimistic one, for Levin provides evidence that a shift from a bureaucratic to an interactive worldview will alter this situation. And we can also understand that shift in worldview as associated with a shift to our reconstructed scientific method. Just as a bureaucratic scientific method is embedded within a bureaucratic worldview, so is an interactive scientific method embedded within an interactive worldview. Changing that method can help us to change our worldview.

Chapter 8

Prejudice: The Levin Experiment

Bernard Phillips

Ethnocentrism, or the favoring of one's own ethnic group over all others, is one kind of prejudice widely seen as a social problem. Whereas ethnocentrism is about hierarchical behavior relative to ethnicity, other "isms" focus on other hierarchies. We have racism, sexism, ageism and classism, and we can add other types of prejudice rarely studied, such as weightism, heightism, handicapism, uglyism and anti-intellectualism. They all have in common a persisting prejudice against any member of a given group, often accompanied by acts of discrimination. Such prejudice generally involves the stereotyping of individuals based on visible characteristics yet it generally proceeds invisibly, where the individual using such isms remains unaware of this fact. And increasing emphasis on the cultural value of equality in modern society, which directly opposes such isms, tends to make them even more invisible. The impact of such prejudice on the individual is difficult to measure, yet generally it appears to be profound. Efforts to understand the forces generating prejudice and to develop procedures for reducing it, based as they have been on a traditional approach to the scientific method, appear to this writer to have largely failed. The question I pose here is whether the web approach to the scientific method described and illustrated in this volume can do better. Are our efforts to understand isms in fact based on a too-narrow range of knowledge relative to the breadth of the web orientation? When we invoke that breadth, can we uncover forces behind such prejudice which otherwise would remain invisible? Forces which we can begin to address? Can that breadth be applied to other fundamental social problems like war, terrorism and poverty?

Following the general approach within this volume, we shall focus on a secondary analysis of Jack Levin's study of ethnocentrism, based on an experiment he performed as a requirement for his doctoral dissertation in sociology at Boston University (1968; see also Levin, 1975; Phillips, 1979: 185-188, 2001: Chapter 3). We shall begin with a description of Levin's 1968 dissertation, including the background to the study, the experiment he mounted, the results he obtained and the conclusions he drew. We follow this with a secondary analysis of that study with the aid of this volume's reconstructed approach to the scientific method. Our focus is on whether such an analysis can succeed in building useful bridges connecting the Levin study to the analysis of social change illustrated by Figure 1-2 in Chapter 1. Conceivably, any study whatsoever could have been selected, given the general nature of this reconstructed methodology, but the analysis in Chapter 1 is particularly useful because of its availability to the reader. Also, it contrasts sharply with the Levin study in its emphasis on society as a whole as well as very long-term processes of change. Yet such bridge-building constitutes only an initial step in any effort to assess the utility of our reconstructed methodology. This assessment will be made in the final section of the chapter. It will take into account credibility, new insights obtained, new directions for research, reflexivity and contribution to theory and methods in the discipline as a whole. And far beyond this bridge-building exercise, we hope to demonstrate the possibility of a web of bridges connecting sociology's the forty Sections of the American Sociological Association.

THE INFLUENCE OF SOCIAL FRAME OF REFERENCE FOR GOAL FULFILLMENT ON SOCIAL AGGRESSION

The academic background to Levin's study derives largely from two areas of knowledge: the social psychological literature on the "frustration-aggression" hypothesis stemming mainly from the work of Sigmund Freud and studies of "relative deprivation" and "reference groups" emerging from surveys of the American soldier during World War II (Stouffer et al., 1949). That academic background included a postwar conviction, based in part on the perceived success of those surveys, as to the importance of quantitative procedures coupled with survey procedures for the advancement of sociology. This was a period dominated by the middle-range approach to theory emphasized by Merton (1968), an approach which gave legitimacy to specialization with limited communication across the boundaries of sociology's various fields of knowledge. It is difficult for us moderns to return in memory to those times, given the enormous changes we have experienced. Narrow specialization has advanced substantially so that we have tripled the number of Sections of the American Sociological Association since the time Levin wrote his dissertation. Yet at the same time, with the demise of Parsonian theory's hegemony over sociological theory, those new Sections often represent challenges to earlier unquestioning commitments to the efficacy of surveys and quantitative analysis along with functionalist theory. And with the rise of postmodernist thinking, granting its frequent irrationality, we also have challenges issued about the fundamental assumptions behind our methods and theory. Nevertheless, let us attempt to go back in time to that earlier period of the late sixties in order to understand the Levin experiment.

Although Levin's title indicates an interest in "social aggression," which he defines broadly to include homicide along with acts of prejudice against members of minority groups--such as derogatory verbalizations--the literature he cites and the examples he uses suggest a narrower focus on prejudice. Given the civil rights movement in the sixties--not to suggest that prejudice and discrimination are not at the present time extremely important social problems--we can understand Levin's choice of a topic as occurring within that context. Levin was interested in the causes of prejudice or, in the jargon which dominated those years and many subsequent ones, the "independent variables" which might help to explain its origins. His overall approach was most scientific. He would make good use of the literature stemming from Freudian theory relating to the impact of frustration on aggression as well as the displacement of aggression onto people not responsible for that frustration. He would also build on the work of those influenced by the analysis of relative deprivation in the American soldier studies. And he would introduce a new element into the equation alongside of those other elements: the "frame of reference" of the individual, an aspect of the structure of the individual.

As Levin's first reader, I can recall the excitement and anticipation he experienced. And I also recall the lengths he went through to review literatures full of contradictory findings. What were the major findings bearing on Freud's theory of the displacement of aggression? Exactly what theories lay behind those findings? Why weren't those findings confirmed by those studies which yielded contradictory results? What theories might be advanced to explain that lack of confirmation? For example, there were the studies by Miller and Bugelski (1948), by Cowen, Landes and Shaet (1959), by Dollard (1957), and by Henry and Short (1955) supporting the frustration-aggression hypothesis. Yet studies by Stagner and Congdon (1955), by Epstein (1965), and by Rosnow, Holz and Levin (1966]) failed to support it. Levin drew this conclusion:

> The frustration-displacement hypothesis provides an inadequate explanation of social aggression. . .In the first place, frustration may not always lead to aggression as the original hypothesis would suggest. According to Allport, the most common reaction to frustration is a direct attempt to surmount the obstacle which blocks goal-fulfillment]. . . . aggression, when it does occur, is not always displaced, but may take an intropunitive form whereby hostility is turned upon the self or an extropunitive form whereby aggression is directed against the true source of the frustration and not against some innocent target (1968:13-14).

As for the role of relative deprivation in the onset of prejudice, the following is an example of that concept taken from the analysis of the morale of the American soldier during World War II, with a particular focus on the drafted married man:

> Comparing himself with his unmarried associates in the Army, he could feel that induction demanded greater sacrifice from him than from them;   and comparing himself with his married civilian friends he could feel that he had been called on for sacrifices which they were escaping altogether (Stouffer et al., 1949: 125).

A great many studies were stimulated by such findings, studies emphasizing the importance of reference groups in the generation of feelings of relative deprivation (see for example Proshansky and Seidenberg, 1965; Merton, 1957: 283-284; Lipset and Bendix, 1964: 254-259; Lipset, Trow and Coleman, 1962; and Form and Geschwender, 1962). Yet Levin saw in Wrong's article on "The Oversocialized Concept of Man" (1961)--the very first reference in his thesis--support for his view that social scientists were going too far in emphasizing the automatic existence of an outward or social orientation within the individual. And he found further support for this belief in Riesman's contrast of "other-direction" with "inner-direction" (1953). Granting the achievements of reference group theory in understanding the genesis of relative deprivation, something was still missing for an understanding of the genesis of prejudice, just as it was missing from the frustration-aggression studies.

Levin came up with this conclusion about the nature of the missing factor:

> Individuals rarely fulfill their goals in an "absolute" way: Instead, they may compare their successes and failures against a social frame of reference. On the other hand, it is often overlooked that the performances of other individuals and groups need not be employed as a point of reference, but that the individual may rely upon personal performances as a standard of comparison. These alternative frames of reference for goal fulfillment can be identified as *relative evaluation* whereby the individual judges his personal performances relative to the productivity of other persons and groups, and *self evaluation* whereby the individual relies upon his other personal performances, past or present, as a standard of comparison (1968: 20).

Levin's approach here does not negate the importance of frustration in the genesis of social aggression. Neither does it negate the importance of reference groups or individuals as a basis for feelings of relative deprivation and social aggression. Rather, it adds on to those earlier studies. For him, the individual's use of the language of prejudice is a more complex process than those two literatures, even taken together, envisaged. The individual is not an oversocialized being. And neither is she or he necessarily an other-directed being. By contrast with a frame of reference emphasizing "relative evaluation," the individual can develop a frame of reference stressing "self evaluation," where she or he looks inward and compares self with either previous performances or current ones. It is that frame of reference which appeared to Levin to be a key to the genesis of prejudice.

For Levin, feelings of relative deprivation still remain fundamental in the genesis of prejudice, but his concepts of "relative evaluation" and "self evaluation" help us to understand prejudice within a much wider context. He illustrates here how relative deprivation operates outside of the experimental laboratory:

> The appearance of relative evaluation among Negro Americans may be having profound effects on the character of the civil rights movement in the United States and on the expectations which Negro Americans have about it. Even though the actual gains of Negroes have been occurring faster since 1940 than during any other period of Negro American history, the position of Negro Americans assumes a desperately deprived character when contrasted

with the typical conditions of contemporary white Americans (Pettigrew and Back, 1967: 696). The result has been a keen sense of
relative deprivation (1968: 26).

Here, Levin is viewing the achievements of African-Americans
first by comparing those achievements with earlier ones, just as someone engaging in "self evaluation" would do for his or her own
achievements. Then, Levin proceeds to compare those achievements
with the achievements of white Americans, just as an African-
American engaging in "relative evaluation" might do. He saw the latter case, when combined with feelings of relative deprivation, as having the potential for social aggression, but not the former, a view much
the same as one of his experimental hypotheses. In this example, the
shoe is on the other foot and we are examining the social aggression of
African-Americans, but the process involved in the genesis of prejudice is much the same. Similarly, white Americans experiencing relative deprivation --as in the case of the drafted married man--may also
be relative evaluators, with the potential of this combination for social
aggression.

Levin proceeded to develop a 2 x 2 x 3 x 2 factorial design experiment with after-only measurements. This type of design permitted him
to test separately four different kinds of experimental conditions as
well as to test the joint impact of those conditions: (1) failure or success on a potentially frustrating experience; (2) the public or private
nature of the student's learning how well he or she did, suggesting the
potential for a built-in emphasis on relative evaluation; (3) an emphasis
on relative deprivation, relative satisfaction, or no information; and (4)
the student's frame of reference, that is, either relative evaluation or
self evaluation. In this way he was in a position to test for the separate
impact of frustration on increased prejudice, following the literature on
the frustration-aggression hypothesis. He was also able to test for the
separate impact of feelings of relative deprivation versus relative satisfaction on prejudice, following the literature on relative deprivation
and reference groups. In addition, Levin was in a position to test for
the combined impact of the student's frame of reference coupled with
relative deprivation, and also for the combined impact of his built-in
measure of relative evaluation coupled with relative deprivation.
Levin's analysis of the literature suggested the following: (1) failure
or success alone would not yield increased prejudice, given the inadequacy of frustration-aggression theory; (2) relative deprivation alone,
also would not yield increased prejudice, given the inadequacy of relative deprivation theory; (3) when relative evaluation is coupled with
relative deprivation, increased prejudice will result; and (4) when re-

sults of the test are revealed publicly--suggesting a built-in emphasis on relative evaluation--and this is combined with relative deprivation, prejudice increases.

Levin launched an experiment that included a questionnaire and involved 180 freshmen and sophomores enrolled in two sections of introductory sociology at Boston University during the fall semester of 1965. In order to measure social aggression he gave them an initial questionnaire--long before the experiment took place--which included attitudes toward Puerto Ricans measured with a question that followed the format of Osgood's semantic differential. This was his dependent variable. The actual experiment included several series of questions designed to measure whether the individual tended to be a relative evaluator or a self evaluator, the experimental condition getting at the student's frame of reference. He administered a questionnaire with a series of paragraphs like these:

Mary was in her freshman year of high school and had just received a B on her first algebra examination. Joan, who was Mary's best friend, got an A on the same examination. The class average for the exam was C. Last year in junior high school, Mary had received a C in mathematics. This year, Mary's highest exam grade was an A in French.

Without referring back to the paragraph on the preceding page [where the above paragraph was located] what do you think is the most accurate way to describe Mary's grade on her first algebra examination? (check only one)

1___Mary's algebra grade was higher than the class average
2___Mary's algebra grade was lower than her best friend's grade
3___Mary's algebra grade was higher than her last year's grade in mathematics
4___Mary's algebra grade was lower than her grade in French

Those checking 1 or 2--comparing themselves with others--were seen as illustrating relative evaluation. Those checking 3 or 4--comparing themselves with their own previous performances--were seen as illustrating self evaluation.

As for a second experimental condition involving relative deprivation, relative satisfaction or the control situation with no information, one-third of the students were given this note in their test booklets: "In similar groups of undergraduates at Boston College and Syracuse University, the average student was able to correctly complete 143 of the 150 items." This was the condition involving relative deprivation. Under the condition involving relative satisfaction, one-third of the students were informed that "in similar groups of undergraduates at

Boston College and Syracuse University, the average student was able to correctly complete 60 of the 150 items." As for the control or no-information condition, one-third of the sample received no information about the test performances of comparison groups. In yet a third experimental condition, half of the sample were informed that "one week from today, your instructor will post your examination grades on the door of this room," leading the students to believe that other members of the class would be able to see those grades. Levin interpreted this condition as involving built-in relative evaluation, for students could easily compare their grades with those of their classmates. By contrast with this public display of grades, the other half of the students were informed of the private reporting of grades: "One week from today, you will receive your examination grade. At the time, please ask your instructor for the envelope with your name on it (in which you will find your grade report)."

As for his fourth kind of experimental condition--frustration or lack of frustration--Levin arranged for two contrasting experimental situations where students in both the "failure" and the "success" condition were led to believe that they were taking an aptitude test for graduate school. Actually, it was a bogus test requiring them to identify pairs of words as having either the same or opposite meanings, with a severe penalty for guessing in that an incorrect answer on any item would nullify two correct answers.. Those in the failure condition were given 12 minutes to complete a test consisting of 150 items and were informed that less than 120 correct answers would result in automatic failure. Fully 50 of the 150 vocabulary-test items were constructed from nonsense syllables. No student in the failure condition completed more than 100 of the 150 items and, as a result, no one received a passing score. In the success condition, students were told that correct completion of less than 60 of the 150 items would result in automatic failure, by contrast with the cutting point of 120 items in the failure condition. Further, only 23 of the test items contained counterfeit words, by contrast with 50 in the failure condition. Also, instead of being limited to 12 minutes, sufficient time was permitted so that all subjects were able to complete most of the test items and obtain a high score. Immediately following this experience, students were once again given questions measuring their attitudes toward Puerto Ricans--the dependent variable--and this "after" measure was compared with the previous "before" measure to assess changes in levels of prejudice.

Feedback obtained from students after the experiment indicated that students had no idea that they were involved in an experiment. Levin's factorial design, with its 2 x 2 x 3 x 2 components of experimental conditions and one dependent variable, created no less than 24 different experimental experiences for the 180 students involved. For example, half of the students failed the bogus examination, but only half of that half were told their grades would be posted publicly. Only a portion of that group was classified as relative evaluators, and that group of relative evaluators was in turn divided into three subgroups where only in one subgroup were the students given instructions pointing toward relative deprivation. This kind of design might appear to be unnecessarily complex for the purposes at hand. Yet it is in fact a most efficient design, since Levin was able to test a number of hypotheses simultaneously, which he proceeded to do by means of an analysis of variance that revealed clear-cut results. He found that the impact of frustration on prejudice, taken all by itself, was not statistically significant. Granting the limitations of such statistical findings in assessing cause-effect relationships, this supported his previous perspective on the limitations of frustration alone on the displacement of aggression. This is not to claim that frustration has nothing to do with displaced social aggression, but rather that it appears to constitute too simplistic a hypothesis. Freud's idea becomes, then, only a partial truth, since it fails to take into account important additional forces which determine whether or not it in fact leads to displaced aggression.

As for the hypothesis that relative deprivation versus relative satisfaction will, all by itself, yield displaced social aggression or increased prejudice, that hypothesis also was not supported. Here again, Levin's earlier examination of a literature suggesting the validity of this hypothesis resulted in his conclusion that this too was no more than a partial truth. Rather, he had hypothesized that it was when the idea of relative deprivation was combined with a frame of reference emphasizing relative evaluation that increased prejudice would occur under the condition of frustration. Self evaluators, by contrast, would have nothing to gain by putting down--in see-saw fashion--members of a minority group and attempting to raise themselves up as a result. For they appear to be located on their own stairway, looking to their own previous or contemporary performances in an effort to improve on them, and not comparing themselves with others. Levin also had hypothesized that the public reporting of grades would function much like a student's own frame of reference that emphasized relative evaluation: it would influence students to emphasize relative evaluation even if their personal frame of reference was that of self evaluation. Accordingly, he had hypothesized that when such public reporting was combined with instructions emphasizing relative deprivation, the result would be increased prejudice against a minority group. Statistical results indicated confirmation for both of these hypotheses: relative evaluators experiencing relative deprivation increased their prejudice against Puerto Ricans, and those experiencing relative deprivation who were informed that their grades would be publicized (built-in relative evaluation) also increased such levels of prejudice.

Levin recognized the importance of his hypothesis on the individual's frame of reference in the genesis of prejudice, and he attempted to explore the implications of this finding by obtaining data on some of the correlates of frame of reference. For example, Levin's questionnaire included a 29-item version of the California F Scale, based on earlier studies of authoritarianism which implied links with ethnocentrism [Adorno et al., 1950]. Although the F-scale throws together a number of heterogeneous phenomena which take away from its precision, it includes two subscales--"power and toughness" and "conventionalism"--which are homogeneous. The power-and-toughness cluster consists of items such as these, with responses on a five-point scale: "I agree strongly, I agree somewhat, I neither agree nor disagree, I disagree somewhat, I disagree strongly":

Obedience and respect for authority are the most important virtues children should learn.
No weakness or difficulty can hold us back if we have enough will power.
Every person should have complete faith in some supernatural power whose decisions he obeys without question.
An insult to our honor should always be punished.
Sex crimes, such as rape and attacks on children, deserve more than mere imprisonment: such criminals ought to be publicly whipped, or worse.
There is hardly anything lower than a person who does not feel a great love, gratitude, and respect for his parents.
Most of our social problems would be solved if we could somehow get rid of the immoral, crooked, and feeble-minded people.

Levin found that this subscale of power and toughness has a statistically significant relationship to frame of reference.

The subscale of conventionalism--also rated on the same five-point scale--is illustrated by these items:

Young people sometimes get rebellious ideas, but as they grow up they ought to get over them and settle down.
If people would talk less and work more, everybody would be better off.
Nowadays when so many different kinds of people move around and mix together so much, a person has to protect himself especially carefully against catching an infection or disease from them.
No sane, normal, decent person could ever think of hurting a close friend or relative.
Nowadays more and more people are prying into matters that should remain personal and private.

The wild sex life of the old Greeks and Romans was tame compared to some of the goings-on in this country, even in places where people might least expect it.

A person who has bad manners, habits and breeding can hardly expect to get along with decent people.

Here again, Levin found this cluster to have a statistically significant relationship to the individual's frame of reference.

The individual's frame of reference was also tested against a series of questions oriented to measuring a tendency to downgrade the capabilities of the human being, known as the DC scale, a scale illustrated by these questions, rated on the same five-point scale:

The degree of intelligence with which any particular child is endowed determines his general efficiency all throughout life and sets an upper limit to what he can successfully perform.

Science has its place, but there are many important things that can never be understood by the human mind.

The nature of man's achievements is predetermined by his heredity.

Nobody ever learned anything really important except through suffering.

Once again, Levin found a statistically significant relationship between frame of reference and the scale he tested, in this case the DC scale.

Several other items were found to be statistically linked to frame of reference. Students were asked to rate the desirability of competition on a seven-point scale from "highly desirable" to "completely undesirable," with the relationship between relative evaluation and an emphasis on the desirability of competition proving to be statistically significant. Students were also asked: "Which do you generally prefer to deal with in your everyday affairs, ideas or things?" Whereas 43 percent of relative evaluators chose ideas, 56 percent of the self evaluators did so. As for career preference, whereas 58 percent of the relative evaluators chose non-profit institutions, 71 percent of the self evaluators did so. Levin explored this finding further by arranging for twenty graduate students in the Department of sociology to rate schools at Boston University according to whether "their related careers emphasize the pursuit of money and profit." They placed three schools in this category: Business Administration, Engineering and Public Communication. Among the relative evaluators, 27 percent chose majors within those schools by contrast with 17 percent for the self evaluators.

SECONDARY ANALYSIS: LEVIN'S EXPERIMENT ON PREJUDICE AND THE ANALYSIS OF SOCIAL CHANGE IN CHAPTER ONE

In our secondary analysis of Levin's experiment, we shall attempt to build bridges from that experiment to the analysis of long-term social change in Chapter 1, stressing the escalating gap between aspirations and fulfillment portrayed in Figure 1-2. The two studies appear to be worlds apart. Levin emphasized one social problem, that of prejudice, whereas Chapter 1 deals with a wide range of social problems. Levin's analysis centered on the small group, whereas society as a whole is the focus of Chapter 1. Levin was not concerned with long-term social change, yet such change is emphasized in that chapter. Levin's experiment involving primary analysis of data, yet Chapter 1 involves neither experiments nor primary analysis.. Levin's approach did not stress the importance of reflexivity, by contrast with Chapter 1. Also, over thirty years separate the two studies. On the other hand, they have much in common. The author was involved with both, they are committed to the importance of the scientific method, and both are implicitly optimistic about the possibilities of that method for penetrating our deepest problems. Both attempt to build on the results of earlier studies, and both were products of American sociologists. Both attempt to delve deeply into intangible phenomena, such as the individual's "frame of reference" or "worldview." Both took place within a societal context where sociology has very little credibility. Both emphasized new insights not emphasized or available within prior research. Both pointed up directions for further research. Both emphasized the importance of theory, as illustrated by their extensive literature reviews. And both were committed to the importance of methodology, whether of experimental design and analysis or of a reconstruction of traditional methodology.

In building bridges connecting these studies we are also connecting two vast territories: that of the late sixties and that of the beginning of the twenty-first century. Perhaps the greatest difference is a change from optimism about the future of sociology to pessimism and cynicism about that future, given the discipline's and social science's failures to address social problems effectively. Vidich and Bensman's description of the efforts of farmers and businessmen in the 1960s to cope with their long-term failures might well apply to ourselves:

The technique of particularization is one of the most pervasive
ways of avoiding reality. . . .The realization of lack of fulfillment
of aspiration and ambition might pose an unsolvable personal problem if the falsification of memory did not occur (1960: 299, 303).

We sociologists appear to manifest "the technique of particularization" in our multiplication of special fields and relative abandonment
of responsibility for the fate of the discipline as a whole. As for the
"falsification of memory," we can see it in shift of emphasis from the
very difficult problem of prejudice to the easily-visible phenomenon of
discrimination. We can also see that falsification in the shift away from
attempting to understand how to achieve the rehabilitation of criminal
offenders. And the overall impact of the varieties of postmodernist
thought--granting their contribution in raising fundamental questions--
appears to represent an abandonment of earlier ideals in favor of profound pessimism about the possibility of understanding today's complex social problems.

Yet Levin's ideals for sociology's possibilities were tied to his accepting research methods which apparently placed limits on the fulfillment of those ideals. For example, although he investigated the
frame of reference of those he studied, he failed to examine--
reflexively--his own frame of reference. Following Merton's middle-
range orientation to avoid abstract concepts which might have been
used to span a wide variety of fields within sociology, he apparently
assumed that his specialized analysis of prejudice would somehow,
somewhere, become combined with other specialized studies in the
discipline. However, we are now in a position to build conceptual
bridges that tie Levin's concepts to those in Chapter 1, bridges which
Levin failed to build. Yet more than the linkage of concepts at different levels of abstraction is involved here: there is also the relationship
between Levin's findings about the relationships among his concepts,
and the corresponding findings about the relationships among the corresponding concepts in Chapter 1. It is this combination of linking
concepts at different levels of abstraction, along with the relationships
among those concepts based on research in the discipline, which can
yield increased credibility for both the Levin study and that in Chapter
1. Further, it is that linkage which can open up new insights and yield
directions for further research as well as for understanding the scientific method. Yet our web approach is not limited to linking just these
two studies, since it points toward a vast web of other studies which
make use of at least some of the concepts involved. Within our present
approach to the scientific method, by contrast, those other studies are
seen as relatively isolated from one another.

In order to make these linkages, it is essential that we return to Chapter 1 and examine the key finding of that secondary analysis. Here, the reader should bear in mind that this finding is no more than one result of applying the web approach to sociological research. Granting that there are limitations to those substantive conclusions, such limitations should not imply that the web approach itself is not a useful procedure in general. Figure 2, "The Invisible Crisis of Modern Society," presents the key hypothesis of Chapter 1's secondary analysis: the escalating gap between expectations or aspirations and their fulfillment in modern society. This hypothesis sketched in Chapter 1 is based on the more detailed analysis in Chapter 3 of *Beyond Sociology's Tower of Babel: Reconstructing the Scientific Method* (Phillips, 2001). Conceptually, that escalating gap has to do with the full range of cultural values within modern society, and we can tie this lack of fulfillment to Levin's experimental condition of relative deprivation. This gap was in turn linked to the individual's worldview in Chapter 1, corresponding to Levin's concept of frame of reference. More specifically, a bureaucratic worldview corresponds to relative evaluation and an interactive worldview corresponds to self evaluation. Finally, these concepts are tied to social stratification in Chapter 1, corresponding to prejudice against Puerto Ricans in the Levin study. Following this linkage, just as Levin found that relative deprivation coupled with a frame of reference emphasizing relative deprivation yields increased prejudice against Puerto Ricans among 180 B, U. students, so does Chapter 1 suggest that the lack of value fulfillment coupled with a bureaucratic worldview yields social stratification throughout modern society.

What are some of the implications of this linkage between the two studies, one macroscopic and the other microscopic? Looking first to implications for Levin's microscopic study, it suggests the existence of enormous difficulties involved in changing patterns of prejudice in modern society, given their links to our cultural values, our very worldview as well as to our patterns of social stratification in society as a whole. And that same bureaucratic worldview teaches us to oversimplify the problem of prejudice so that we fail to see these difficulties. Given the complexities involved, it is no wonder that efforts to reduce prejudice appear in general to have failed. Yet another implication for Levin's study is more optimistic: given this understanding, it may be possible to make headway on both a more complex analysis of the forces involved in generating prejudice as well as on applied efforts to reduce it. For example, Chapter 1 implies that the origins of relative evaluation lie in a bureaucratic worldview which is in turn linked to a bureaucratic cultural paradigm. Further, Chapter 1 also implies that by shifting from a bureaucratic to an interactive worldview, the individual can also change from relative evaluation to self evaluation. In these ways, Chapter 1 opens up a general direction, albeit an extremely difficult one, for the individual to change from a frame of reference emphasizing relative evaluation to one emphasizing self evaluation. Given the relationships between worldview and the other abstract concepts in Table 1.1, it is a direction that also will point away from anomie, labeling, conformity, alienation and addiction. Generally, it takes into account a great deal of the complexity involved in any given scene, including social structure, aspects of history, the structure of the individual, and momentary phenomena within the scene.

Levin's analysis of some of the correlates of a frame of reference stressing relative evaluation--corresponding in our own terms to a bureaucratic worldview--can give us more assurance as to its simplistic emphasis as well as to the importance of a more complex orientation for moving away from prejudice. Metaphorically, we can see this oversimplification, stereotyping, labeling or prejudice from Ralph Ellison's novel, *Invisible Man*, where the Afro-American protagonist proclaims that he is invisible because those who approach him "see only my surroundings, themselves, or figments of their imagination--indeed, everything and anything except me" (1947:7). For example, questions in the power-and-toughness subscale emphasize the necessity of hierarchy or social stratification to the exclusion of all other factors, such as: "Obedience and respect for authority are the most important virtues children should learn." There is also a carrying of such stratification so far as to reach a point of violence: "Most of our social problems would be solved if we could somehow get rid of the immoral, crooked, and feeble-minded people." We can also see the subscale on conventionalism as also suggesting oversimplification: "Young people sometimes get rebellious ideas, but as they grow up they ought to get over them and settle down." From this conventional perspective, social interaction itself introduces too many questions or problems and should be reduced: "If people would talk less and work more, everybody would be better off." By contrast, self evaluators are less oriented to patterns of stratification and conformity, illustrating the orientation to complexity associated with an interactive versus a bureaucratic worldview.

Other statistical relationships which Levin uncovered also suggest links between frame of reference and worldview. The greater orientation to competition of relative evaluators versus self evaluators once again suggests a hierarchical orientation with winners versus losers. Yet within a more complex perspective with multiple values involved, any winner on one value can be a loser on others, and vice-versa, suggesting the more complex perspective associated with an interactive worldview. Further, Levin found relative evaluators to prefer things to ideas more than self evaluators, and they also chose careers emphasizing the pursuit of money or profit more than self evaluators. This harks back to the subscale on conventionalism, where people should "talk less and work more." From the perspective of the relative evaluator, social interaction can raise too many questions, and it is to be limited, just as "rebellious ideas" should be avoided, corresponding to the bureaucratic worldview discussed in Chapter 1. By contrast, social interaction is a fundamental component of an interactive worldview, where rebellious ideas are welcomed. Overall, Chapter 1 helps us to understand how the diverse relationships Levin uncovered between frame of reference and other factors can all be understood as illustrating different facets of a contrast between two worldviews, one of which is more oriented to complexity than the other. In this way, we can understand more clearly the genesis of Levin's two contrasting frames of reference. For example, worldview is itself tied to social structures such as anomie, cultural values and social stratification, helping us to understand its genesis in society and history.

When we understand Table 1-1 as suggesting that it is scientifically fruitful to take into account all nine cells in researching any phenomena, then we open up to the complexity involved within an interactive worldview or a frame of reference emphasizing self evaluation, by contrast with a bureaucratic worldview and relative evaluation. That figure is itself based on far more than a set of abstract categories linked by still broader categories, for it derives from a wide range of studies showing relationships among those concepts that have been derived from research. By illustrating those relationships we are able to gain further insight into Levin's experiment on prejudice and come up with additional hypotheses for future research. Given enough space we might range widely over those nine cells of Table 1-1, but our limited space requires more focus, so we shall center simply on cultural values. We have already seen the lack of fulfillment of cultural values as linked to patterns of relative deprivation in the Levin study. We have also noted above that by opening up to the range of cultural values we also open up to the complexity associated with an interactive worldview and a frame of reference emphasizing self evaluation. And following the analysis in Chapter 1, as depicted in Figure 1-2, we have noted the revolution of rising expectations for a wide range of cultural values associated with the scientific and industrial revolutions of the last four centuries.

Yet all of this by no means exhausts the relevance of cultural values--given the abstract or broad nature of this concept along with its links to other basic concepts--for understanding the forces producing prejudice or suggesting directions for confronting prejudice effectively. For example, we might look to a growing inability to fulfill the cultural value of equality, paralleling the more general growing gap between aspirations and fulfillment sketched in Figure 1-2, as implied in that same figure. If individuals are alerted to this gap for equality in a situation where they are compared with others, then that situation would encourage relative evaluation, just as the Levin experiment encouraged relative evaluation by informing students that their grades would be posted. As for relative deprivation, the individual could be alerted to failings with reference to commitment to the cultural value of equality. But instead of this resulting in increasing prejudice against a minority group, the individual could be given an opportunity to show commitment to that cultural value, thus reducing his or her feelings of relative deprivation. If individuals in fact seize that opportunity and show increased commitment to the cultural value of equality, then this is evidence both for Levin's findings as well as for the secondary analysis of cultural values, worldviews and stratification in Chapter 1. In other words, we are conceiving here of two specific studies of prejudice as well as a bridge having to do with cultural values that connects them. One study is the Levin study. The other study, yet to be described, has to do with the impact of awareness of the individual's lack of fulfillment of the cultural value of equality. The bridging study connecting the two is the secondary analysis in Chapter 1. We should bear in mind that these studies can be related by means of the interactive scientific method described and illustrated in this volume, but that they would remain separated if we employed the traditional approach to the scientific method.

The second study, the one centering on the individual's fulfillment of the cultural value of equality, is actually an entire research program conducted over a thirty-year period by Milton Rokeach and a number of others (Greenstein, 1989). Rokeach had become interested in going beyond the work on attitudes revealing cognitive dissonance (Festinger, 1957), believing that a focus on long-term values would be more fruitful than the current emphasis on short-term attitudes (1967, 1968; see also 1964). He devised a series of experiments having to do with the cultural value of equality which he believed would yield long-term behavioral changes. These experiments would confront the individual with a failure to rank the importance of equality close to the importance of the cultural value of freedom, that is, experiments which would introduce what he called "self-confrontation." Students at Michigan State University--during the late sixties when the civil rights movement had gathered momentum--were asked to rank eighteen values in order of their "importance to you, as guiding principles in your life," values that included freedom and equality. They were then informed that students who were active in the civil rights movement had ranked freedom first and equality second, whereas students not sympathetic to that movement had ranked freedom first and equality eleventh. This announcement was followed by this interpretation:

> This raises the question whether those who are against civil rights are really saying that they care a great deal about their own freedom but are indifferent to other people's freedom. Those who are for civil rights are perhaps saying that they not only want freedom for themselves, but for other people too (quoted in Greenstein, 1989: 400-401).

When students in the experimental group were given another opportunity to rank those 18 values at time intervals up to seventeen months after the experiment, they tended--with statistical significance--to increase their ranking of equality, and those who had declared favorability to civil rights tended to increase that ranking more than others. Further studies going beyond these paper-and-pencil tests supported the findings. For example, some three to five months after the initial study, students in the experimental group were more than twice as likely to respond favorably to a solicitation to join the NAACP than students in the control group. Also, experimental subjects were more likely to enroll in a special program of coursework on ethnic studies fully twenty-one months after the experiment. In addition, those subjects who changed majors were more likely than control subjects to shift to either a social science or education. A non-experimental study based on a special television program on February 27, 1979 in eastern Washington State was designed to test whether that medium could yield similar results. Although no statistically significant changes in value rankings occurred in mailed questionnaires, changes did occur in the predicted direction. But statistical significance was obtained for reactions to requests for donations to organizations dealing with racism as well as sexism. And these effects were strongest for those who had viewed the entire program without interruption. These studies provide evidence supporting not only Rokeach's thesis and Levin's thesis but also the analysis in Chapter 1 of the link between worldview, the lack of fulfillment of cultural values, and stratification.

Up to this point in our secondary analysis, our focus has been on gaining further understanding and support for the Levin study with the aid of the analysis of long-term change in society as a whole in Chapter 1. Now let us turn around and look in the other direction: What

can our secondary analysis of the Levin study do for further understanding of Chapter 1? For one thing, the Levin study gives us concrete examples and measurement procedures for key abstract concepts
in that chapter. For example, we can measure a bureaucratic and an
interactive worldview by using Levin's measures for relative evaluation and self evaluation. And the same is true for understanding the
concrete nature of social stratification, given Levin's measurement of
prejudice against Puerto Ricans. Further, Levin's analysis of the
power-and-toughness and conventionalism subscales of the F-scale
yield ways of measuring and understanding the oversimplification associated with a bureaucratic worldview. This also supports the complex approach to understanding suggested by Figure 1-3, with its
orientation to taking into account--for any given phenomena--social
structure, individual structure and the situation. Also, Levin's linkage
of a frame of reference emphasizing relative evaluation with interest in
competition--as well as in things versus ideas along with careers emphasizing money and profit--fleshes out still further our understanding
of the nature of a bureaucratic worldview. In other words, Levin's
study helps us to move down language's ladder of abstraction from the
abstract concepts located in Chapter 1 to the concrete ones he used in
his experiment. And his study adds credibility to that chapter.

Once we use Chapter 1 as a bridge connecting the Levin experiment with the Rokeach experiment, we can begin to understand the
potential of our research approach for shedding further light on that
chapter. For example, granting the importance of one's worldview,
and granting the links between that concept and the other concepts in
Table 1.1, how is one's worldview to be changed? Or, more specifically, how might we shift from a bureaucratic to an interactive worldview? Rokeach's analysis suggests that we bring up to the surface
contradictory values within the bureaucratic worldview, or contradictions between cultural values and patterns of behavior or social organization. And his analysis further suggests that we open up a direction
for alternative patterns of behavior which resolve that contradiction,
just as he offered students another chance to rank cultural values and
repair the contradiction they felt about their downgrading the importance of the value of equality. Yet this is exactly what was done in
Chapter 1, although in an extremely general way. The accelerating gap
between aspirations and fulfillment depicted in Figure 2 is an instance
of a contradiction between basic cultural values like equality and patterns of social organization which limit the fulfillment of those values.
And the discussion of an interactive worldview suggests a direction for
resolving that contradiction. Thus, the Rokeach study suggests that the
approach taken in Chapter 1 is exactly what is needed for changing

cultural paradigms: unearthing contradictions within a cultural paradigm, and describing an alternative cultural paradigm within which those contradictions are resolved.

The Rokeach experiment, strengthened by its links to the Levin experiment, also adds credibility to the web approach to the scientific method presented in Chapter 1 and helps us understand it further. A key to that web approach is the definition of a fundamental problem, an approach that follows Rokeach's approach to encouraging behavioral change: locate basic contradictions and bring them up to the surface. And just as Rokeach offered students a way of resolving this contradiction with another chance to rank values, so does the scientific method offer the researcher specific procedures for resolving the problem or contradiction they define. Rokeach helps us to understand the importance of the link between that external scientific definition of a problem and the internal contradiction or problem within the researcher: the latter, it appears, is most important if the procedures of the scientific method are to be sustained. By contrast, the bureaucratic approach to the scientific method stresses the importance of limited emotional involvement on the part of the researcher, given the possibility that emotional involvement can work to bias the results obtained. The interactive approach cannot eliminate the possibility of such bias, but it can open up to the reader the commitments of the researcher, assuming that such research embodies a reflexive component. In this way, interactions between the researcher and the phenomena under investigation are opened up to the reader, and he or she moves in a position to assess the impact of those interactions on the research process. The result is not the elimination of bias, but it does allow for intense emotional commitment by the researcher and an opportunity for the reader to assess the results.

It should be noted that the web approach also opens us up to any and all studies which can help us to learn about the researcher's impact on the research process. For example, there are the studies by Retzinger (1991, 1995; see also Retzinger and Scheff, 2000) and Scheff (1990, 1994, 1997) which help us to understand how shame and anger work--both separately and together in a continuing cycle--in a small-group situation. We social scientists are not accustomed to turning the microscope back on ourselves, yet we can learn to do so. Of course, it is our ideas and actions along with our emotions which are clues to our potential impact on the research process. The foregoing analysis of the nature of an individual's worldview and how it might be measured could also be aimed at the investigator to help determine her or his impact on that process. These studies by Retzinger and Scheff suggest the utility of videotaping the researcher during aspects of the research.

They indicate the importance of visual markers no less than the detailed examination of verbal expressions--as noted in Chapter 2 of this volume--for the detection of emotions. Yet all of this would be no more than a beginning in any effort to assess investigator effect. Retzinger and Scheff would agree, given their emphasis on the complexity of social interaction.

In the above secondary analysis we have employed the reconstructed approach to the scientific method sketched in Chapter 1. It is an approach that has involved the definition of fundamental problems, problems that are sufficiently important to capture the commitment of the researcher and engage the interest of his or her audience. This is aided by the ability to link social problems to one another, just as the problem of prejudice can be linked to general problems such as an accelerating gap between aspirations and fulfillment throughout modern society. That approach has involved very abstract concepts, like worldview, cultural values and patterns of social stratification. And it has also involved concrete concepts like relative and self evaluation and prejudice against Puerto Ricans. Those abstract concepts are linked systematically to one another, as in Chapter 1, just as the concrete concepts are linked, as in the Levin experiment. Those links carry us beyond simply categorizing concepts to a quest for cause-effect relationships. Finally, there is a reflexive orientation within this interactive approach to the scientific method. Such reflexivity is illustrated by the very process of engaging in a secondary analysis. It is also illustrated by returning to the concepts and propositions developed throughout the history of the discipline and attempting to build on them. This procedure is given lip service within a bureaucratic approach to the scientific method, but it generally fails due to a middle-range approach to levels of abstraction as well as concern for value neutrality. By contrast, within an interactive approach the investigator reveals personal assumptions insofar as possible.

ASSESSING THE UTILITY OF THE WEB APPROACH

Credibility

Looking back at the foregoing analysis, we have attempted to illustrate the utility of a reconstructed scientific method in several ways. As for credibility, we have attempted to build bridges connecting a microscopic with a macroscopic study, a primary experiment with a secondary analysis, a relatively static study with one stressing long-term social change, a study centered on one social problem with one focused on a wide range of problems, a study with few abstract concepts to a study with many, and a relatively non-reflexive study with one that is relatively reflexive. Along the way, our bridge has extended to another experiment, one linked to prejudice but also involving efforts to modify values and behavior through self-confrontation. Neither this one secondary analysis nor all of the secondary analyses within this volume is sufficient to establish the credibility of our research approach, a task that can only be fulfilled over time and on the basis of a great deal of research. Our goal in employing this reconstructed scientific method extends far beyond building bridges connecting these three studies. We hope that these bridges will demonstrate the fruitfulness of building a web of interlocking bridges connecting the literatures within the forty Sections of the American Sociological Association, just as the concepts in Chapter 1 extend widely within social structure, the structure of the individual, and phenomena within the situation. The credibility of the web approach depends on whether it can help us sociologists to fulfill what Mills called "the promise of sociology." This involves both the rapid cumulative development of our knowledge as well as the ability to use that knowledge as a solid basis for addressing the mammoth social problems of modern society.

New Insights and Directions for Research

We are now able to see the Levin experiment as a microcosm of the macrocosm of modern society outlined in Chapter 1, giving us a clearer view not only of the concept of worldview but also of the other abstract concepts located in Table 1.1. Although much of the secondary analysis has centered on cultural values, including the introduction of the Rokeach experiment, we might equally have examined the other concepts in that figure more fully. One implication of our analysis is the incredible difficulty involved in understanding or addressing the social problem of prejudice, given its ties to our worldview, cultural values and patterns of social stratification. Within a bureaucratic worldview or relative evaluation, complexities become invisible just as Ralph Ellison discussed in his *Invisible Man*. Also, competition oriented to hierarchy along with a focus on things and materialistic values become the order of the day. And we learn along with the Springdalers the techniques of particularization and the falsification of memory as devices for achieving some degree of satisfaction in life. In our research we learn to avoid tackling the large problems of society with all of their complexity. Yet the Levin experiment coupled with the Rokeach experiment also point to a possible direction for addressing the mammoth problem of prejudice, linked as it appears to be with both the problem of changing our cultural worldview and our research paradigm within the social sciences. For example, the Levin experiment gives us a clearer view and an approach to measurement of the bureaucratic and interactive cultural paradigms. And the Rokeach experiment gives us a direction for altering paradigms--meshing with Kuhn's analysis--by making value contradictions visible and providing an alternative paradigm within which those contradictions promise to be resolved.

Reflexivity

For an extended treatment of the importance of reflexivity, the reader might consult Chapter 2 of this volume. What is involved is the enormous problem of opening up to one's own worldview, based on the prevailing cultural paradigm, a situation much like that of the goldfish attempting to see the water in the goldfish bowl. If Kuhn suggested the enormous difficulties involved in challenging one's research paradigm, then the difficulties here are many-fold greater. His suggestion--that we require an alternative research paradigm which resolves the contradictions within the old paradigm if we are to challenge the latter--meshes with our analysis of the Rokeach study, where fundamental contradictions are brought to the surface and the individual has an opportunity to resolve them. Our secondary analysis of the Levin study helps us to understand mere clearly just what it is that we are bringing up to the surface, as well as the nature of a direction that will resolve those contradictions. In a sense we are all reflexive simply by using language, and the social sciences carry that reflexivity further by helping us all to understand ourselves. But the web approach to reflexivity requires much more: to probe so deeply that we are able to bring up to the surface our very worldview. To the extent that we can achieve this, we can communicate to one another the nature of a fundamental force that profoundly influences every aspect of the research process. And in this way we are able to follow the ideals of the scientific method. Failing this openness, it becomes difficult or impossible to achieve much cumulative development of knowledge, since we are continuing to hide powerful forces which shape every aspect of our research procedures.

Implications for Theory and Methods

It is for the reader to assess whether our reconstructed scientific method--with its theoretical implications--not only follows scientific ideals but is also a fruitful or useful reconstruction. Does it in fact build bridges, increase credibility, yield new insights, yield directions for further research, encourage a useful reflexive orientation, and advance theory and methods within the discipline as a whole? Does it appear to help us sociologists achieve rapid cumulative development by helping us to integrate our knowledge and build on that knowledge more effectively? Does it also point toward the development of a platform of knowledge on the basis of which we might address fundamental social problems more effectively? And might such a platform provide a better basis for all of us to develop a sociological imagination? Such questions are best answered not by those of us involved with this volume but by sociologists throughout the discipline. It is you, the reader, who are in the only position to determine the utility of this approach to theory and methods. Do you believe that you can go beyond the relative simplicity of our traditional specialized and subspecialized approaches to the scientific method? Are you convinced to a degree that human behavior involves greater complexity than such approaches are able to handle? Can you find the time to study this approach to methods and theory carefully and develop links to a relatively unfamiliar literature? Only a few of us are involved in this volume, and our own convictions and research do not go very far, considering the vastness of our discipline. Yet if you, the reader, join us, we all will be able to learn quite soon whether or not this reconstruction of the scientific method is indeed worth pursuing.

END NOTE

In looking back over this chapter, a thread of optimism about sociology's possibilities may be found throughout it. It is no accident that the concepts of anomie and alienation have been used here, for they suggest the optimism of classical sociologists like Durkheim and Marx as to those possibilities. Levin's study somehow manages to exude optimism even in a century which had experienced two devastating world wars as well as the holocaust and a great deal more to encourage pessimism. And the Rokeach experiment exudes optimism as well, with its direction for bringing basic contradictions or problems to the surface and charting a direction for resolving them. There is also the optimism contained in Chapter 1 as well as the present chapter, written in a new century and following decades during which pessimism and cynicism about sociology's possibilities have escalated throughout the discipline, accompanied by escape to narrow Sections within sociology. It appears that our traditional and bureaucratic research paradigm is nested within a bureaucratic cultural paradigm, creating incredible difficulties for shifting to this reconstructed scientific method even should we desire to do so. Yet it also appears that we sociologists are by far in the best position, given our breadth, our classical heritage, and our commitment to the promise of sociology, to show the way. Will we be able to take this responsibility--to ourselves, to our discipline, and perhaps to the world--seriously? Will we be able to make good use of the window of opportunity that present controversies within the discipline over fundamental matters give us? Will we be able to do this before that window closes down on all of us?

REFERENCES

Adorno, T. W., et al. 1950. *The Authoritarian Personality.* NY: Harper & Row.

Cowen, E., J. Landes, and D. E. Schaet. 1959. "The Effects of Mild Frustration on the Expression of Prejudiced Attitudes." *Journal of Abnormal and Social Psychology* 58(1959):33-38.

Dollard, John. 1957. *Caste and Class in a Southern Town.* New York: Doubleday.

Ellison, Ralph. 1947. *Invisible Man.* New York: Signet.

Epstein, Ralph. 1965. "Authoritarianism, Displaced Aggression, and Social   Status of the Target," *Journal of Personality and Social Psychology* 2: 585-588.

Festinger, Leon. 1957. *A Theory of Cognitive Dissonance.* Stanford: Stanford University Press.

Form, William H., and James A. Geschwender. 1962. "Social Reference Basis of Satisfaction." *American Sociological Review* 27:228-237.

Gorer, Geoffrey. 1964. *The American People.* New York: W. W. Norton.

Greenstein, Theodore N. 1989. "Modifying Beliefs and Behavior through Self-Confrontation," *Sociological Inquiry* 59 (November):396-408.

Henry, Andrew F., and James F. Short, Jr. 1954. *Suicide and Homicide.* Glencoe: The Free Press.

Levin, Jack. 1968. "The Influence of Social Frame of Reference for Goal   Fulfillment on Social Aggression." Ph.D. dissertation, Boston University. Ann Arbor, Michigan: University Microfilms, catalog number 6818171.

Levin, Jack. 1975. *The Functions of Prejudice.* New York: Harper & Row.

Lipset, Seymour Martin, and Reinhard Bendix. 1964. *Social Mobility in Industrial Society.* Berkeley: University of California.

Lipset, Seymour Martin, Martin Trow, and James Coleman. 1962. *Union Democracy.* New York: Doubleday.

Merton, Robert K. 1968. *Social Theory and Social Structure.* Glencoe: Free Press.

Miller, Neal E. and Richard Bugelski. 1948. "Minor Studies of Aggression: II. The Influence of Frustrations Imposed by the In-Group on Attitudes Expressed Toward Out-Groups." *Journal of Psychology* 25:437-442.

Pettigrew, Thomas F., and Kurt W. Back. 1967. "Sociology in the Desegregation Process: Its Use and Disuse." In *The Uses of Sociology* (ed. by Lazarsfeld, Sewell and Wilensky). New York: Basic Books, pp. 692-722.

Phillips, Bernard. 1979. *Sociology: From Concepts to Practice.* New York: McGraw-Hill.

Phillips, Bernard. 2001. *Beyond Sociology's Tower of Babel: Reconstructing the Scientific Method,* Hawthorne, NY: Aldine de Gruyter.

Proshansky, Harold, and Bernard Seidenberg. 1965. *Basic Studies in Social Psychology.* New York: Holt, Rinehart, and Winston.

Retzinger, Suzanne. 1991. *Violent Emotions: Shame and Rage in Marital Quarrels.* Newbury Park, CA: Sage.

Retzinger, Suzanne. 1995. "Identifying Shame and Anger in Discourse." *American Behavioral Scientist* 38(August):1104-1113.

Retzinger, Suzanne, and Thomas J. Scheff. 2000. "Emotion, Alienation, and Narratives: Resolving Intractable Conflict." *Mediation Quarterly* (Fall): 71-86.

Riesman, David (with Nathan Glazer and Reuel Denney). 1953. *The Lonely Crowd.* New York: Doubleday.

Rokeach, Milton. 1964. *The Three Christs of Ypsilanti.* New York: Knopf.

Rokeach, Milton. 1967. *Value Survey.* Sunnyvale, CA: Halgren Tests.

Rokeach, Milton. 1968. *Beliefs, Attitudes, and Values.* San Francisco: Jossey-Bass.

Rosnow, R. L., R. F. Holz, and Jack Levin. 1966. "Differential Effects of Complementary and Competing Variables in Primacy-Recency." *Journal of Social Psychology* 69:135-147.

Scheff, Thomas J. 1990. *Microsociology: Discourse, Emotion, and Social Structure.* Chicago: University of Chicago Press.

Scheff, Thomas J. 1994. *Bloody Revenge: Emotions, Nationalism, and War.* Boulder, CO: Westview.

Scheff, Thomas J. 1997. *Emotions, the Social Bond, and Human Reality: Part/Whole Analysis.* Cambridge, MA: Cambridge University Press.

Stagner, R., and C. S. Congdon. 1955. "Another Failure to Demonstrate Displacement of Aggression," *Journal of Abnormal and Social Psychology* 51:696-697.

Stouffer, Samuel et al. 1949. *The American Soldier, Volume 1.* Princeton: Princeton University Press.

Vidich, Arthur, and Joseph Bensman. 1960. *Small Town in Mass Society.* Garden City. NY: Doubleday.

Wrong, Dennis H. 1961. "The Oversocialized Concept of Man." *American Sociological Review* 26:183-93.

Introduction to Chapter 9

A 1954 analysis of a psychiatric interview of "Roberta" by "Dr. B."--available on an LP record--is the basis for Retzinger's secondary analysis. Retzinger develops a highly systematic and detailed procedure for analyzing the transcript so as to take into account the many verbal and paralinguistic ways in which shame is expressed. She finds that there is a close relationship between the expression of shame and the nature of the interaction between doctor and patient, where shame is often linked to conflict between the two. For example, she finds Dr. B. almost completely oblivious to Roberta's expressions of shame in his total commitment to categorize her with a diagnosis. And he also seems oblivious to his own feelings of shame, brought on by Roberta's question, "Am I boring you? You keep looking at the clock." Retzinger offers us a methodology for taking into account much of the complexity involved in any given situation where social interaction is taking place. From the perspective of Table 1-1, this involves an ability to analyze the situation. Yet at the same time she makes use of very abstract sociological concepts that mesh with the sociological literature, such as "alienation," "labeling" and "social interaction." We can also see from her analysis indications of the narrowness of the orientation of the profession of psychiatry, for Dr. B.--with all of his training--is unable to take into account the impact of his patient's shame and his own shame. That inability to be "reflexive" in Gouldner's terms also extends to traditional research methods within the social sciences, a limitation which can be changed by a shift to our reconstructed approach.

Chapter 9

Alienation, Labeling, and Stigma:

Integrating Social and Emotional Aspects of Mental Illness

Suzanne M. Retzinger

I use a single case to show the dynamics of labeling and maintenance of mental illness. This chapter suggests interpersonal sources of rejection and labeling produce iatrogenic symptoms. My purpose is to explain mental illness in terms of both primary and secondary residual deviance (Lemert, 1951; Scheff, 2000). A conventional view of mental illness can oppress those who are deviant. I use a method that undercuts the conventional view, and links abstract concepts with case material in order to get a clearer understanding of labeling, alienation, emotions and mental illness.

Labeling theory (Scheff, 1966, 2000) has given rise to intense debate (Crocetti, et al., 1974; Gove, 1982; Gove and Fain, 1973; Huffine & Clausen, 1979). The critics' claim that the overall impact of discrimination and stigma related to labeling is small, and that the consequences of rejection by others is of little importance. It has become customary to consider that internal systems alone, particularly biological, biochemical or psychodynamic ones, produce the symptoms of mental illness. Critics posit the cause of the illness within the individual; society intervenes only later after the causes of mental illness are already present.

For understanding sub-disciplines within sociology, a web of concepts is useful (Phillips 1988, 2001). As well as having a web of concepts, learning to be "multi-lingual" within the discipline as well as between disciplines is useful in understanding concepts on a working level as well as using material available to solve social problems. The integration of the sub disciplines within sociology is crucial for sociology as a whole. Phillips (1988, 2001), and Scheff (1990, 1997) discuss the necessity of applying the language of sociology to case material. Emphasis in this chapter is on using and linking abstract sociological concepts and applying them to a concrete phenomenon--a psychiatric interview. I use case material for understanding labeling of mental illness and the effect of labeling. I use discourse analysis and word count to get a better understanding of the labeling phenomenon. The value of discourse analysis is that it penetrates deeply into the case material in a way that quantitative methods cannot.

A single case, taken from Gill, Newman and Redlich (1954), is used to analyze the dynamics of the labeling process. In *The Initial Interviews in Psychiatric Practice* they analyze 3 interviews to demonstrate interviewing processes. The purpose of their 'microscopic' analysis of patient-therapist interaction was to look at the dynamics and interviewing technique (10). Although Gill et al. specifically state that "Humiliation of the patient must be avoided at all costs" (54), this is not addressed in either the actual interview or in the analysis of the interview. Word count and discourse analysis are used to get at the underlying dynamics of labeling.

Discourse is analyzed during an actual therapeutic dialogue; sequences of emotion are traced prior to a moment of relapse. Sequences within and between therapist and patient alternate from emotional alienation and shame, to disrespect and labeling, to further alienation and shame, and so on. The method here differs from other sociological methods for studying emotion in that it is interdisciplinary and multilevel. While most studies on emotion use survey or field methods, I use sequential analysis of discourse as it occurs in interaction. This method of analysis may lend itself well to expanding studies of emotion, in addition to or in conjunction with any type of research method.

POWER OF SOCIAL-EMOTIONAL BONDS

I begin with the premise that the individual does not exist outside his or her social context. Many theorists of mental illness, including psychiatrists, psychologists and sociologists, have viewed human beings as individuals outside the social context, even though early social psychologists such as James (1910), Cooley (1902), McDougall (1908), and Mead (1934) proposed a thrust toward sociability:

> [We have an] innate propensity to get ourselves noticed, and noticed favorably, by our kind. No more fiendish punishment could be devised. . .than that one should be turned loose in society and remain absolutely unnoticed by all the members thereof. . .as if we were non-existing things, a kind of rage and impotent despair would ere long well up in us. . .(emphasis added) (James, 1910: 179).

> [The individual] finds in the praise of his fellows evidence that his emotions are shared by them, their blame or disapproval makes him experience the pain of isolation. . .this sense of isolation, of being cut off from the habitual fellowship of feeling and emotion, is, no doubt, the source of the severest pain of punishment; and moral disapproval, even though not formally expressed, soon begins to give them this painful sense of isolation; while approval . . .makes them feel one with their fellows. (emphasis added). (McDougall, 1908: 173).

Studies of social isolation and confinement (e.g., Bowlby, 1973; Spitz, 1946; Harlow, 1962) support the conjectures about the importance of human sociability. Baumeister and Leary (1995) suggest that the need to belong has strong effects on our emotional life, and that alienation is linked to a variety of ills. Although a biosocial view of human behavior is not a new idea, what is new is the systematic, microscopic analyses based upon the observation of complex interactive processes between the neonate and caregiver. Human beings appear to be biologically geared toward limbic resonance (Lewis and colleagues, 2000).

Evidence indicates that the infant is much more competent and socially responsive than was thought in the past, coming into the world equipped to interact and respond. The affective system is a primary means by which the infant monitors itself and modulates its behavior in relation to others. These studies show the human with innate capacities for sociability and affection. Human beings appear to be social by biological origin.

The importance and power of the social bond occurs not only in infancy but over the lifespan. Shaver (1987) shows the similarities between adult romantic love relationships and attachment in infants, following Bowlby (1969). The concept of the social bond can help explain how mental illness develops and how it is maintained. The emotions associated with threatened or broken bonds (in the context of social isolation) may play a central role in both primary and secondary residual deviance.

In a biosocial framework, a primary motive is securing important bonds; emotions play a central role--secure bonds are accompanied by feelings of joy and happiness; threatened, damaged or severed bonds are accompanied by feelings of insecurity, sadness, anger and shame. One function of these emotions is to serve as signals to readjust in relationship to others. Human survival is dependent on social bonds. Shame plays a prominent role in the maintenance of bonds; it is a signal of threatened or damaged bonds.

The source of shame is a perceived injury to self: criticism, rejection or fear of rejection, rebuff, devaluation, discrimination, discredit, moral condemnation, inattentiveness and unrequited love. It can be imagined as well as real, or a combination.

ROLE OF SHAME

In her analysis of mental illness, Lewis (1971, 1981, 1983) proposed that unacknowledged shame leads to the formation of symptoms and this needs to be analyzed. She (1981) argued that virtually any therapeutic intervention might be experienced by the patient as an exposure of his or her inadequacy. She suggests "unanalyzed shame in the patient-therapist interaction fosters the sudden development of negative therapeutic reactions. . ." (204).

Shame symbolizes mutual social involvement, and at the same time reminds us of our separateness. Shame tells us that we are both separate and social beings, and guards the boundaries of privacy and intimacy (Lynd, 1958). For shame to occur we must care in some way about the other. To neglect to acknowledge damaged or threatened bonds, or the shame that is evoked, leaves relationships open to disruption. Shame occurs when persons are not connected --either too close or too distant. Being too close is engulfment, being too distant is isolation; both can involve violation of boundaries. Shame is about alienation. In Buber's words there is no "I-thou" relationship.

A working concept of shame (Lewis, 1971) includes these relationships between self and other: 1) The self is the object of scorn, contempt, ridicule; the other is the source. 2) The self feels paralyzed, helpless, passive, etc.; the other appears to be ridiculing, powerful, active. 3) The self is flooded with noxious stimuli such as rage, tears, blushing, fluster, blankness; although the other may also be in a state of shame, he/she appears intact. 4) One feels childish, small, insignificant, etc., while the other appears adult, going away, abandoning. 5)

Both self and other are focal in awareness. The self may split or think they are being observed. The other appears to be the observer. 6) The self may begin to function poorly as agent. He/she is divided between imaging her self and the other simultaneously. The boundaries are permeable, and there may be a vicarious experience of self and other. The other appears intact. 7) There will be an increase in cues for shame (Retzinger 1991, 1995). 8) The reaction may be anger or withdrawal, denial, repression of ideas, affirmation of the self, affect disorder such as depression, negation of other, conflict and violence.

Lewis considered shame to be a family of emotions with particular characteristics in common. Shame includes many variations, from mild embarrassment and social discomfort to intense forms such as humiliation or mortification. Shame always involves self and other; it is the most social of emotions. Shame involves concern about other's images of self. It occurs within and between persons, often unacknowledged by all parties. Shame arises out of threat or damage to social bonds.

Goffman (1965) defined stigma as "the situation of the individual who is disqualified from full social acceptance." With labeling, segregation and stigmatization, the social bond is no longer intact but in a state of disconnection; the person feels, and may actually be, isolated from others.

Disqualification isolates the deviant from others: it involves inadequate deference. Goffman (1967) showed that each person is acutely aware of the exact amount of deference he or she receives. If one receives either too much or too little, embarrassment results. In this way Goffman's and Lewis's work complement each other. Where Goffman describes outer ritual behavior, Lewis provides the corresponding inner dynamics, as well as observable markers for identifying shame states. Social disconnection with its associated disrespect is primary contexts for shame.

PRIMARY RESIDUAL DEVIANCE:
SHAME AND SYMPTOM FORMATION

In her analysis of Freud's work, Lewis (1971, 1981, 1983) pointed out discrepancies between his clinical and theoretical work. She showed that at the time there was no feasible theory of the social nature of human behavior and no viable theory of emotion. Among his important contributions are precise accounts of his cases, which Lewis re-analyzed in light of recent theory and research.

Beginning with a biosocial view of human nature, Lewis reinterpreted Freud's cases, showing the role of shame in psychopathology. Another of Lewis's (1981) contributions is a systematic study of psychotherapy sessions (1971). In her extremely detailed moment-by-moment analysis, Lewis (1971) used hundreds of cases, illustrating sequences from evoked shame into symptoms. She demonstrated that shame is transformed into symptomatic behavior.

In this paper I view primary residual deviance as a manifestation of the shame process; residual deviance can be viewed as thwarted attempts to retrieve lost affectional ties. Failure to reinstate bonds (isolation from meaningful social contact) is a primary context for shame and may disturb the self-other monitoring system. Shame can be seen as a governor of this system.

The presence of frequent and intense unacknowledged shame is derived from continual failure of social connection. Under this condition distortion may take place, rendering one unable to function, resulting in behavior that cannot be easily explained in conventional terms. Like any self-monitoring system that has lost its governor, it spirals endlessly (Bateson, et al., 1956).

In the above sense, shame is a thermostat. If it fails to function, it is difficult to regulate behavior. This model may account for many types of symptoms (residual deviance). In some cases of schizophrenic behavior, one has the sense of a constant state of acute embarrassment. With the intense sequences of emotion generated by shame, it may become excessively difficult to regulate self in relation to other, leading to "strange" behavior.

If shame is evoked but not acknowledged, a further sequence of emotions is likely to occur. Shame is often perceived as an attack coming from the other. A sequence of emotions follows:

> [H]hostility against the rejecting other is almost always simultaneously evoked. But it is humiliated fury, or shame-rage, ...Hostility against the other is trapped in this directional bind. . .Shame-rage is readily turned back on the self (Lewis, 1976: 193).

Shame, when suffered in isolation, may cause primary residual deviance (e.g. symptoms). I suggest that the dynamics involved in the labeling process on a societal level parallel the shame dynamics in interpersonal process.

SECONDARY RESIDUAL DEVIANCE

The labeling process is viewed as a continuation and extension of the shame system. Both parties have bought into the underlying societal view regarding deviant behavior. Deviant behavior leads to emotional arousal in witnesses--fear, anger and/or shame. If these feelings are not acknowledged, they often lead to demeaning, degrading, or rejecting behavior toward the deviant, which shames the deviant further as an attempt to soothe the labeler. Even subtle or covert criticism can produce feelings of isolation, leading, in time, to further shame and its transformation into symptoms. Intensified deviant behavior will lead the others to be more critical and rejecting. Each person's behavior serves to reinforce the behavior of the other in a reciprocating chain. The dynamics underlying the labeling process help explain how escalation of emotions can result in madness.

Shame is not only an intrapsychic process but also an interpersonal one. It occurs within persons as a shame-rage spiral (Retzinger, 1987) as well as between them, in a triple spiral (Scheff, 1987). Each emotion, shame and rage, serves as a stimulus for further response as it is manifested in disrespect (criticism, derogation, etc.) or social isolation.

Below are 5 propositions which link alienation, labeling, shame and stigma:

1) A major cause of mental illness (primary residual deviance) is unacknowledged shame in a context of alienation.

2) Mental illness is a process occurring within and between persons: when shame is evoked and not dispelled, it touches off chains of emotion within and between persons.

3) When shame is not acknowledged, the bonds we be weak, which can lead to the belief that a person is somehow unlike oneself or conventional others; normalization is hindered.

4) The labeling process contains shame dynamics on an interpersonal and societal level.

5) Labeling as a shaming process is a cause of secondary residual deviance.

METHODOLOGY

In the last 50 years it has become customary to use large samples and aggregate data in studying social phenomena. Large-scale studies can lead to generalizations but only at the expense of richness and understanding. With the complexity of human behavior and the wide range of areas that have been left unexplored, more intense analyses may prove valuable. Case studies such as Gill, Newman and Redlich's are under-analysed with lay language that does not lead to an in-depth understanding of what occurs in interaction. The value of their work is the transcribed interviews and long-playing record that goes along with it. Intensive case studies are perhaps an endangered species that fill a knowledge gap. But studies such as Piaget's and Cooley's with children, and Freud's with case histories provided major contributions in the understanding of human behavior. Case studies of sequences of behavior may lead to more adequate concepts and hypotheses. The price we pay for intensive case analyses is that they are tedious, time-consuming and expensive.

While most studies of emotion use surveys (Thoits, 1989), field methods (Hochschild, 1983), or experimental methods (Gottman, 1979), intensive case studies using sequential analysis may provide a significant contribution. Rather than relying on anecdotal material, an intensive method detects emotions in discourse. A rich source of information can be drawn from actual discourse, which reveals recurring patterns of behavior in moment-by-moment sequences. A single case of escalation between therapist and patient can be investigated for hidden patterns. The framework for analysis can be built around a theory of the social bond, labeling and emotion theory.

My analysis utilizes many of the procedures and insights of the established methods (e.g., Heritage, 1985; Labov and Fanshel, 1977; Mishler & Waxler, 1968), but it has combined them in a new way; it is not traditional conversation analysis. Rather, it is eclectic, combining several approaches which deal with more than one channel of communication (verbal, facial, paralinguistic). It is intensive rather than extensive. While there are strengths and weaknesses to any method, intensive case studies have been all but neglected in contemporary human science. From the rich information provided by case studies, a gap can be filled with information relevant to many aspects of social interaction.

The method used here for identifying shame involves both context and cues. The context is the source of shame, the position of self in relationship with other. The relationship between the therapist and patient, the situation under analysis, and the party's verbal statements can be used to determine the context. Cues involve words and gestures (paralinguistic and visual). This method does not strip away context, but instead explicitly relies on contextual understanding; it has been developed in order to observe particular cues and to infer sequences second-by-second. This method can be particularly useful in exploratory studies where the quest is to develop a testable theory and to develop hypotheses rather than to test them.

Table 9.1 shows the conventions used to transcribe the tapes.

P.	= Patient (Roberta)
T.	= Therapist (Dr. B)
boldface	= anger
italics	= shame
boldfaced italics	= shame-rage
[ ]	= interruptions
- between words	= rapid condensed speech
(inaud)	= inaudible
< >	= words laughed
CAPITAL LETTERS	= heavy emphasis
()	= untimed pause (under 1 second)
(0.0)	= timed pause (seconds 1/100
::	= previous syllable drawn out
*	= a counterfactual (hypothetical statement)

Table 9.1. The conventions of transcription

The categories used for coding involve the verbal and non-verbal cues. Verbal behavior includes explicit naming of emotions and indirect references to emotion, as well as thought processes involved in emotional experiences (Gottschalk & Gleser, 1969; Lewis, 1979). Non-verbal activities include paralanguage such as voice tone, loudness, and pitch (Labov and Fanshel, 1977; Pittinger, et al., 1960), and facial and bodily behavior (Ekman and Freisen, 1978; Izard, 1971). All three categories can be used for identifying sequences of emotions and are explained in detail.

Verbal behavior

1) Gottschalk-Gleser's (1979) content analysis scale, and Lewis's (1971, 1979) analysis are models: detecting emotion through spoken words, which indicate emotion.

Gestures

2) paralinguistic cues--vocal behavior that is not symbolic: tone, pitch, loudness, speed, etc. (Labov and Fanshel, 1977, and Pittenger, et al. 1960).

3) visual cues--facial and bodily behavior. Methods for detecting facial expression of emotion are derived from the work of Ekman and Freisen (1979), Izard (1977), Darwin (1872), and Tomkins (1963).

Identifying Verbal References to Shame

This category includes reference to the self as ridiculed, inadequate, ashamed, embarrassed, humiliated, exposed, deficient, or threatened. It may also include reference to one's self in relation to another, with a negative evaluation placed on self, as well as references to disconnectedness to significant others, e.g., rejection, desertion, abandonment, ostracism, loss of support or love, etc. Negative ideation about one's appearance in relation to another, or obsessive ideation about what one might have said or done may indicate shame.

Cue words used to describe shame

There are hundreds of words that refer to shame without calling it such. These words have been found to occur frequently in the basic shame context (viewing self negatively in the eyes of the other; Lewis, 1971). Some of these include:

alienated: rejected, dumped, deserted, rebuff, abandoned, estranged, deserted, isolated, separate, alone, disconnected, disassociated, detached, withdrawn, inhibited, distant, remote, split, divorced, polarized.

confused: stunned, dazed, blank, empty, hollow, spaced giddy, lost, vapid, hesitant, aloof.

ridiculous: foolish, silly, funny, absurd, idiotic, asinine, simple-minded, stupid, curious, weird, bizarre, odd peculiar, strange, different, stupid.

inadequate: helpless, powerless, defenseless, weak, insecure, uncertain, shy, deficient, worse off, small, failure, ineffectual, inferior, unworthy, worthless, flawed, trivial, meaningless, insufficient, unsure, dependent, exposed, inadequate, incapable, vulnerable, unable, inept, unfit, impotent, oppressed.

uncomfortable: restless, fidgety, jittery, tense, anxious, nervous, uneasy, antsy, jumpy, hyperactive

hurt: offended, upset, wounded, injured, tortured, ruined, sensitive, sore spot, buttons pushed, dejected, intimidated, defeated

Labov & Fanshel (1977) provide further methods for identifying shame in verbal behavior. Some of these include such behaviors as oblique, suppressed references, e.g., "they"; denial and verbal withdrawal also imply shame states. Each of these behaviors implies presence of shame through verbal hiding behaviors. That is, an important issue or feeling is hidden behind words and behaviors:
mitigation--to make less severe or painful, e.g., "It's just my mother who rejected me."
oblique, suppressed reference--e.g., "they", "it", "you" ("you get really nervous in front of a group" - when speaking of your own nervousness).

indifference--acting "cool" in an emotionally arousing context.
vagueness
denial
defensiveness
verbal withdrawal--lack of response.

Shame

   Temporal expansion/condensation or generalization--:"you always. . .", "you never. . ."; other kinds of expansion include "all,"
"everything," or "nothing."

   Triangles--bringing up an irrelevant third party or object: "Why are
you asking me to mow the lawn? You never make 'ittle brother' do
anything."

   "Triangle" is a term used by Bowen (1978) to describe how families often behave when tension gets too high between persons; a third
party or object is brought in. Triangles involve third parties (persons
or things) drawn into a conversation to distract or hide from the immediate relationship. Expansion and triangulation both involve hiding
behaviors, as well as hostile acts toward the other.
   Emotions can be detected in non-symbolic verbal gestures as well
as in words. Labov & Fanshel (1977) and Pittenger, et al. (1960) provide paralinguistic cues:
Vocal withdrawal/hiding behaviors, disorganization of thought.--
   over soft
   rhythm irregular
   hesitation
   self interruption - censorship
   filled pauses (-uh-)
   long pauses ()
   silences
   stammer
   fragmented speech
   rapid speech
   condensed words
   mumble
   breathiness
   incoherence--lax articulation
   laughed words

monotone

Visual cues

Gestural data involves facial and body behavior (Ekman and Freisen, 1978; Izard, 1971). Although we are able to hear our own audi-
tory messages, we cannot see our own facial changes. Many of these
changes occur outside awareness and are usually good indicators of an
emotional state. Nonverbal analysis involved observing facial and
body movements in conjunction with verbal and paralanguage analyses.

Shame can be detected by bodily manifestations (Darwin, 1872;
Tomkins, 1963; 1971, 1977; Lewis, 1979; Retzinger, 1985, 1991).

1. Hiding behavior:
  a) The hand covering all or parts of the face.
  b) Gaze aversion, eyes lowed or averted
2. Blushing
3. Control:
  a) Turning in, biting, or licking the lips, biting the tongue
  b) Forehead wrinkled vertically or transversely
  c) False smiling (Ekman & Freisen, 1982); or other masking
    behaviors
  d) fidgeting

According to Izard, #3b would have to be associated with another
indicator. The other cues, above, can occur alone or in any combination. Often they occur in sequences of events such as biting the lip >
false smiling > cover face with hand. Sometimes one event follows
another, but they may occur simultaneously. In an independent study,
Edelmann (1987) found these behaviors to be associated with embarrassment across cultures.

The cues are context-related; that is, their relevance to shame depends on the relationship between self and other. The more categories
(e.g., visual, verbal, paralanguage, etc.) that are involved, and the
greater the number of cues from each category, the stronger the evidence for the particular emotion. For instance, if a person is talking
about feeling small or helpless, is averting his or her eyes, and if his or
her speech is oversoft, fragmented and hesitant--the evidence that
shame is occurring is stronger than if the person were only averting his
or her eyes. In order to provide strong evidence for any particular

emotion, the cues need to occur in combination. Based on constellations of cues, I infer emotions being expressed and exchanged between persons. Numeric codes have been applied to each of the categories listed above (e.g., Patterson, 1982; Gottschalk & Gleser, 1969). A sequential analysis provides a holistic picture of the interactive process between persons, charting gestural communicative processes.

Word count of emotion words is also used in this case. Although word count is systematic, it is also too basic in itself with a mixture of strengths and weaknesses. I use a word count to match the occurrence of emotion words used by the therapist to indicate where he may empathize with the patient. That is to find occurrences of interaction type 1 (see below).

I have classified different types of interaction that occur in interview 3 (see Table 9.2). I specify Dr. B's goals at various points in the interview and the patient's responses, whether or not labeling is occurring, and describe the emotions of both patient and therapist.

1) Normalization: therapist and patient are responsive to each other-- they are connected.

2) Neutral: therapist asks diagnostic questions; patient responds with answers--absence of conflict.

3) Conflict: therapist asks diagnostic questions; patient responds by protesting/rejecting--marked by occurrence of shame and rage (a triple spiral).

4) Secondary deviance: patient accepts label/stigma-- connection is lost; marks a last resort at social connection. Solidification of mental illness.

Table 9.2.   Types of interaction.

Interaction type #1: illustrates social connection and empathy necessary for normalization. Types #2, #3, #4 are steps in the labeling process. They involve what Balint (1957) called "apostolic function," with the therapist inadvertently causing the patient to display symptoms of illness. These steps occur in the context of negotiation about diagnosis. The patient makes proposals that are rejected by the doctor, who makes counter-proposals until an acceptable illness is found. The outcome, according to Balint, is for the patient to "settle down" to an "organized illness" (corresponding to interaction type #4 in the scheme).

The patient responds either by answering the question (type 2), or attempts to normalize the situation (type 3) The patient's protests might be viewed as any attempt to retain self-respect. I hypothesize that in this phase the patient will show an increase in "delusional" or "fantasy" behavior as an attempt to escape from intense shame. Type 4 involves accepting the diagnosis and agreeing with the therapist. The acceptance of the label occurs as the patient's self-respect decreases. It can be seen as a last hope of connecting with an authority figure. In the session as a whole, the proportion of the four types of interactions are shown in Table 9.3.

					Total Exchanges
Type #1	Type #2	Type #3	Type #4	Misc.	
36 (11%)	94 (28%)	64 (19%)	1 (< 1%)	137 (41%)	332 .

Table 9.3 Interaction types in interview 3.

"Misc." refers to types of interaction that were either ambiguous or mixed. Interaction Type #1 consists of those exchanges where one, the other or both persons are responsive. Only 18 of the 36 exchanges in this category include interaction where both parties are responsive at the same time.

The interactions in the miscellaneous category are mixed or unclassifiable. At least 47% of the exchange involved negotiating the patient's illness, compared with 11% involving normalization. Category #2 occurs in greater frequency at the beginning of the interview. As the interview progresses, #3 becomes prevalent, peaking between exchanges 300 and 331, and declines with increasing symptomatic behavior.

Dr. B responds only to utterances which might be interpreted as indicators of delusions. Although Gill et al. state that the agenda should be explicit between therapist and patient (55), in the third interview the therapist has a hidden agenda: He assumes that Roberta is psychotic; he wants to know whether she realizes it. All her behavior is seen through this lens. Both Dr. B and the editors support their beliefs with behavior that might, in other circumstances, be considered normal. For instance, when Dr. B makes an error he says, "I hardly knew myself I was looking at the clock" (T. 291), Roberta responds,

"You don't realize it. I don't either" (P. 291). Gill, Newman and Redlich suggest that Roberta is using T. 291 to rationalize her delusional thinking. Perhaps she is only being gracious.

Another example occurs in exchange 80, where the editors discuss literalness in the use of the word "call" (T.80: "Although you call her mother"; P.80: "No, I call her mom"). One might make the same argument about the editors in their commentary. Roberta makes an error in speech (she says "fisht" and corrects herself--"fist"). The literalness of the commentary ("the patient says her head is being attacked by a fist-fish"--347) could be used to suggest that the editors were delusional. Looking through lenses such as the ones used here, any mistake might appear psychotic.

THE INTERVIEW

To illustrate social-emotional process I use a transcript (Gill, Newman and Redlich, 1954) and its LP record. This recording is readily available; the reader can check my interpretation as grounds for validity (Scheff, 1986). In this case the patient had been already committed to a mental hospital before the initial interview. The interview goes well in parts, but two thirds of the way through there is a flagrant increase in symptomatic behavior. This chapter attempts to explain this relapse by describing the dynamics within and between doctor and patient.

In the detailed analysis below, I use two segments (exchanges 297-300 and 324-331) which include all the interaction types except #4; segment 2 is marked by intense attempts at labeling, ending with the patient escaping into fantasy. This is not the only point in the interview where symptomatic behavior occurs, but it is the most flagrant.

Both segments occur in the second half-hour, 24 exchanges apart. I call the therapist Dr. B and the patient Roberta. Ten exchanges before the first segment (P. 286) Roberta notices Dr. B looking at the clock. She confronts him, catching him off guard: "Am I boring you?" she explains, "you keep looking at the clock." Dr. B seems embarrassed: instead of a brief explanation, he perseveres, even though Roberta has let the matter drop.

There is evidence that Dr. B is in a state of shame: 1) The editorial commentary states: "he was obviously feeling uneasy about this," and "is a good example of how a therapist's preoccupation with his own anxious feelings can be disturbing in an interview" (T.289-291: page 379). The words in italics refer to shame markers (Gottschalk and

Gleser, 1969; Lewis, 1971, 1979; Retzinger, 1991, 1995). 2) That the feeling refuses to subside suggests shame (the conversation continues on the topic of the clock for 8 exchanges). 3) His speech becomes fragmented at this point as compared to other parts of the interview: "Did I? Yes. You didn't...you don't bore me at all. No." Because of Dr. B's preoccupation with the clock, a role switch occurs; Roberta becomes therapist and Dr. B patient. Roberta interprets and empathizes with Dr. B's behavior. Segment #1 occurs two exchanges after the clock incident:

Segment 1

P. 297   . . .Are you confused?
T. 298 I'm a little confused now. Yes.
P. 298 Th-That's what I wanted to know.
T. 299 But I can see how you must feel.
P. 299 Its awful.
T. 300 (10 sec pause) You said before you don't think this
          is anything mental.
P. 300 No.

Beside switching roles, Segment #1 begins with empathy (interaction type 1), but changes abruptly ending at T.300, beginning a series of exchanges in which Dr. B investigates her "insight" into her illness (T.300-329).

In between segment 1 (before segment 2) Dr. B continues with questions which hint at mental illness, e.g., "But would you. . .would you say that you are not right in your mind?" (T.319), questions too numerous to include (approximately 13). From here on I focus on segments just prior to Roberta's increase in symptomatic behavior.

Segment #2 occurs 24 exchanges after segment 1, following the same pattern of questioning as the exchanges not included:

Segment 2

T. 324   so there is something which is not right
P. 324/5 yes I think it it jis isn't my head and my body
T. 325/6 [But you call it   amnesia]
P: 326   And duh () na-I could pass right to my own

(2.5)   There are scientific explanations besides
(1) other explanations for it () I don't see why
I should go back tu living with a family I don't
wanna be with () I-en't-see why I should have a
Daddy if I don't want him () He doesn't seem to
want me () An that in itself hurts me very much.

T. 327   who is he

P. 327   I don't know

T. 328   You'd like you have no idea

P. 328   [I see him (inaud)] clearly in my mind
              sometimes

T. 329   but you don't know who he is

P. 329   Mmm no I'm not gonna say if I do

T. 330   Mmm

P. 330   I-I be I'd feel silly if f-found out the opposite

T. 331   [don't say it] if you don't want to.

P. 331   (6.22) And I jis love everything they do? (3.18)
              When I'm myself I-I enjoy my life. I enjoy sports
              and ballet and () everything I knew how to do.

T. 332   [Mmm]

P. 332   And nothing came too hard with me. Everythings
              simple. Maybe my father has a good mind? probably
              inherited it from him. But I do I love a great mind
              I () I love being a little bit small-minded, I love
              everything I am. I don't see why I should spend ()
              ALL my life being what I'm not?

Segment #2 begins, and continues, with questions about Roberta's
sanity; it ends with an increase in symptomatic behavior, "the patient
escapes to her fantasy" (commentary, page 395).

One context for shame includes Roberta's encounter with Dr. B
when he is rendered inept. Although he does not experience shame
overtly, I suggest that he is in a bypassed state of shame--he is uncomfortable being too close with a psychotic patient. Roberta is also
watching him intently; he is caught under the watchful gaze of the
other. They move though a period where she appears intact and he is
assailed by noxious stimuli; he is helpless (in a sense), while she is
active in empathizing and mitigating his discomfort. To take himself
out of the primary focus, he attempts to focus on Roberta's keen perception. In the face of this he functions poorly as agent and regroups
by reverting to technique.

Absence of I-Thou (alienation) and shame mark their interaction;
the therapist does not acknowledge Roberta's shame, although the pa-

tient tries to express it. In the first third of the interview Dr. B responds to Roberta's emotional statements 3 times. In the second third he responds to her emotion statements 8 times. In the third part of the interview he does not respond to her emotion statements. In the third portion of the interview Dr. B makes an error, but does not acknowledge his own shame. When the bond deteriorates, Roberta relapses.

In this particular interview there is ample evidence that shame is not addressed. Although Roberta brought up feelings about the interview, Dr. B ignores them. Roberta makes ten explicit, undisguised attempts to state how she feels about discussing her problem with a psychiatrist (e.g., P. 12, 56, 75, 141, 156, 157, 159, 314, 330, 240): (P. 12: "I feel very ridiculous speaking about it, a little bit ashamed, I guess"). These types of feelings are never investigated or even acknowledged by Dr. B.

To determine the emotional content of the interview, I used techniques developed by Gottschalk & Gleser (1969), Lewis (1971, 1979) and Labov & Fanshel (1977). Because of the availability of both record and transcript, the reader can check my interpretation.

ANALYSIS OF TWO SEGMENTS

The segments are broken down into 7 excerpts for detailed analysis. My analysis begins after the clock incident, just before intense conflict. Excerpt 1 begins with Roberta questioning Dr. B about his mental state:

Excerpt 1

P. 297 . . .Are you confused? <affectionately)

T. 298 I'm a little confused now. Yes.
P. 298 Th-That's what I wanted-tu know <very softly)

T. 299 But I can see how you must fee::l <empathically)
P. 299 Its AW::ful <softly).

Excerpt 1 illustrates both Dr. B's and Roberta's empathic abilities (interaction type #1). Rather than redirecting the question P.297 back onto Roberta, as he has been doing (e.g., T.169, 179), Dr. B simply answers the question; he momentarily steps out of role. This is one place in the interview where attunement occurs.

Other examples of empathy occur at 32, 33 (T.33: "That must be very puzzling" (T116: "That upsets you a great deal"). Roberta responds with acknowledgement ("yes, it does"); T:211-212: "That must be very upsetting").

Although they appear to be attuned at times, Roberta's utterance in P.298 is ambiguous. She may be saying she appreciates him responding on a human level, or may be echoing what she had said earlier in 297 ("that's what I want-u know"). A third possibility is that she is speaking to herself, in a sense withdrawing from his response. It is like a little dance: Roberta approaches Dr. B; instead of turning her question around, Dr. B responds empathically, approaching Roberta. In P.298, Roberta withdraws: unaccustomed to his approach, her voice sounds as though it is far away as if speaking to herself; it is almost inaudible. Dr. B does not withdraw but continues to try to connect; T.299 indicates feelings of empathy--his pitch rises gently on the word "feel," she responds with her feelings ("Its AW::ful"). For a moment they appear connected (T.- P.299).

The course of events takes a sharp turn with a sudden shift in Dr. B's approach. Although Roberta and Dr. B are momentarily attuned, there is a dramatic change in excerpt 2 after a long pause (10 seconds):

Excerpt 2

T. 300   (10) **You said before you don't think this is anything mental**.
P. 300 No.

In excerpt 2 Dr. B "grasps at the psychiatric framework" (indicated by the editors' commentary; T.300; page 381). Dr. B leaves an empathic approach for a labeling one (interaction type 2). The abrupt shift in Dr. B's tone marks the beginning of a series of attempts at diagnosis. Roberta protests. This series is marked by intense conflict. It ends with Roberta fantasizing.

Excerpt 2 illustrates dynamics in the labeling process; Dr. B also has unacknowledged feelings. He is 'uncomfortable' as indicated, in part, by the long pause. Instead of investigating his feelings (even in his own mind, which could connect him and the patient), he projects onto the outer world: *"Even though we seem alike at this moment, we are not alike, you are psychotic (I am not) and this is what needs to be investigated." _

The abrupt shift shows disregard for Roberta; Dr. B does not make any transition into this topic (abruptness marks anger, as pausing marks "discomfort" [shame]). Evidence for Dr. B's shame is twofold. 1) Dr. B abruptly grasps at the "psychiatric framework;" 2) there is a very long preceding pause, followed by the sudden shift. Perhaps Dr. B still feels uneasy (i.e., ashamed) about the error 12 exchanges earlier, the clock incident.

Identification with a mental patient, as in excerpt 1, may have caused Dr. B shame, as suggested in an earlier commentary (T. 295-297; page 381):

The patient has told Dr. B that he is right when he says his mind wanders and he is not aware of what he does--that he and she are alike. *This may be felt by a therapist as an attack.* To the patient it was a friendly identification (emphasis added).

The series of events which occur from 300-331 are too numerous to state: 25 instances of labeling on Dr. B's part; Roberta makes 21 attempts at protesting, rejecting or otherwise normalizing. I use exchanges 324-331 to illustrate alienation, labeling, shame, and the conflict that results in a 50-second time span. Excerpt 3 occurs after Roberta complains about being sick of life.

Excerpt 3

T. 324 **so there IS something which is not right**
P. 324/5 yes I-thing-it it jis isn't my head and my BO::dy
T. 325/6 **[But you call it   amNE::SIA]**
P: 326   And duh () na-I could pass right to my own
         <volume softens) (2.5)] There are scientific
         explanations besides (1) other explanations for
         it <over soft) () I-don't-see-why-I-should-go
         -back-tu-living-with-a-family **I don't wanna be**
         with () I-en't-see why I should have a Daddy if
         I don't wan-im () He doesn't seem to want
         me:/: () An that-in itself HURTS me very much.

Commentary (T.324-326) states that Dr. B:

Is trying to convince her it is something he knows about and that she is psychotic. We are trained to do this: to see if a patient is crazy, not to see what a patient thinks about it. We are trained to think that if a patient sometimes admits he is crazy it is insight and that the possibilities of therapy are better.

Excerpt 3 exemplifies interaction type 3; this excerpt as well as the editors' commentary illustrate the apostolic function. Dr. B's tone (T. 324) is *"AHA! so you do have a problem." In the context of everyday interaction, his statement would be discourteous, even hostile; he implies that she is psychotic and ignores her demurrers. There is disrespect for Roberta's perception. Even if her perspective were wrong, respect could be shown. The implication is that she is psychotic, unlike himself, and therefore not entitled to an opinion.

Roberta protests in P.324/25. Dr. B continues speaking, interrupting Roberta, to make his point that she is wrong: "but...amNE::SIA" (* "If you think it's amnesia you MUST be nuts"). There is a rising volume and drawing out of the word "amnesia"; Labov and Fanshel call this contour "heavy emphasis", indicating not only disrespect, but possible anger, even contempt. In P.326 Roberta continues to protest and normalize, explaining her understanding of what has happened. She concludes with a very strong emotional expression of "hurt." This and other strong expressions of emotion are ignored. Dr. B changes the subject abruptly:

Excerpt 4

T. 327 **who is he**
P. 327 **I don't know**

Empathic in excerpt 1 (T.299), Dr. B lacks even ordinary courtesy here. He does not address Roberta's last set of utterances about her feelings. There is no rising intonation on "he" (T.327); it is not a real question. The implication is *"I'm checking to see how psychotic you are." Roberta withdraws by denying that she knows anything, expressing both shame and anger: anger by withdrawal, shame by denial. The quarrel continues; Dr. B presses further:

Excerpt 5

T. 328 **You'd like-you have no idea**
P. 328 [I see-im (inaud)] clearly in my mi::nd
       sometimes
T. 329 **but you don't know who he is**
P. 329 **Mmm no <very soft> I'm not gonna say if I <do**
      <laughs the word do)

Dr. B rephrases and repeats his statement twice again (T.328, 329). There is no rising intonation in his utterance to mark a question. Repeated questions are challenging (Labov & Fanshel, 1977); Dr. B challenges Roberta's competence, showing further disrespect. She interrupts Dr. B, reciprocating the disrespect, as she attempts to answer. Dr. B repeats the question, she refuses to answer the third time he asks the same question (P.329).

P.329 indicates that Roberta is in a state of both shame and rage. Her statement is very soft (shame): she won't give Dr. B what he has asked for. Her statement is like a child's*"Nah!-Nah!-Nah!-Nah!-Nah! I'm not gonna tell you, because you donít care!" She laughs the last word of the sentence ("do"), indicating further embarrassment. She goes on to explain:

Excerpt 6

T. 330 Mmm
P. 330 I-I be-I'd feel SILLY if-f-found out the o::pposite

Roberta manifests further shame, evidenced in the fragmented speech and in the statement "I'd feel SILLY," a code word for shame. There is also the possibility of being mistaken, a shame context. Roberta tells him about a very vital part of herself. Dr. B misses the point. Roberta reverts to symptomatic behavior as the conflict intensifies and social connection fails:

Excerpt 7

T. 331 [DON't say it] if you don't want to < softly trails
      off).

P. 331 (6.22) And I jis love everything they do::? (3.18)
        When I'm myself I-I enjoy my life. I enjoy sports
        and ballet and () everything I knew how to do.
T. 332 [Mmm]
P. 332 And nothing came too HAR:D with me. Everythings
        simple. Maybe my father has a good mind? probably
        inherited it from him. But-I-do-I-love a great mind
        I () I love being a little bit small-minded, I love
        everything I am. I don't-see why I should spend ()
        ALL my life being what I'm not?

In excerpt 7 there is dramatic change. Dr. B may notice Roberta regressing and softens his approach. After intense questioning he tells her she doesnít have to say. At this point not only does Roberta suddenly change the topic, the tone changes, emotion markers disappear. Instead, there are words of temporal expansion: "everything," "nothing," and "all." She withdraws. The editors note: "The patient escapes to her fantasy." Excerpt 7 suggests that labeling leading to symptoms is a shame process. The increase in symptomatic behavior is, at least in this case, directly linked to the patient's increasing unacknowledged shame, and alienation between the two.

During the interview Dr. B demonstrates that he has the capacity to connect with Roberta, but he fails to do so for much of the session. When he does empathize with Roberta, her shame is reduced, or at least does not increase. She seems to appreciate Dr. B's genuine responses, and is quite responsive in return. Instead of continuing in this vein, he gets caught in labeling, particularly after his error, which is a source of shame. In this case they switch roles and Roberta becomes the observer and Dr. B the observed. He becomes flustered and begins to function poorly as agent. Both he and Roberta are focal in Dr. Bís awareness at the time of the error. He is divided between imaging her self and the other simultaneously. The boundaries are permeable. There is an increase in shame cues (Retzinger 1991, 1995). He reverts to technique as a defense against the shame. It is at this point that he tests Roberta for understanding of her illness with an agenda in mind. The agenda is unknown to Roberta because it is never explicitly expressed.

WORD COUNT

The interview was divided into three equal parts based on the number of exchanges: first, second and third parts of the session (see Table

9-4). In the first part Roberta uses 16 words which are indicative of shame, Dr. B uses six. By looking at the location of the words for Dr. B, they indicate empathic responses from Dr. B toward Roberta. That is, when Roberta uses an emotion word it is matched or responded to by Dr. B. He responds three times to Roberta's emotional states in the third portion of the interview; then there is a push toward a labeling approach, in part indicated by the absence of further reflection about what Roberta is saying. Indicated by percentage

	First Third	Second Third	Third Third
Roberta			
Total words	1869	1977	3033
Shame words	16 (8/10%)*	23 (1.16%)	29 (1%)
Dr. B			
Total words	819	782	838
Shame words	6 (7/10%)	4 (5/10%)	3 (4/10%)

* percent per 100 words

Table 9.4. Count for shame words.

of words per 100, Dr. B becomes less empathic as the interview progresses. Roberta's references to shame appear to increase in the second third of the interview. As she begins to relapse she becomes more verbal (more than a 1000 more words than in the first two-thirds), with the proportion of shame words decreasing slightly. As Dr. B's shame increases following the clock incident, it is bypassed as he pursues labeling. His labeling can be seen as a defense against his own shame. The word count and their location in the interview supports the analysis of discourse.

DISCUSSION

I have illustrated the connection between the Lewis-Goffman shame construct and Scheff's labeling theory. Hidden shame is present in labeling and stigmatization. The analysis by the authors of *Initial Interviews in Psychiatric Practice* (1954) only began to touch the surface of what was occurring during the interview between Roberta and Dr. B.

My analysis of a single case illustrates four of the five propositions, showing the role of emotion in labeling. Dr. B views himself unlike the patient (he is normal, she is crazy--social disconnection). Patient and therapist are increasingly alienated, particularly in the third portion of the interview. As Dr. B's shame increases he pushes to get Roberta to admit to mental illness. His empathy decreases. The relapse which occurs in this interview is preceded by a series of exchanges between Dr. B and Roberta marked by conflict. The relapse that occurs is an interpersonal rather than individual phenomenon set off by chains of emotion within and between persons.

Patient and therapist engage in intense but quiet conflict as Dr. B attempts to label the patient as psychotic, and attempts to secure her agreement. The patient protests. Disrespect and shame mark their interaction; Dr. B does not acknowledge Roberta's explicit and implicit shame, although the patient tries to tell him. When Dr. B's shame increases as a result of the clock incident, the conflict about her "illness" peaks, and the patient fantasizes.

The dynamics of labeling, as illustrated here, occur on an interpersonal level, fueled by societal beliefs (i.e., admitting mental illness shows insight). Secondary residual deviance is not indicated in this session, since Roberta continues to protest that there is some other explanation as to what has happened to her. She never admits to being "crazy."

Although shame is often trivialized, it is a powerful human mechanism at the roots of alienation. The contradiction of how important the shame experience is to the self and how trivial the event that caused it appears in the outer world is enough to drive a person up the wall.

Shame that is expressed by mental patients (as in this case) may not be a symptom of pathology. Shame is an essential part of the interaction order. Labeling, segregation and stigmatization breed shame. When left unacknowledged, in conjunction with social isolation (a context for further shame), a chain reaction of emotion can occur, escalating into symptomatic behavior.

As well as integrating Scheff's labeling theory (2000) with Lewis's shame theory (1971), my analysis extends the work of others: Balint (1957), Link (1987), and Hooley (1987). To Balint's notion of the apostolic function I add the emotional dimension involved in negotiation. In his work on labeling, Link (1987) describes beliefs about mental patients that become personally applicable, leading to "self-devaluation and/or the fear of rejection by others." His analysis comes very close to my own in his description of demoralization. Although he describes the shame process, he does not identify it as such; in demoralization, Link notes:

> . . .the erosion of self-esteem, along with feelings of help-lessness and hopelessness, and a pattern of confusion of thought process...reduce adaptive thinking (p. 98, emphasis added).

In her work on expressed emotions, Hooley comes close to my analysis in her attempt to explain the recurrence of symptoms. She refers to shame process without naming it. One of the best predictors of recurrence of psychiatric symptoms, she states, is criticism of the patient by significant others. She wonders how expressed emotion could lead to symptoms; my analysis helps answer her question. Criticism usually involves disrespect, which is a primary context for shame. Much of the research on mental illness describes shame process without naming it; shame appears as an 'invisible' force.

My results are tentative; three further steps are needed: First, checking my analysis of this interview against the record and transcript. Second, additional cases need to be analyzed, utilizing a similar method. Third, ultimately, each proposition should be tested with many cases. Before that can be done, more work on single cases may be needed to further specify the causal process and markers.

REFERENCES

Balint, M. 1957. *The Doctor, His Patient, and the Illness*. New York: International Universities Press.

Bateson, G., D. D. Jackson, J. Haley and J. Weakland. 1956. "Toward a Theory of Schizophrenia." *Behavioral Science* 1:251-64.

Baumeister, R., and M. Leary. 1995. "The Need to Belong: Desire for Interpersonal Attachments as a Fundamental Human Motivation." *Psychological Bulletin* 117:497-529.

Bowen, M. 1978. *Family Therapy in Clinical Practice*. New York: Jason Aronson.

Bowlby, J. 1969. *Attachment and Loss, Vol. 1*. New York: Basic Books.

Bowlby, J. 1973. *Attachment and Loss, Vol. 2: Separation*. New York: Basic Books.

Cooley, C. H.. [1902] 1970. *Human Nature and the Social Order*. New York: Schocken Books.

Crocetti, G. M., H. Spiro and I. Siassi. 1974. *Contemporary Attitudes Toward Mental Illness*. Pittsburg, PA: University of Pittsburgh Press.

Darwin, C. [1872] 1965. *The Expression of the Emotions in Man and Animals*. London: John Murray.

Edelmann, R. J.., J. Asendorf, A. Contarello, V. Zammuner et al. 1989. "Self-reported Expression of Embarrassment in Five European Cultures." *Journal of Cross Cultural Psychology* 20:357-371.

Ekman, P., and W. Freisen. 1978. *Facial Action Coding System*. Palo Alto, CA.: Consulting Psychologists Press.

Ekman, P., and W. Freisen. 1982. "Felt, False and Miserable Smiles." *Journal of Non-verbal Behavior* 6:238-252.

Gill, M. R. Newman, and F. C. Redlich. 1954. *The Initial Interview in Psychiatric Practice*. New York: International Universities Press.

Goffman, E. 1965. *Stigma.* New Jersey: Prentice-Hall.

Goffman, E. 1967. *Interaction Ritual.* New York: Anchor.

Gottman, J. M. 1979. *Marital Interaction.* New York: Academic Press.

Gottschalk, L,. and G. Gleser. 1969. *Manual of Instruction for Using the Gottschalk-Gleser Content Analysis Scales.* Berkeley: University of California Press.

Gove, W. 1982. *Deviance and Mental Illness.* Beverly Hills: Sage.

Gove, W., and T. Fain. 1973. "The Stigma of Mental Hospitalization: An Attempt to Evaluate Its Consequences." *Archives of General Psychiatry* 29:494-500.

Harlow, H. 1962. "The Heterosexual Affectional System in Monkeys." *American Psychologist* 17:1-9.

Heritage, J. 1985. "Recent Developments in Conversational Analysis. " *Sociolinguistics* 15, 1-19.

Hochschild, A. 1983. *The Managed Heart.* Berkeley, CA: University of California Press.

Hooley, J. 1987. "The Nature and Origins of Expressed Emotions." In Hahlweg, K & M. J. Goldstein (eds.), *Understanding Major Mental Disorder: The Contribution of Family Interaction Research.* New York: Family Process Press.

Huffine, C., and J. Clausen. 1979. "Madness and Work: Short- and Long-term Effects of Mental Illness on Occupational Careers." *Social Forces* 57:1049-62.

Izard, C. 1971. *The Face of Emotion.* New York: Appleton-Century-Crofts.

Izard, C. 1977. *Human Emotion.* New York: Plenum.

James, W. 1910. *Psychology.* New York: Henry Holt & Co.

Labov, W., and D. Fanshel. 1977. *Therapeutic Discourse.* New York: Academic Press.

Lemert, E. M. 1951. *Social Pathology*. New York: McGraw-Hill.

Lewis, H. B. 1971. *Shame and Guilt in Neurosis*. New York: International Press.

Lewis, H. B. 1976. *Psychic War in Men and Women*. New York: New York University Press.

Lewis, H. B. 1979. "Using Content Analysis to Explore Same and Guilt in Neurosis." In L. A.. Gottschalk (ed.), *The Content Analysis of Verbal Behavior*. New York: Halstead Press.

Lewis, H. B. 1981. *Freud and Modern Psychology, Vol. I: The Emotional Basis of Mental Illness*. New York: Plenum Press.

Lewis, H. B. 1983. *Freud and Modern Psychology, Vol. II: The Emotional Basis of Human Behavior*. New York: Plenum Press.

Lewis, Thomas, Fari Amini, and Richard Lannon. 2000. *A General Theory of Love*. New York: Random House.

Link, B. G. 1987. "Understanding Labeling Effects in the Area of Mental Disorders: An Assessment of the Effects of Expectations on Rejection." *American Sociological Review* 52: 96-112.

Lynd, H. 1958. *On Shame and the Search for Identity*. New York: Harcourt.

McDougall, W. 1908. *An Introduction to Social Psychology*. New York: University Paperbacks.

Mead, G. H. 1934. *Mind, Self, and Society*. Chicago: University of Chicago Press.

Mishler, E. and N. Waxler. 1968. *Interaction in Families*. New York: Wiley and Sons.

Patterson, G. 1982. *Coercive Family Process*. Eugene, OR: Castalia Publishing.

Phillips, Bernard S. "Toward A Reflexive Sociology." *The American Sociologist* 19 (Summer 1988):138-151.

Phillips, Bernard S. 2001. *Beyond Sociology's Tower of Babel: Reconstructing the Scientific Method*. Hawthorne, NY: Aldine de Gruyter.

Pittenger, R., C. Hockett, and J. Danehy. 1960. *The First Five Minutes*. New York: Paul Martineau.

Retzinger, S. M. 1985. "The Resentment Process: Videotape Studies." *Psychoanalytic Psychology* 2:129-151.

Retzinger, S. M. 1987. "Resentment and Laughter: Video Studies of the Shame-Rage Spiral." In H. B. Lewis (ed.), *The Role of Shame in Symptom Formation*. Hillsdale, NJ: Lawrence Erlbaum Assoc.

Retzinger, S. M. 1991. *Violent Emotions*. Newbury Park, CA: Sage.

Retzinger, S. M. 1995. "Identifying Shame and Anger in Discourse." *American Behavioral Scientist* 38:104-113.

Scheff, T. J. 1966. *Being Mentally Ill*. New York: Aldine (Third Edition, 2000).

Scheff, T. J. 1986. "Toward Resolving of Controversy over "Thick Description." *Current Anthropology* 27:408-9.

Scheff, T. J. 1987. "The Shame-rage Spiral: A Case Study of an Interminable Quarrel. In H. B. Lewis (ed.), *The Role of Shame in Symptom Formation*. Hillsdale, NJ: Lawrence Erlbaum Assoc.

Scheff, T. J. 1997. *Emotions, the Social Bond, and Human reality: Part/whole Analysis.* NY: Cambridge University Press.

Shaver, F.   1987. "Love and Attachment: The Integration of Three Behavioral Systems." In Sternberg, R. J. and M. Barnes (eds.), *Anatomy of Love*. New Haven: Yale University Press.

Spitz, R. A.. 1946. "Anaclitic Depression: An Inquiry into the Genesis of Psychiatric Conditions in Early Childhood II. *Psychoanalytic Study of the Child* 2:313-332.

Thoits, P. 1989. "The sociology of emotions." In Scott, W. R.   and J. Blake (eds.), *Annual Review of Sociology* Vol 15.

Tomkins, S. 1963. *Affect/Imagery/Consciousness, Vol. II.* New York: Springer.

Introduction to Chapter 10

Sennett's and Cobb's 1972 book, *The Hidden Injuries of Class*, has much in common with Willis' 1977 book, *Learning to Labor*. Both books describe emotional and relational problems suffered by working-class individuals. Scheff embarks on a secondary analysis of those books, employing the broad approach to the scientific method described in his own part/whole approach, similar to the web approach described in Part One. This involves detailed content analyses of the words and phrases those authors used as well as the words and phrases used by their working-class subjects, analyses employing the systematic procedures developed by Retzinger (see Chapter 9). In both studies Scheff finds shame to be central to both the emotional life of the working-class individuals as well as to the ways in which they relate to others. It is not only their class situation which keeps them in place within the social stratification system: it is their own behavior as well, based on the shame or shame/anger or anger resulting from shame that they have learned. More specifically, it is unacknowledged versus acknowledged shame which proves to be fundamental. This has relevance not just for working-class individuals but also for all of us, since shame appears to be pervasive throughout society and to have similar impacts when we fail to acknowledge it. There also appear to be implications for large-scale social change, given that the behavior of working-class individuals works to keep them in place within the system of social stratification. Scheff suggests that his analysis also has implications for confronting violence in the schools, given the linkage he found among working-class boys between shame and anger.

Chapter 10

Working Class Emotions and Relationships:

Secondary Analysis of Sennett and Cobb, and Willis

Thomas J. Scheff

Most approaches to class dominance award more agency to the ruling class, less to the ruled class. Often the working class is portrayed as the victim of machinations of the ruling class, or as pawns in the structural reproduction of hierarchy. Such approaches are pessimistic; they seem to imply that there is no way out.

There are studies, however, that propose an emotion dynamic in the reproduction of social class, the generation of pride in the ruling class and shame in subordinate classes. In this paper I flesh out this idea using two classic studies: Sennett's and Cobb's *The Hidden Injuries of Class* (1973), and Paul Willis' *Learning to Labor* (1977). My analysis concerns the emotional/relational world of these men. It suggests that working class men participate in the reproduction of class because they are ashamed, but fail to acknowledge their shame, and that their relationships are alienated. This hypothesis suggests that contrary to the tone of both books, it is possible that social and psychological initiatives might help restore authentic pride, and therefore full participation in governance.

The ruling class also may have a problem with acknowledging shame, one that could have even more destructive consequences than in the working class. The idea of ruling class shame seems to be implied in two other classic texts: Weber's *Protestant Ethic and the Spirit of Capitalism* (1906),   and Veblen's *Theory of the Leisure Class* (1899). In the discussion section, below, I will return to this issue.

FRAMEWORK

Renewing Sociology and Social Science

This essay is written in the spirit of reforming sociology and the social sciences by integrating concepts, data, and application into a single approach (Scheff, 1990, 1997; Phillips, 2001). Here I emphasize capturing a three dimensional image of human beings, by including action, emotion, and cognition as integral parts of the whole; in Phillips's (1988) phrase, "hand, heart, and head". I also suggest an application of the findings to the real world.

Both my earlier work (1990, 1997) and Phillips's (2001) framework emphasize connecting abstract sociological concepts to actual data, and applying the results to practice in the real world. Modern theory tends to shy away from concrete details and from practice, just as research and practice usually pays lip service, if that, to abstract theory. I show connections between abstract sociological and social psychological theory, on the one hand, and dialogue and other textual material in the Sennett and Cobb (1973), and the Willis (1977) studies.

A major antinomy in social science, agency and structure, can be resolved by inferring structure from process, the actions of living persons. Several hundred years ago, the philosopher Spinoza proposed that in order to understand the complexity of human beings, one needs to connect the "least parts (concrete particulars) to the greatest wholes (concepts or theory). That is, we need to understand theories in terms of words and gestures in social interaction, and these same words and gestures in terms of a relevant theory. I call this approach "part/whole" (Scheff 1997). Phillips's (2001) develops a similar idea in terms of what he calls the "web of concepts."

In this study I show the relationship between structure (social class) and process (emotion chains and alienation) and between structure (social stratification) and agency (the subjects' techniques of hiding emotion). In this way I approach the Holy Grail of social science: relating structure and process, and showing agency. My approach combines theory, method, and data, moving back and forth between least parts and greatest wholes.

Emotional/Relational Dynamics and Social Class

Currently there are psychological and sociological literatures that propose two paths for unacknowledged shame: it can lead either to aggression (false pride) or withdrawal/silence.[1] These same studies suggest that acknowledgment of shame can restore true pride. But these emotions generate, and are generated by relationship dynamics. Solidary relationships are reciprocally related to pride, and alienated relationships to shame. This paper will explore the implication of these hypotheses for class politics.

Both hypotheses can be illustrated by two studies of working class males: the lack of acknowledgment of shame leads either to ineffectual aggression (Willis) or withdrawal from conflict (Sennett and Cobb). Similarly, collective aggression is associated with one type of alien-ation, engulfment. Withdrawal is associated with the other pole of alienation, isolation. My analysis suggests that learning to acknowl-edge shame and alienation might help build pride and solidarity in the working class, and make for more effective challenges to the class sys-tem. The first step will be to state a theory of shame and alienation.

Alienation and Shame as Basic Sources of Conflict

According to the theory to be outlined here, intractable conflict is generated by alienation and emotions hidden in the interaction between individuals and between groups. To understand this thesis, it is first necessary to explain the relationship between alienation and shame.

More perhaps than any other sociologist, Goffman fleshed out Cooley's idea of the looking glass self. In his later work, this theme received less attention. But in most of the earlier work (1959, 1959a, 1963, 1963a, 1967) Goffman provided many concrete examples that convey the look and feel of continually seeing one's self through the eyes of the other(s).

Before describing Goffman's contribution to emotion dynamics in relationships, I will define the way I use the word shame. Goffman referred to embarrassment in social interaction, but seldom to shame. Even in the book Stigma, in which shame is a central subject, he used the word shame only twice, both times casually and in passing. More frequently and much less casually, Goffman not only referred to embarrassment but also theorized about it (1967).

By my definition, however, embarrassment is one particular type of shame. Humiliation is another. There are many words that are used as substitutes or cognates, that is, for the feeling that results from seeing one's self negatively in the eyes of the other, such as feeling "self-conscious, rejected, unworthy, or inadequate." I will define shame as a class name for a large family of emotions and feelings that arise through seeing self negatively, if even only slightly negatively, through the eyes of others, or even for only anticipating such a reaction.

My definition is in conflict with vernacular usage, in which shame is defined narrowly, as an extreme crisis emotion, what might be called disgrace shame. But in my usage, most shame does not involve crisis or disgrace. It is rather routinely available in the interior theatre of the imagination: modesty, shyness, self-consciousness, or conscience (Schneider, 1977 calls it discretion-shame). Since my usage of the word includes both disgrace and discretion-shame, perhaps I should call this class name SHAME, to distinguish it from ordinary usage. Goffman's most powerful contribution to our knowledge of relationships was that SHAME, or much more frequently anticipation of SHAME, is a continuing presence in most social interaction.

There were four other sociologists, in addition to Goffman and Cooley, who stated or implied that shame was a pervasive motive in social behavior: Simmel (1904), Norbert Elias (1994), Helen Lynd (1968), and Richard Sennett (1972, 1980). But much more than any of these other authors, more even than Lynd (1968), Goffman implied that what I am calling SHAME was the dominant emotion of social interaction.

Goffman's idea of impression management, which formed the core of much of his work, made the avoidance of shame and embarrassment the central motive of interpersonal behavior, but without naming shame directly, as Cooley did. In his early work on presentation of self, embarrassment and avoidance of embarrassment is the central thread. Goffman's Everyperson is always desperately worried about her image in the eyes of the other, trying to present herself with her best foot forward to avoid shame. This work elaborates and vivifies Cooley's abstract idea of the way in which the looking glass generates shame, giving the idea roots in the reader's imagination.

Goffman also made the key sociological point about embarrassment: it arises out of disparities, real, anticipated, or just imagined, in the amount of deference, NO MATTER HOW SLIGHT the disparity. Everyone is extremely sensitive to the exact nuance of deference they receive. This is Goffman's key contribution to SHAME dynamics. It is this idea that gives rise to treating SHAME as the central emotion in social interaction. As already indicated, this usage differentiates my conception of shame from the vernacular one, which considers only crisis and disgrace.

Goffman affirmed Cooley's point on the centrality of the emotions of shame and pride in normal, everyday social relationships. In Goffman's language: "One assumes that embarrassment is a normal part of normal social life, the individual becoming uneasy not because he is personally maladjusted but rather because he is not; embarrassment is not an irrational impulse breaking through social prescribed behavior, but part of this orderly behavior itself" (1967, pp. 109 and 111).

Goffman's method of approaching emotions also made a crucial advance over the work of Mead and Cooley, in that Goffman based most of his work on the analysis of actual instances of behavior. This approach differentiated him from the highly abstract formulations of Mead and Cooley.

In his theoretical statements, Mead allowed for the importance of the nonverbal components of communication, when he referred to the "conversation of gestures." But he didn't examine empirical instances. Both in his theoretical work and his analysis of instances, Goffman noted the importance of the gestural components of interaction. But his analysis of instances was not detailed. Like most analysts of texts and most ethnographers, he didn't try to identify all of the gestures in dialogue and the precise details of context, and therefore ignored most of the emotional content. Nor did he examine the context in detail, especially the extended context, what happened before and after the episode. Since SHAME is elaborately hidden and disguised in Western civilization, an extremely close examination of the verbal, gestural, and contextual details is needed to uncover it.

In traditional and Asian societies, the central importance of SHAME is taken for granted. Indeed, in some Asian societies, such as Japan, it is seen as the central emotion. In a traditional society like the Maori, SHAME (they call it whakamaa) is also treated as the key emotion. Indeed, the whole approach to SHAME and relationships in this essay would be seen as platitudinous by the Maori, news from nowhere (Metge, 1986). But in Western societies, treating SHAME as highly significant in everyday life is counter-intuitive and even offensive.

Western societies focus on individuals, rather than on relationships. Emerson, because of his emphasis on self-reliance as an antidote to blind conformity, was one of the prophets of individualism: When my genius calls, I have no father and mother, no brothers or sisters." In extreme contrast, in a traditional society, there is NOTHING more important than one's relationships. Freeing up the individual from her relational/emotional world has been at the core of modernization. Since one's relationships and emotions don't show up on a resume, they have been de-emphasized to the point of disappearance. But SHAME and relationships don't disappear, they just assume hidden and disguised forms.

Individualism is the dominant theme of all relationships in Western societies. This focus disguises the web of personal and social relationships that sustain all human beings. The myth of the self-sustaining individual, in turn, reflects and generates the suppression and hiding of SHAME and pride. Since pride and SHAME, or at least their anticipation, are the predominant emotions in social interaction, suppression supports the status quo, the myth of the self-contained individual. But the obverse is that as we become aware of the massive amounts of emotions and disguising of emotion that occur in social interaction, we can make visible what is otherwise invisible, the state of any given relationship.

It is of some interest that in Western societies, the word pride, when unqualified by such adjectives as genuine, true, or justified, has come to connote arrogance or hubris. I prefer to call this affect "false pride," an indication of defense against SHAME. Because the emotion lexicon in Western societies is small and ambiguous, it is necessary to clearly define the meaning of emotions terms, as I have attempted to do in the case of disgrace and discretion shame, and true and false pride.

In my approach, manifestations of true pride, like those of embarrassment and SHAME, can be used as indicators of the state of the interpersonal bond. Markers of true pride indicate a secure bond (solidarity), and markers of SHAME indicated a threatened bond. Although pride is given theoretical parity with SHAME in most approaches to emotion dynamics in relationships, virtually all research in this domain concerns SHAME only. For this reason, the remainder of this article will also focus only on shame. Hopefully, future studies will fill this gap in our knowledge of true pride.

When SHAME and pride markers are suppressed or ignored, one has trouble sensing whether one's distance from the other is too great or too small. Under these conditions, dialogue becomes stiff and stilted, as in most university lecturing to large classes. Since emotion markers are direct observables in dialogue, they can be use to identify the "temperature" of a relationship, as a thermometer is used to identify the presence or absence of fever. Since the markers are known, SHAME, even when it is hidden, it is the key emotion for this purpose. Anger is also a part of the picture, since it is often linked to hidden SHAME.

How does one detect hidden SHAME and anger? Drawing upon the literatures on both verbal and nonverbal indicators, Retzinger has developed a decoding system. Following the work of Lewis (1971) and others, Retzinger has shown that there are many common words and gestures which may be used to identify hidden SHAME and anger, if these indicators are interpreted in the social context in which they are embedded (Retzinger, 1991, 1995).

SHAME as the Master Emotion

I call SHAME the master emotion because it has many more social and psychological functions than other emotions.

1. SHAME is a key component of conscience, the moral sense, since it signals moral transgression even without thoughts or words. SHAME is our moral gyroscope. Since this function is well understood, I will give most of my attention to two others, both less well understood.

2. SHAME arises in an elemental situation in which there is a real or imagined threat to our bonds; it signals trouble in a relationship. Since an infant's life is completely dependent on the bond with the caregivers, this emotion is as primitive and intense as fear. The point that SHAME is a response to bond threat cannot be emphasized too strongly, since in psychology and psychoanalysis there is a tendency to individualize SHAME, taking it out of its social matrix. Typically in these disciplines, SHAME is defined as a product of the individual's failure to live up to her own ideals. But one's ideals, for the most part, are usually a reflection of the ideals of one's society. Mead's idea of the generalized other captures this notion perfectly. If one feels that her behavior has been inadequate or deviant, not only an internal gap has been created between behavior and ideals, but also a gap between group ideals and ones self, a threat to the bond. The sociological definition of the source of SHAME subsumes the psychological one, pointing to the source in shared ideals.

3. Finally, SHAME plays a central role in regulating the expression, and indeed, the awareness of all of our other emotions. Anger, fear, grief, and love, for example, are not likely to be expressed outwardly to the degree that one is ashamed of them. One can be so ashamed of one's emotions that they can be repressed almost completely, to the point that only unusual circumstances will allow them to come to awareness. In Western societies, SHAME is almost completely re-

pressed and hidden, because one would be embarrassed that one was in a state of grief, fear, anger, or even embarrassment.

Two Paths for Unacknowledged SHAME

The path of overt, undifferentiated shame, withdrawal and silence, corresponds to our vernacular sense of shame. We are not surprised to find a link between shame and silence. But the other path of bypassed SHAME, leading to anger and aggression, is counter-intuitive, at least in Western societies. For that reason, I will describe this path in greater detail.

In interminable quarrels SHAME/anger spirals (humiliated fury, helpless anger) within and between the disputing parties, with the SHAME component hidden from self and other, cause intractability (Retzinger, 1991).[2] Both Gaylin 1884 and Gilligan 1996 propose shame as the cause of rage. In impasse, both shame and anger are hidden. In both cases it is the hidden shame that does the damage, because hidden shame blocks the possibility of repair of damaged bonds. To the extent that shame is hidden from self in others, one cannot bring one's self to connect with the other side, leading to more alienation, and so on, around the loop. Hidden shame and alienation are the emotional and relational sides of the same dynamic system, a cycle of violence.

I suggest that rage is a composite affect, a sequence of two elemental emotions, SHAME and anger. This idea has been advanced by other authors, notably Heinz Kohut (1971), and Helen Lewis (1971). Kohut proposed that violent anger of the kind he called "narcissistic rage" was a compound of shame and anger. Helen Lewis suggested that shame and anger have a deep affinity, and that it might be possible to find indications of unacknowledged shame occurring just prior to any intense hostility.

This sequence has been demonstrated to occur in marital quarrels by Retzinger (1991), and in Hitler's writings and speeches (Scheff, 1994), exactly as Lewis proposed. With all sixteen of the episodes of escalation of verbal violence in her data, Retzinger was able to demonstrate that prior to each episode, there had been first an insult by one party, indications of unacknowledged SHAME in the other party, and finally intense hostility in that party. This sequence can be seen as the motor of violence, since it connects the intense emotions of SHAME and anger to overt aggression.

Although there has been little research focused explicitly on pure, unalloyed anger, there are indications from the studies of discourse by

Lewis (1971), Retzinger (1991) and my own work, (such as Scheff 1990) that pure anger is rare and unlikely to lead to violence or even social disruption. On the contrary, anger by itself is usually brief and instructive. A person who is frustrated and unashamed of her anger is mobilized to tell what is going on, and to do what is needed, without making a huge scene.

In my own personal case, I can testify that most of my experiences of anger have involved SHAME/anger, either in the form of humiliated fury, or in a more passive form, what Labov and Fanshel (1977) call "helpless anger." Both of these variants are long lasting and extremely unpleasant, especially for me. SHAME-induced anger was unpleasant while happening, and even more unpleasant when it was over, since I inevitably felt foolish and out of control.

But in the very few episodes of what seems to have been, in retrospect, pure anger, the experience was entirely different. I did not raise my voice in any of them, nor did I put any one down or any other kind of excess. I simply told my view of what was going on directly, rapidly and with no need of calculation or planning. I was overcome with what I call "machine gun mouth." Every one who was present to one of these communications suddenly became quite respectful.

As for me, I did not feel out of control, even though my speech was completely spontaneous; on the contrary, I was wondering why I had not said my say before. It would seem that anger without SHAME has only a signal function, to alert self and others that one is frustrated. When anger has its source in feelings of rejection or inadequacy, and when the latter feelings are not acknowledged, a continuous spiral of SHAME/anger may result, which is experienced as hatred and rage. Rather than expressing and discharging one's SHAME, it is masked by rage and aggression. One can be angry one is ashamed, and ashamed that one is angry, and so on, working up to a loop of unlimited duration and intensity. This loop is the emotional basis of lengthy episodes or even life-long hatred and rage.

SHAME is pervasive in conflictful interaction, but usually invisible to interactants (and to researchers), unless Lewis's (or Gottschalk; and Gleser's; [1969]) approach is used. That is, SHAME is pervasive but invisible because it is not acknowledged. Unacknowledged SHAME takes two forms: bypassed and overt, undifferentiated shame.

The two forms are polar opposites in terms of thought and feeling. Overt shame; involves painful feeling with little ideation; bypassed shame, the opposite pattern: rapid thought, speech, or behavior, but little feeling. The two forms correspond to a distinction in Adler's (1956) theory of personality: children lacking a secure bond; at critical junctures respond in two different ways, either with an inferiority complex (chronic overt shame), or the drive to power (behavior masking bypassed shame). Lewis's analysis parallels Adler's;, but also represents an immense advance over it. Unlike Adler, she described observable markers for the theoretical constructs, and specified the causal sequence, the unending spiraling of emotion in feeling traps.

Overt shame is marked by furtiveness, confusion and bodily reactions: blushing, sweating and/or rapid heartbeat. One may be at a loss for words with fluster or disorganization of thought or behavior, as in states of embarrassment. Many of the common terms for painful feelings appear to refer to this type of SHAME, or combinations with anger: feeling peculiar, shy, bashful, awkward, funny, bothered, or miserable; in adolescent vernacular, being freaked, bummed, or weirded out. The phrases "I felt like a fool," or "a perfect idiot" may be prototypic.

Bypassed shame is manifested as a brief painful feeling, usually less than a second, followed by obsessive and rapid thought or speech. A common example: one feels insulted or criticized. At that moment (or later in recalling it), one might experience a jab of painful feeling (producing a groan or wince), followed immediately by imaginary but compulsive, repetitive replays of the offending scene. The replays are variations on a theme: how one might have behaved differently, avoiding the incident, or responding with better effect. One is obsessed.

Lewis (1971) referred to internal SHAME-rage process as a feeling trap, as "anger bound by SHAME", or "humiliated fury." Kohut's (1971) concept, "narcissistic rage", appears to be the same affect, since he viewed it as a compound of SHAME and rage. Angry that one is ashamed, or ashamed one is angry, then one might be ashamed to be so upset over something so "trivial". Such anger and shame are rarely acknowledged, difficult to detect and to dispel. SHAME /rage spirals may be brief, a matter of minutes, but can also last for hours, days, or a lifetime, as bitter hatred or resentment.

Brief sequences of SHAME /rage may be quite common. Escalation is avoided through withdrawal, conciliation, or some other tactic. In this article a less common type of conflict is described. Watzlawick et al. (1967, 107-108) call it "symmetrical escalation." In this theory, unacknowledged SHAME is the cause of revenge-based cycles of conflict [this formulation was anticipated in the work of Geen (1968) and Feshback (1971). SHAME-rage may escalate continually to the point that a person or a group can be in a permanent fit of SHAME /rage, a kind of madness.

Studies of Shame and Aggression

The theory outlined here is supported by several exploratory studies. Katz (1988) analyzed descriptions of several hundred criminal acts: vandalism, theft, robbery, and murder. In many of the cases, Katz found that the perpetrator felt humiliated, committing the crime as an act of revenge. In some of the cases the sense of humiliation was based on actual insults: [A] typical technique [leading to a spouse being murdered] is for the victim to attack the spouse's deviations from the culturally approved sex role. For example, a wife may accuse her husband of being a poor breadwinner or an incompetent lover, or the husband may accuse his wife of being "bitchy," "frigid" or promiscuous (Ch. 2, p.8).

In other cases it was difficult to assess the degree to which the humiliations were real and/or imagined. Whatever the realities, Katz's findings support the model of the shame /rage feeling trap. In his analysis of the murder of intimates, he says: "The would-be-killer must undergo a particular emotional process. He must transform what he initially senses as an eternally humiliating situation into a blinding rage "(p.ll). Rather than acknowledging his or her shame, the killer masks it with anger, which is the first step into the abyss of the shame /rage feeling trap, which ends in murder. Katz reports similar, though less dramatic findings with respect to the other kinds of crimes he investigated.

One issue which Katz's study doesn't address is the conditions under which humiliation is transformed into blind rage. Since not all humiliations lead to blind rage, there must be some ingredient that is not indicated in Katz's cases. Studies of family violence by Lansky suggest this extra ingredient. In order to lead to blind rage, the shame component in the emotions that are aroused must be unacknowledged.

Lansky has published three papers on family violence. The first paper (1984) describes six cases, the second (1987), four. The third (Lansky, 1989) analyzes one session with a married couple. In most of the cases, he reports similar emotional dynamics: violence resulted from the insulting manner that both husbands and wives took toward each other. Although some insults were overt, in the form of cursing, open contempt and disgust, most were covert, in the form of innuendo or double messages.

Underhanded disrespect gives rise to unacknowledged shame, which leads in turn to anger and violence, in the way predicted by Lewis. It is difficult for the participants to respond to innuendo and to double messages; these forms of communication confuse them. Instead of admitting their upset and puzzlement, they answer in kind. The cycle involves disrespect, humiliation, revenge, counter-revenge, and so on, ending in violence.

The way in which both spouses seem to be unaware of the intense shame that their behavior generates can be illustrated in one of the cases (Lansky, 1984: 34-35, emphasis added):

> A thirty-two year old man and his forty-six-year-old wife were seen in emergency conjoint consultation after he struck her. Both spouses were horrified, and the husband agreed that hospitalization might be the best way to start the lengthy treatment that he wanted. As he attempted to explain his view of his difficult marriage, his wife disorganized him with repeated humiliating comments about his inability to hold a job. These comments came at a time when he was talking about matters other than the job. When he did talk about work, she interrupted to say how immature he was compared to her previous husbands, then how strong and manly he was. The combination of building up and undercutting his sense of manliness was brought into focus. As the therapist commented on the process, the husband became more and more calm. . .After the fourth session, he left his marriage and the hospital for another state and phoned the therapist for an appropriate referral for individual therapy. On follow-up some months later, he had followed through with treatment.

The disguising of the wife's humiliation of the husband in this case is not through innuendo, since her disparagement is overt. Her shaming tactics are disguised by her technique of alternately praising her husband, by stating how "strong and manly" he was, then cutting him down. Perhaps she confused herself with this tactic as much as she did her husband.

Lack of awareness of shaming and shame can be seen in Lansky's report of a conjoint session with a violent man and his wife (1989). In this session, Lansky indicates that the hwife was dressed in a sexually provocative way, and that her bearing and manner was overtly seductive toward the interviewer. Yet neither spouse acknowledged her activity, even when the interviewer asked them whether the wife was ever seductive toward other men. Although both answered affirmatively, their answers concerned only past events. The lack of comment on what was occurring at that very moment in the interview is astounding. It would seem that blind rage requires not only shaming and shame, but blindness toward these two elements.

The relationship between collective violence and unacknowledged SHAME is suggested by an analysis of the Attica riots (Scheff, Retzinger, and Ryan, 1989). The violence of the guards toward the inmates began with a series of events which the guards perceived as humiliating: without consulting the guards, a new warden intent on reform increased the rights of the prisoners, which resulted in a series of incidents with prisoners which guards experienced as humiliating. Since the guards did not acknowledge their humiliation, their assault on the prisoners follows the sequence predicted by the Lewis's theory: insult, unacknowledged SHAME , rage, and aggression.

This formulation does not discount the importance of the topic of conflict, be it scarce resources, cultural differences, or any other issue. But it argues that in the absence of unacknowledged SHAME, human beings are resourceful enough to be able to find a compromise to any dispute, one that is most beneficial to both parties, or least harmful. If SHAME is evoked in one or both parties, however, and not acknowledged, than the content of the dispute becomes less important than the hidden emotions, which take over. Unacknowledged SHAME seems to be the basis of what Goffman (1967) called "character contests," conflicts in which the topic of dispute becomes subordinate to the issue of "face."

The last part of the theory presented here draws on the work of Elias (1987). I have suggested that his analysis of figurations can be construed as a theory of alienation that is linked to empirical indicators in discourse (Scheff, 1997). He typified relationships as either independent, dependent, or interdependent. I have shown that these three categories correspond to those used by many other sociological and psychological theorists (101-104). Unlike the other theorists, however, Elias provided links to data; he proposed that what he called "the I-We balance" could be assessed through the analysis of personal pronouns in discourse (Introduction, 1987). That is, independence would have the highest ratio of lst person pronouns (I, me, mine, my) to We pronouns (we, us, our, ours), dependence the lowest, and interdependence somewhere between, a balance between I and we. But Elias didn't take his scheme to the point of applying it to actual discourse.

In an earlier study (1994), I showed how Elias's scheme could be used to assess types of relationships by counting pronouns in the verbatim text recorded from four marital quarrels (Ch. 1). However, I use different names for the three types of relationships. Terms for relationships are scarce and somewhat awkward in English, since it favors descriptions of individuals. English also wants to make an absolute distinction between personal, interpersonal, and collective levels. I find the terms that Elias chose, particularly independence and dependence, so fraught with unwanted connotations that I have employed another set, taken from family systems theory: isolation (independence), engulfment (dependence), and a secure bond (interdependence).

The terms I chose are also awkward, but less evocative of unwanted meanings, and better poised between interpersonal and social levels. I proposed (1997, Ch. 4) that these terms can be understood as the essential elements in a theory of social integration (solidarity/alienation). Isolation represents one pole of alienation (bond too loose), engulfment the other (bond too tight). Seeman (1975) found evidence of engulfment (he called it self-estrangement) in his review of studies based on alienation scales. The third category, secure bonds, corresponds to solidarity in the theory of social integration.

This formulation has a number of advantages over existing ones. Rather than being based on the assumption that groups are made up of isolated individuals, it assumes a structure/process involving social relationships and emotional reactions. It is not static, since it proposes that the degree of conflict at any moment is based on successive momentary states of social bonds. The formulation is exceedingly complex, since it suggests an analysis of solidarity and alienation in terms of actual social relationships and emotions between and within the parties to a conflict.

Unlike many theories of conflict, this one offers a description of the causal chain which links social and psychological conditions to the generation of conflict. Communication practices which serve to deny alienation and emotion generate spirals in which emotions escalate to the point of intolerable tension, explaining the origin of "war fever" and other highly irrational behaviors by individuals and groups.

Finally, this theory is potentially testable, since it provides detailed descriptions of its elemental components, alienation and emotion. For this reason, it might be seen as a "grounded theory" (Glaser and Strauss, 1967). In our study of videotapes of game shows, Retzinger and I (1991) have shown that markers of solidarity and alienation can be rated systematically, and that alienation interferes with the ability of contestants to cooperate, and therefore, to win.

SECONDARY ANALYSIS
OF SENNETT AND COBB, AND WILLIS

1. The Path of Hostility and Aggression

Many people, including myself, believe that Willis's (1977) study of working class boys in an English high school is one of the best ethnographies ever written. Willis spent years observing and talking with the "lads" in one particular school, and also, more briefly, other boys in comparable schools. He followed the lads around and visited their classes, recording their actions and, at great length, their conversations.

The question that interests Willis is the reproduction of social class: why do a huge majority of these lads wind up taking working class, rather than middle class jobs? Willis is somewhat surprised by the answer that his data suggest. Although he acknowledges that these boys tend to be routed into working class jobs by their teachers, he finds that the boys themselves play a large part in the process. They perceive their teachers to be middle class, and perceive them to be rejecting towards working class persons like themselves.

Because of the feeling of rejection, the boys are defiant toward the teachers, and, more generally, toward education itself. The boys vehemently reject the teachers and their values, and in doing so, sabotage their own education. The rejection of education, Willis finds, plays a major role in the job futures of the lads.

There is a parallel in studies of the US prison system in the 1950's and 60's. They investigated the different kinds of pain that imprisonment causes. One of the most intense pains, they argued, was the loss of status (degradation). They go on to suggest that prisoners react to their loss of status by forging a prisoner culture that attempts to restore at least some of their damaged status. These studies propose that since prisoners feel rejected by their keepers and by their society, they unite in a culture which "rejects the rejecters (McCorkle and Korn 1954). Hostility from the guards and from society is met by counter-hostility from the prisoners:

> The acute sense of status degradation that prisoners experience generates powerful pressures to evolve means of restoring status. Principal among the mechanisms that emerge is an inmate culture- a system of social relationships governed by norms that are largely at odds with those espoused by the officials and the conventional society. In other words, prisoners are led to seek from within their own numbers what the outside world so fully withholds: prestige; But a lofty state for some presupposes that the many in lowly states will accord legitimacy to these invidious distinctions; if eminence is to be enjoyed by some, then deference and homage must be secured from the lesser ranks.

But deference is not so easily secured, especially in the prison. If, as Veblen said, prestige is always in short supply, it is the more so in the prison because so many are deprived of it. Consequently, these disenchanted individuals are forced into bitterly competitive relationships through which the essential superiority of one or another criminal status over other criminal statuses is asserted. Thus it is hardly surprising to find that the upper echelons of the inmate world come to be occupied by those whose past behavior best symbolizes that which society rejects and who have most fully repudiated institutional norms. For those who succeed in asserting the superiority of their particular criminal status, a sense of worth and dignity is the reward. According to McCorkle and Korn,

> "Observation suggests that the major problems with which the inmate social system attempts to cope center about the theme of social rejection. In many ways, the inmate social system may be viewed as providing a way of life which enables the inmate to avoid the devastating psychological effects of internalizing and converting social rejection into self-rejection. In effect, it permits the inmate to reject his rejecters." [McCorkle and Korn, 1958; Cloward, et al., 1960).

Although SHAME is not explicitly mentioned in these studies, they imply a SHAME/anger dynamic. Rather than acknowledge the SHAME of rejection, the prisoners mask it with anger and hostility, much like the "lads" in Willie's book react to their teachers. Although class analysis is not an explicit feature of these prison studies, they seem to assume that almost all of the prisoners are working class rather than middle class. To the extent that is the case, there is a second parallel with Willis's study of working class boys.

2. The Path of Withdrawal[3]

My study of elderly working class mental patients in England in 1965[4] suggests a parallel with Sennett and Cobb's study of older working class men at about the same period. I was struck at the time how every one of the older male patients presented at their intake interview as withdrawn: eyes cast down and slumping in their chair, their speech usually soft almost to the point of inaudibility. Another feature was their virtual unanimity that they themselves were to blame for their problems, again parallel to Sennett and Cobb's subjects. It was clear that all of these men were rejected by their society. But rather than acknowledging SHAME, or hostility directed outward, they withdrew.

The hidden injuries that Sennett and Cobb discovered might be paraphrased in this way: their working class men felt that first, because of their class and occupational position, they were not accorded the respect that they should have gotten from others, particularly from their teachers, bosses, and even from their own children. That is, these men have many complaints about their relationships. Secondly, a more subtle injury: these men also felt, in some ways, that their class and occupational position was at least partly their own fault. Sennett and Cobb imply that social class is responsible for both injuries. They believe that their working men did not get the respect they deserved because of their social class, and that the second injury, lack of self-respect, is also the fault of class, rather than the men's own fault, as most of them thought.

Sennett and Cobb argue that in American society, the respect one receives is largely based on one's individual achievement, the extent that one's accomplishments give one a unique identity that stands out from the mass of others. The role of public schools in the development of abilities forms a central part of Sennett and Cobb's argument. Their informants lacked self-respect, the authors thought, because the schooling of working class boys did not develop their individual talents in a way that would allow them to stand out from the mass as adults. In the language of the sociology of emotions, they carry a burden of feelings of rejection and inadequacy, which is to say chronic low self-esteem (SHAME).

Sennett, who did the participant-observation part of the study, reported most fully on a particular grammar school, "Watson School," that he observed. He suggests that "teachers act on their expectations of the children in such a way as to make the expectations become reality" (p. 81). One of his observations concerns a second-grade class:

> In this class there were two children, Fred and Vincent, whose "clothes were pressed and seemed better kept" than the other children's clothes." In a class of mostly dark Italian children, these were the fairest skinned. From the outset the teacher singled out these two children. To them he spoke with a special warmth in his voice. He never praised them openly but a message that they were different, and better, was spontaneously conveyed (p. 81).

Sennett and Cobb argue that teachers single out for attention and praise only a very small percentage of the students, usually students who are either talented or middle class or closest in actions and appearance to middle-class. This praise and attention allows the singled-out students to develop their potential for achievement. The large majority of the boys, however, are ignored and, in subtle ways, rejected. "by the time the children are ten or eleven the split between the many and the few who are expected "to make something of themselves" is out in the open. "[The mass of] boys in class act as though they were serving time, as though schoolwork and classes had become something to wait out, a blank space in their lives they hope to survive" (pp. 82-83).

This statement is a damning indictment of public schools. There are a few working class boys who achieve their potential by virtue of their superior academic or athletic talents. But the large mass does not. For them, rather than opening up the world of culture and accomplishment, public schools close this vision off. Education, rather than becoming a source of personal and cultural growth, provides only SHAME and rejection. For the majority of students in public schools, surviving the days and years of large classes means running a gauntlet of shame and embarrassment every day. These students learn by the second or third grade that is better to be silent in class rather than risk ridicule or humiliation of a wrong answer. Even students with the right answers must deal with having the wrong accent, clothing or physical appearance. For most students, schooling is a vale of SHAME.

Word Counts in Three Texts.

In order to further support my hypothesis about SHAME dynamics and class, I undertook a content analysis of the Willis, and the Sennett and Cobb texts discussed above, and for the sake of comparison, a third text, *The Theory of the Leisure Class*, by Veblen (1899). This later text was available as an electronic file on the net, and has emotion content somewhat parallel to the two texts in question. But because it is entirely analytical, the theory predicts that it should have fewer anger and SHAME cues than the other two texts, which contain both authorial analysis and discourse by subjects.

The theory used here predicts that SHAME cues should be the greatest in the Sennett and Cobb text, because the emotion path followed by these men was withdrawal and silence. By the same token, anger and SHAME/anger should be the greatest in the Willis text, because the lads followed the path of false pride and hostility directed outward. I have used the Retzinger (1991; 1995) coding system to locate words that are indicative of SHAME, anger, and SHAME/anger in the three texts.

For the Willlis text, I added two slang phrases and a word the lads used that are not found in Retzinger's word lists: "aving a laff, "us and them," and "pisstake." As Willis pointed out, all three are indicative of the lads' defiance of authority. Both "aving a laff" and "pisstake" refer to pranks, usually at a teacher's expense. "Us and them" refers to the distance that separates the lads from authorities. All three are indicative of aggressive rejection of the rejecters (SHAME/anger). The count of all three indicators together is 27, which is 14% of the SHAME/anger indicators found in the Willis text.

Hypotheses and Data

The following hypotheses, if they are supported by the data, would undercut the truth of the theory outlined above.

1. There will be more SHAME and anger cues in the Veblen text than in the other two texts.

2. There will be more SHAME cues in the Willis text, and more anger and SHAME/anger cues in the Sennett and Cobb text.

3. The I-we ratio will be higher in Sennett and Cobb's subject discourse than in Willis's subject discourse, expressing alienation in the engulfed form in the Sennett and Cobb subjects, and in the isolated form in the Willis subjects.

Emotion in Three Texts

WILLIS	SENNETT/COBB	VEBLEN
Total words		
108k	75.3k	106k
□		
Shame words		
1.92 cue words/k	3.19 cue words/k	1.76 cue words/k
Anger and shame/anger words		
2.36 cue words/k	1.47 cue words/k	52 cue words/k

Table 10.1. Emotion in Willis, Sennett and Cobb, and Veblen

As the table shows, none of the null hypotheses were supported. Instead, the data supports all of the theoretical predictions. As suggested above, the largest amount of SHAME cues is found in Sennett and Cobb: 240 SHAME words (.32 %). The Willis text is next, with 209 SHAME words (.19%). Last is the Veblen text, with 186 SHAME words (.18 %). Although the lowest in rank compared with the other two texts, the Veblen text has only a slightly lower rate of SHAME words than the Willis text. The high rate of SHAME-related words is not surprising, considering the subject matter: Veblen's volume is centrally concerned with social honor, pride, and invidious social comparisons.

As suggested in the discussion of theory above, the text with the highest rate of anger and SHAME/anger words (255; .24 %) is Willis. According to the theory, aggressive pranks and ridicule ("aving a laff") are ways of masking SHAME with anger. In terms of the theory, the SHAME is "bypassed," not experienced as such.

Next in rank is the Sennett text (111; 15%). The middle-aged and older working men expressed relatively little anger and SHAME/anger. According to the theory, their way of managing SHAME was withdrawal and silence, rather than angry protest.

Finally, the Veblen text has the fewest expressions of anger and SHAME/anger (55; .052 %). The social behavior described by Veblen masks anger by symbolic actions. Veblen was a master of satirical expression, which is too subtle for my method of counting words. Separate counts for the authors' and the subjects' language in the Willis and the Sennett texts had an unexpected result. There was little difference between subject's speech and the authors' language in the proportion of SHAME, anger and SHAME/anger cognates. I had thought that subject's language would contain more emotion cues than of the authors', but it was not the case. Apparently both use a language of indirection equally, when it comes to emotions.

Although content analysis through the use of word counts is systematic, it is also somewhat crude, and therefore leads to errors. For example, the word "different" is one of the cue words for SHAME in the Retzinger coding system. As used by the lads in the Willis study, and the men in the Sennett and Cobb study, it usually does have this meaning, as in "feeling different" from the teachers and middle class persons. However, in the authorial commentary, it usually is not an indicator of SHAME. Similarly, the words always and never, when used in dialogue, are usually indicators of SHAME/anger, as assumed by the Retzinger coding method. But in authorial commentary, they seldom have this meaning. I have removed these words from the coding of the authorial commentary, therefore.

Like all systematic methods, word counts bring with them a mixture of strengths and weaknesses. On the one hand, it is reassuring to find that a mechanical method yields data, independently of the researcher's point of view, that supports the thesis. On the other hand, the word lists are culture dependent. For this reason, I have had to add some words for the Willis study of English school boys that weren't present in Retzinger's US based word count, and to remove some words from the counts in the authorial commentary, since they have a different meaning there than in dialogue.

Relational Indicators In Two Texts

I counted pronouns only om the subjects discourse in Willis and in Sennett and Cobb. I didn't count pronouns in the author text of either book or in Veblen, since the authorial voice favors objectivity, meaning very few I pronouns.

WILLIS	SENNETT/COBB
Subject Pronoun Count	
Total Words 19.4k	Total Words 6.0k
I-Words	
629 (3.2%)	252 (6.3%)
We-Words	
203 (1.0%)	31 (.5%)
I-We Ratio	
3.0	15

Table 10.2. I-We ratio in Willis and in Sennett and Cobb.

The I-We ratio for the Sennett subjects is 15, fivefold that of the Willis subjects (3.0). The null hypothesis is not support by the data. The words of the old men in the Sennett and Cobb study point towards the isolated form of alienation. Those of the boys in the Willis study point toward the engulfed form of alienation. Since I have no marker for the ratio that would indicate a secure bond, I am unable to determine which group appears to be more alienated.

DISCUSSION

Hopefully, future studies of working class emotions will support the thesis developed here. If that is the case, what kinds of social change might be indicated? Building pride in the working class by acknowledging SHAME would not be a simple matter. According to the theory, to the extent that one acknowledges, rather than masks one's SHAME, then there is less compulsion to act out, whether by aggression or withdrawal. However, the same theory recognizes that unacknowledged SHAME is largely outside of awareness. For this reason, helping working class men to become aware of their own SHAME would require considerable effort, skill, and good will all around. The vehicle for such a movement has yet to be developed.

Of course, all classes, not just the working class, have problems with SHAME. My guess is that in the ruling classes, unacknowledged SHAME takes the form of false pride or aggression. Covering up hidden SHAME with ostentatious displays of consumption, as implied by Veblen, is one such vehicle. Attacks on racial and class minorities by the reactionary rich would be an example of the SHAME/anger path. In my experience, effecting changes in upper class management of SHAME might be even more difficult than in the working class, since the rich show obvious gains from their current practices.

There also may be a link between the motive to acquire capital and SHAME implied in Weber's analysis of *The Protestant Ethic* (1907). Weber focused only on the cognitive link between belief in a religious elect and strenuous effort to show worldly success. That is, Weber thought that the correlation between capitalism and ascetic Protestantism suggested that these believers could show that they were probably predestined for heaven in the next world by acquiring capital in this world.

But Weber's analysis also implies an accompanying emotional motive, as well. Showing that one is a member of a religious/economic elect can also be a way of showing oneís superiority over the poorer classes, a defense against shame. As in Veblen's idea of conspicuous consumption, members of the ruling class can bypass shame by external behavior of being superior. Since the bypassing of shame can lead to anger and aggression toward others, it may be a more destructive form than overt, differentiated shame. This latter form leads only to withdrawal and silence, as in the case of the working class men studied by Sennett and Cobb.

But my data concerns working class men, not the rich or even the middle class. Of course it is possible that initiatives for social change in the management of SHAME might touch upon all classes, not just the working class.

An example of such a vehicle would be the inauguration of classes in public grammar and high schools on conflict resolution. Such classes could help students learn that when they are ashamed or humiliated, there are other options besides aggression or withdrawal. In Western societies, children, especially male children, are often socialized to grin and bear it rather than voicing their needs and their suffering.

Having taught some thirty classes on conflict at the university level for many years, I have a sense that only certain kinds of classes would have real effects. Classes organized around lectures and information would probably have little effect, since the changes that are necessary in dealing with conflict concern hidden emotions, for the most part.

My own classes were organized around role-playing and discussion. I could see intense effects on the majority of the class arising out the role-plays of conflicts from the student's own experience. Even students who were too shy to role-play their own conflicts seemed to grasp the emotional meaning of demonstrations by other students.

To be fair, there was always a substantial minority of students who didn't seem to understand the class, and a tiny minority who protested. These latter sometimes complained that the class was more like group psychotherapy than education. But their protests were rejected by the majority of the class.

Conflict resolution classes could be a first step toward changing destructive class emotions. Such classes would benefit children of all social classes, and hopefully, their parents also. In the present climate of frequent shooting outrages in the schools and elsewhere, the likelihood that this option or a similar one will be tried seems to be increasing.

CONCLUSION

This chapter has sought to implement a new direction in sociology and social science by integrating various approaches to theory, method, data, and applications. I have sought to include the least parts (words and gestures in discourse) and abstract concepts and theory, as per Spinoza's dictum. My approach includes both sociological and psychological theory, and balances both by including the analysis of subject's talk, even their actual comments. Finally, I have used both a qualitative method, discourse analysis, and a quantitative method (word counts), suggesting that the strengths of one method provide some check to the limitations of the other.

This approach, it seems to me, offers the potential for resolving the seeming opposition between structure and process, between structure and agency. By demonstrating the reproduction of social class in dialogue in two studies of working class males, this study suggests that agency can be located in the microprocess and microstructure in the lives of the subjects.

NOTES

1. See studies by Hammond, 1990, 1999; James, 1997; Lamont, 2000; Scheff and Mahlendorf, 1989; and Wilkinson, 1996, 1999. James, Wilkenson, Scheff and Mahlendorf suggest pride and shame as the key emotions generated by inequality. Hammond does not name these emotions, but his analysis implies them. The link between inequality and pride/shame is still weaker in Lamont, but her use of words like self-esteem and dignity are hints in this direction. The classic study of resentment by Scheler (1972) also implies, somewhat indirectly, the same emotion dynamic.

2. See clinical studies by Lewis (1971), Kaufman (1989), and Morrison (1996).; and also sociological studies by Retzinger (1991); Scheff and Retzinger (1991), and Scheff (1990, 1994, 1997).

3. This section is based on one part of Scheff (2000).

4. This section is based on one part of Scheff (1994, Chapter 3).

REFERENCES

Adler, A. [l907-37] l956. *The Individual Psychology of Alfred Adler*. New York: Basic Books.

Cloward, Richard, et al. 1960. *Theoretical Studies in Social Organization of the Prison*. New York: Social Science Research Council.

Cooley, C. H. ,l922. *Human Nature and the Social Order*. New York: Scribners.

Coser, L. A.. 1956. *The Functions of Social Conflict*. Glencoe: Free Press.

Elias, Norbert. 1994 *The Civilizing Process*. Oxford: Blackwell.

Gaylin, Willard. 1984. *The Rage Within: Anger in Modern Life*. New York: Simon and Schuster.

Gilligan, James. 1996. *Violence: Reflections on a National Epidemic*. New York: Vintage.

Glaser, B., and A. Strauss. l967. *The Discovery of Grounded Theory*. Chicago: Aldine.

Goffman, E. 1959. *The Presentation of Self in Everyday Life*. Garden City, NY: Doubleday Anchor.

Goffman, E. 1959a. *Asylums*. New York: Anchor.

Goffman, E. 1963. *Behavior in Public Places*. New York: Free Press.

Goffman, E. 1963a. *Stigma*. Englewood Cliffs, NJ. Prentice-Hall.

Goffman, E. l967. *Interaction Ritual*. New York: Anchor.

Gottschalk, L., and G. Gleser. 1969. *Manual for Using the Gottschalk-Gleser Content Analysis Scales*. Berkeley: University of California Press

Hammond, Michael. 1990. "Affective Maximization: A New Macro-theory in the Sociology of Emotions." In Kemper, Theodore D. (ed.),

Research Agendas in the Sociology of Emotions. Albany, NY: State University of New York Press, pp, 58-81.

Hammond, Michael. 1999. "Arouser Depreciation and the Expansion of Social Inequality. In   Franks, David D., Thomas S. Smith, et al (eds.), *Mind, Brain, and Society: Toward a Neurosociology of Emotion, Vol. 5*. Stamford, CT: Jai Press, pp. 339-358.

James, Oliver. 1997. *Britain on the Couch: Why We're Unhappier Compared with 1950 Despite Being Richer*. London: Century.

Jervis, R., N. Lebow, and J. Stein. 1985. *Psychology and Deterrence*. Baltimore: Johns Hopkins U. Press.

Katz, J. 1988. T*he Seductions of Crime*. New York: Basic Books.

Kaufman, Gershen. 1989. *The Psychology of Shame*. New York: Springer.

Kohut, H. E.. 1971. *Thoughts on narcissism and   narcissistic Rage: The Search for the Self*. New   York: International University Press.

Lamont, Michele. 2000. *The Dignity of Working Men*. New York: Russell Sage.

Lansky, M.   1984. *Violence, Shame, and the Family*. International Journal of Family Psychiatry 5:21-40.

Lansky, M. 1987. "Shame and Domestic Violence." In Nathanson, D. (ed.), *The Many Faces of Shame*. New York: Guilford

Lansky, M. 1989. "Murder of a Spouse: A Family System's Viewpoint." *International Journal of Family Psychiatry*. 10:159-178.

Lewis, Helen B. 1971. S*hame and Guilt in Neurosis*. New York: International Universities Press.

McCorkle, Lloyd, and Richard Korn. 1954. 'Resocialization within Walls.' *The Annals*. 293:(May), 88.

Morrison, Andrew. 1996. *The Culture of Shame*. New York: Ballentine.

Phillips, Bernard S.   1988. "Toward A Reflexive Sociology."   19: (Summer), 138-151.

Phillips, Bernard S. 2001. *Beyond Sociology's Tower of Babel: Reconstructing the Scientific Method.* New York: Aldine.

Retzinger, Suzanne. 1991. *Violent Emotions.* Newbury Park, CA.: Sage.

Retzinger, Suzanne. 1995. "Identifying Shame and Anger in Discourse." *American Behavioral Scientist* 38:104-113.

Scheff, Thomas J. 1990. *Microsociology: Emotion, Discourse, and Social Structure.* Chicago: Univ. of Chicago Press.

Scheff, Thomas J. 1994. *Bloody Revenge.* Boulder: Westview Press.

Scheff, Thomas J. 1997. *Emotions, the Social Bond, and Human Reality: Part/Whole Analysis.* Cambridge; Cambridge University Press.

Scheff, Thomas J. 2000. "Shame and the Social Bond: A Sociological Theory." *Sociological Theory* 18:84-99.

Scheff, Thomas J., and Suzanne Retzinger. 1991. *Emotions and Violence.* Lexington, MA: Lexington Books.

Scheff, Thomas J., and Ursula Mahelendof. 1989. "Emotions and False Consciousness: An Incident from Werther." T*heory, Culture, and Society* 5: 57-88.

Scheff, Thomas J., Suzanne M. Retzinger and M. Ryan. 1989. "Crime, Violence and Self-Esteem: Review and Proposals." In Mecca, A., N. Smelser and J. Vasconcellos (eds.), *The Social Importance of Self-Esteem.* Berkeley: University of California Press.

Scheler, Max. (1972). *Ressentiment.* New York: Schocken.

Sennett, Richard, and Jonathan Cobb. 1972. *The Hidden Injuries of Class.* New York: Knopf.

Simmel, Georg. 1955. *Conflict & the Web of Group-Affiliations.* New York: Free Press of Glencoe.

Simmel, Georg. 1950. *The Sociology of Georg Simmel*. Glencoe: Free Press.

Veblen, Thorstein. [1899] 1953. *The Theory of the Leisure Class*. New York: Mentor.

Weber, Max. [1906] 1958. *The Protestant Ethic and the Spirit of Capitalism*. New York: Scribner.

Wilkinson, R. G. 1996. *Unhealthy Societies*. London: Routledge.

Wilkinson, R. G.   1999. "Income Inequality, Social Cohesion, and Health: Clarifying the Theory." *International Journal of Health Services* 29:525-543.

Willis, Paul. 1977. *Learning to Labor*. 1977. New York: Columbia University Press.

Introduction to Chapter 11

Howard Becker's analysis of Goffman's essay on total institutions centers on Goffman's ability to confront "our unthinking acceptance of the constraints of conventional thinking." A crucial question is whether the social scientist accepts people's conventional categories or vernacular language. To do so, however, is to take on perspectives and assumptions which the social scientist might well find to be problematic. Goffman's approach to analyzing the organized practices of degradation in total institutions is to use neutral language versus a language of denunciation, as illustrated by "echelon" versus "domination." By using neutral language to describe what most people think are despicable acts, Goffman is able to place those acts under a microscope. Here, Goffman's neutral language parallels the neutral language to be found in this volume's Table 1-1, Chapter 1. Further, Goffman constructed his own abstract categories: "total institution" linked mental hospitals with prisons, concentration camps, military establishments, ships at sea and religious retreats. Becker shows here Goffman's understanding --as well as his own--of the importance of moving far up and down language's ladder of abstraction, and of the use of abstract categories to yield awareness of fundamental problems throughout society. By juxtaposing those establishments, Goffman helped us to see problems we would otherwise fail to see. Becker's insights into Goffman's procedures, when coupled with Becker's own reflexive approach to Goffman's work, thus illustrate the central elements of the web approach to the scientific method. And they also illustrate links between Goffman's approach to the scientific method and the approach taken in this volume.

Chapter 11

The Politics of Presentation: Goffman and Total Institutions[1]

Howard S. Becker

THE PROBLEM OF CONVENTIONAL CATEGORIES

Goffman's essay "On the Characteristics of Total Institutions" is a classic example of the relation between methods of presenting research and scholarship and their political content. This connection, never simple and direct, exemplifies Goffman's presentational solution to a problem which has always plagued social science writing and research: how to avoid the analytic flaws and failures which arise from our unthinking acceptance of the constraints of conventional thinking.

When social scientists study something--a community, an organization, an ethnic group--they are never the first people to have arrived on the scene, newcomers to an unpeopled landscape who can name its features as they like. Every topic they write about is part of the experience of many other kinds of people, all of whom have their own ways of speaking about it, specialized words for the objects and events and people involved in that area of social life. Those special words are never neutral objective signifiers. Rather, they express the perspective and situation of the particular kinds of people who use them. The natives are already there and everything in that terrain has a name, more likely many names.

If we choose to name what we study with words the people involved already use, we acquire, with the words, the attitudes and perspectives the words imply. Since many kinds of people are involved in any social activity, choosing words from any of their vocabularies thus commits us to one or another of the perspectives already in use by one or another of the groups there. Those perspectives invariably take much for granted, making assumptions about what might better be treated, social scientifically, as problematic.

Take the topic of marijuana. People who use it have a language for talking about it. They speak of "getting high." They have many synonyms for marijuana, speaking of it, for instance, as "grass." They might speak of the person they buy marijuana from as a "connection." Other people, whose worlds also contain marijuana--physicians, lawyers, police--will have other words for the same things, perhaps speaking of "addiction" and "cannabis" and "pushers." The language of users suggests that use is voluntary, pleasurable, innocent; the language of some others suggests that it is involuntary, harmful, evil.

What things are called almost always reflects relations of power. People in power call things what they want to and others have to adjust to that, perhaps using other words of their own in private, but accepting in public what they cannot escape. Whatever my friends and I might think, marijuana is called a narcotic drug by people who can make that name and the perspective associated with it stick.

The social scientist's problem, simply, is what to call the things we study. If I study marijuana, do I speak of "marijuana addiction" or, as I chose to do years ago, in a minor linguistic variation that connoted a serious shift in perspective, of "marijuana use"? Do we speak of "getting high on," of "being intoxicated by," or of "being under the influence of" this substance?

If I choose the terms used by the people who "own" the territory, and therefore choose the perspectives associated with those terms, I let my analysis be shaped by conventional social arrangements and the distribution of power and privilege they create. This has both technical and moral consequences.

The technical consequence is that the class of phenomena I want to generalize about is made up of things which have in common only the moral attitudes toward them of powerful people and groups in the society, and the actions that have been taken toward them in consequence. The result of that is a tremendous difficulty in finding anything general to say about the phenomena, other than things associated with those moral attitudes. You can talk about the results of being thought about that way--that's what the labeling theory of deviance did. But you can't find anything to say about how people get that way, underlying causes, or similar matters, because there is nothing related to those matters which all the cases in the class have in common. You can't make science if you can't find anything to generalize about.

The moral consequence of adopting existing language and perspectives toward the phenomena we study is that we accept, intentionally or not, all the assumptions about right and wrong contained in those words and ideas. We accept, in the case of drugs, the idea that addicts are people who have lost control of themselves and therefore cannot help doing things which are inherently bad.

This was Goffman's problem as he began to write about the mental hospital he had studied. The existing language for discussing the people confined in such institutions embodied the perspectives of the people who were able to confine others in them--the professional staff who ran them, the legal professionals who assigned people to them, the families who had solved their problem with an unruly family member, the police for whom those unruly people were what is sometimes called a public nuisance. How could he avoid taking such categories as "mental illness' and the perspectives associated with them for granted?

THE LINGUISTIC SOLUTION

To make clear how Goffman found a workable solution to the problem of conventional categories, I'll begin with a simple observation. No reader of Goffman's essay on total institutions can be unaware of the considerable disparity between the social reality he is talking about and the way he talks about it. He describes and analyzes social practices which are quite common, whose existence and character are known to most adults, if not through their personal experience then through the experience of others they know and through secondhand descriptions in the press, films, drama, and fiction. He describes and analyzes organized social practices of incarceration and degradation which repel and even disgust many readers, and which arouse feelings of shame in us for living in a society in which such things have happened and continue to happen. His detailed and comprehensive descriptions make it impossible to ignore the continued existence of these organized, socially accepted activities, and may have, on occasion, helped instigate attempts at their reform.

The disparity I mentioned exists, first, in the descriptive language he uses, in his penchant for inventing concepts, for giving names to things, for creating categories and sub-categories and classifications.

Every page reveals a set of distinctions: three kinds of this and four kinds of that and they all have names..

Unlike some other theorists (such as Talcott Parsons, who wrote many of his most influential works during the period in which Goffman wrote), Goffman's concepts have names which come from the common language. He did not coin new words based on Latin or Greek roots. Instead, he used words from the common language of life, perhaps not everyday household life, but words which were not esoteric (for instance, "house rules," or "echelon management").

He names the phenomena he observed in this kind of language so often and so consistently that it might seem an affectation or mannerism, a stylistic tic designed to call attention to the author's cleverness. You might even think that he is doing something social scientists are often accused of: making up fancy names for commonplace things which already have names.

You can't criticize Goffman that way. The way he named social phenomena lies at the heart of his approach and, when we consider this characteristic feature of his writing, we uncover some methodological principles he followed but never spoke of.

To begin with, many of the things he gives names to are well known to us, his readers. We recognize them immediately; they are familiar experiences we have had or events we have witnessed. But, and this is a very important but, we don't have names for these experiences and events. Goffman appropriates common language to name things previously unnamed. We have all, for instance, participated in what he calls "face work," the ritual gestures by which we help people who have revealed themselves to not be quite what they had claimed to be to recover their composure, to regain their sense of being, after all, competent adult participants in normal adult interaction. Having participated in these collective attempts to repair the social harm that people do to themselves and that we, and the organizations in which we act, do to them, we know such a situation when it happens, We "instinctively" feel the obligation to deliver this service, to help others "save face," just as we feel the right to expect that service from others. And when Goffman points to such occurrences we know just what he means and are grateful for the word which now allows us to talk about it. We feel that we have always known it but, until Goffman gave it to us, did not know its name. Much of what goes on in social life is like that.

Other things for which he coined new terms already had names, but these names were euphemistic and misleading, designed to hide some aspects, we might even say the true nature, of what is actually going on. Thus, in a usage Goffman liked, Dwight MacDonald spoke of mental hospitals as places in which unwanted people, particularly older people, were systematically and routinely killed. MacDonald did not call these places "mental hospitals." He called them "death camps," arguing that "mental hospital" was a euphemistic way of talking about the killing of old people which could easily be seen to be the real function of such places—easily seen when one looked at the actual facts about how many people entered them and how they left.

I said above that, when Goffman gives us a word for some until now unnamed and therefore undiscussable phenomenon, we feel grateful. But that is only partly true. In fact, though he intended to write about these matters in a neutral (even technical) way, reading Goffman is frequently a morally uncomfortable experience.

Goffman was more original than Dwight MacDonald. Despite the repellent nature of many of the activities he describes, he did not call mental hospitals death camps. No. He called them "total institutions." Most readers think it obvious that he disliked the authoritarian organizations he encompassed in that term, but he did not use openly judgmental language. Nor did he use adjectives and adverbs which betray a negative assessment of these organizations (although he occasionally comes close, as when he describes "total institutions" as "forcing houses for changing persons") He did not express his dislike as social scientists often do, by a tough, direct, harsh denunciation. He did not call people or organizations bad names. He did not even, in the style of the great iconoclast Thorstein Veblen, do it in an elaborate scholarly sarcasm.

Instead, he used a neutral, technical language. When he talked about mental hospitals and prisons, he used language that might just as well be used to describe an ant hill or a bee hive as to describe a common form of social institution which treats some people (never forget, with the complicity of the rest of society, and that does mean us) in such a way that their lives resemble those of members of those insect societies: regimented in an inflexible and humiliating caste system without regard for their own feelings or wishes. His detailed description of what we might find in such places brings us to the sort of conclusion the language I have just used expresses, though he doesn't say anything quite like that himself.

Here are some of the ways Goffman used language to avoid built-in judgments. He used the word "echelon" (instead of, for instance, "domination") to describe the typical authority system of a total institution: "*any* member of the staff class has certain rights to discipline *any* member of the inmate class, thereby markedly increasing the probability of sanction" (42). The word "echelon" is neutral. Since it is not commonly used to name the phenomenon Goffman is pointing to, it does not have the immediately negative connotations a term like "domination" would have. It simply describes one way among many of organizing authority relations, just as Weber's distinction between charismatic, bureaucratic, and traditional describes three other ways.

I will note, without providing argument or examples, that it is far easier to find examples of "echelon control" than of "domination." The former simply requires demonstration of an observable fact--who gives orders to who--while the latter includes, scarcely beneath the surface, a judgment as to the moral suitability of the order-giving arrangement, which is always more arguable.

Some further examples of this kind of neutral language Goffman used to describe matters many readers would probably have strong negative feelings about are:

"role dispossession," to describe how new recruits are prevented from being who they were in the world they previously inhabited;

"trimming" and "programming," to describe how "the new arrival allows himself to be shaped and coded into an object that can be fed into the administrative machinery of the establishment, to be worked on smoothly by routine operations" (p. 16);

"identity kit," to indicate the paraphernalia people ordinarily have with which to indicate who they are but which is routinely denied in total institutions;

"contaminative exposure," to indicate ways inmates are humiliated and mortified in public;

"looping," to indicate how an inmate's attempt to fight mortification leads to more mortification;

"privilege system," to indicate the way withheld ordinary rights become privileges used to coerce conformity;

"secondary adjustments," to refer to "practices that do not directly challenge staff but allow inmates to obtain forbidden satisfactions or to obtain permitted ones by forbidden means" (p. 54);

a variety of "personal adjustments," such as "situational withdrawal," which (he notes) psychiatrists might call "regression."

He also used words that have negative overtones, but used them in a neutral way, so that they lose their negative charge. For instance, he spoke of new recruits being "mortified," but examples of this include officer candidates in military organizations.

He discussed institutional staff by treating what they do as a kind of work (thus showing himself the student of Everett Hughes he often claimed to be), to be seen as part of a class that includes many other kinds of work. He emphasized that the work of a total institution's staff deals with people, rather than inanimate stuff, and that this creates distinctive problems:

> The multiplicity of ways in which inmates must be considered ends in themselves, and the large number of inmates, forces upon the staff some of the classic dilemmas that must be faced by those who govern men. Since a total institution functions somewhat as a state, its staff suffers somewhat from the tribulations that beset governors (77).

Here too he used the linguistic devices I have discussed, speaking "objectively" of staff work as dealing with "human objects" or "human material."

THE COMPARATIVE SOLUTION

The disparity I spoke of--between the reality Goffman talks about and the way he talks about it--also exists in the comparative procedure he used to arrive at the ideal type of the total institution. He created this type, remember, by comparing a variety of organizations found in modern societies which have an important distinguishing characteristic, and abstracting from them their common features.

He first defined the general class of "social establishments" as consisting of "places such as rooms, suites of rooms, buildings or plants in which activity of a particular kind regularly goes on," and spoke of the difficulty of classifying members of this class. Nothing could be more "neutral" or "scientific." He then classified establishments, roughly, by their relations to the lives of the individuals who participate in them. Some institutions will not accept people of certain kinds at all. Many institutions have a changing population of customers or workers. Others, like families, change their personnel less frequently. Some institutions house activities their participants take seriously; others are for more frivolous activities.

This dispassionate sorting of social organizations in the essay's first paragraph--treating families, leisure time activities, and workplaces as all equal, simply establishments which vary along one or more dimensions--warns us that Goffman will not be engaging in social science as usual. Ordinary social science, unlike Goffman, typically uses as classificatory categories the words, and their associated judgments of moral and social worth, common in the organizations being analyzed. The distinction, for instance, between "deviant' and "normal" activities contains just such judgments, common in the legal and therapeutic organizations which deal with the matters conventionally so classified. So do classifications of organizations and activities as "functional" or, more clearly, "dysfunctional." And these are categories that intend to be scientific and dispassionate. The judgmental character of social science categories is clearer yet in more politically and ethically engaged research and writing, which routinely use terms like "repressive" or "corrupt" to describe the phenomena they analyze.

Goffman treated theories in social science and related areas as raw material, whose analysis would reveal the basic character of the institutions which use them, rather than as "science," as in his offhand discussion of psychiatric thinking:

> Mental hospitals stand out here because the staff pointedly establish themselves as specialists in the knowledge of human nature, who diagnose and prescribe on the basis of this intelligence. Hence in the standard psychiatric textbooks there are chapters on "psychodynamics" and "psychopathology" which provide charmingly explicit formulations of the "nature" of human nature (89).

Needless to say, he explained that the purpose of these theories is to validate the methods used to accomplish the end of managing large numbers of people under the conditions of a total institution.

Having defined social establishments, Goffman immediately proposed yet another principle for their classification, one which would separate out a group whose "members appear to have so much in common. . .that to learn about one of [them] we would be well advised to look at the others." He then isolates the defining characteristic of this class this way:

> Every institution captures something of the time and interest of its members and provides something of a world for them; in brief, every institution has encompassing tendencies. When we review the different institutions in our Western society, we find that some are encompassing to a degree discontinuously greater than the ones next in line. Their encompassing or total character is symbol-

ized by the barrier to social intercourse with the outside and to de-
parture that is often built right into the physical plant, such as
locked doors, high walls, barbed wire, cliffs, water, forests, or
moors. These establishments I am calling *total institutions*, and it is
their general characteristics I want to explore (4).

So: institutions take up varying amounts of the time and interest of
the people who participate in them, from a little to a lot. Some take up
so much of their participants' time and lives that they are "discontinu-
ous" with others in this array. They are "total institutions." He distinguished among the institutions this single criterion as isolating according to whether people are confined in them because they can't take care
of themselves, because they are a danger to others, or both, or whether
they are so isolated in order to better accomplish some important work
or as a retreat from the world for religious or similar purposes. His
analysis then looked for the other features which commonly accompany this sort of total control over the lives of institutional participants,
who he soon starts calling "inmates," thus adopting for the whole class
(including nuns, priests, soldiers, and others not usually thought of as
being incarcerated) the demeaning term typically used in mental hospitals.

Goffman's analytic tack emphasized the disparity between the kind
of place he talked about and the way he talked about it. Though he
discusses, through most of the essay, places about which we routinely
make strongly negative judgments--mental hospitals, concentration
camps, prisons--he treated them as members of the same class as organizations about which we usually make no such simple negative
judgments--military establishments, ships at sea, or religious retreats.
This creates what seems to be a moral confusion at the heart of his
method, for we are confronted with a classification that combines and
treats as equivalent things which, as morally competent members of
our society, class, and profession, we "know" are morally quite disparate. We may be anti-militarist, but most of us do not think that army
camps are concentration camps. We may have little sympathy for organized religion, yet not be ready to say that monasteries or convents
are prisons.

The comparative method works by establishing, as we have seen, a
common dimension along which a variety of cases can be ranged. So
there is a dimension of how much of the person's time an establishment
controls, and organizations vary widely in this respect. Some--a tennis
club one belongs to, for instance--control very little while others--a
family--control more. There is a general problem or question of how
people's time is divided among the groups they participate in. The

total institution takes its place as providing one of the many possible resolutions of this question. The total institution no longer stands out as aberrant--as though the social world was divided into institutions and practices which are "ordinary" or "normal" and do not ask for an abnormal commitment from a person, and then there is this strange one, completely different, which requires total control. No longer different and strange, it is now just a different reading on a dial, another of the possible positions on this scale. This is not a trivial result.

As an example, he describes how three classes of total institutions give differing rationales for "assaults on the self": religious institutions say such assaults are good for people, assisting them to reach a goal they aspire to; prisons and concentration camps do it for the sake of mortification itself; others excuse themselves on the grounds that it is necessary for some other important purpose to be achieved (e.g., military readiness or security). Then he says that, in all three classes, these rationales are rationalizations "generated by efforts to manage the daily activity of a large number of persons in a restricted space with a small expenditure of resources" (46-7).

THE TECHNICAL AND MORAL RESULT

The avoidance of built-in judgment is not evidence of a moral confusion on Goffman's part. He was not a moral dope (to adapt Garfinkel's famous description of the homunculus in most sociological theorizing as a "cultural dope)". Far from it. Any careful reader feels, beneath the cool, unemotional language of Goffman's essays in *Asylums*, the beating heart of a passionate civil libertarian. By adopting this method, which entailed both antiseptic "scientific" language and a non-judgmental comparison of cases, Goffman found a solution to the problem of the assumptions built in to conventional thinking.

If you accept the conventional categorizations built into ordinary language and the ordinary way that institutions and practices are sorted out in conventional thought, if you unthinkingly refer to people who drink a lot of alcohol as alcoholics, if you refer to people who smoke marihuana as addicts, then you accept the ideas that those words more or less oblige you to accept, ideas built in to the words themselves and into the perspectives associated with them. If a person who smokes marihuana is an "addict," then that person will smoke it uncontrollably, will be a "slave" to the practice, will engage in crimes in order to pay for the drug, and so on. If you use these words to define the class you are studying, as I have argued above, you will not find empirical regularities to make scientific generalizations about.

By using the neutral language he constructs to discuss total institutions, Goffman isolates a class of social objects which have well-defined characteristics in common, characteristics which are empirically observable and can be connected to one another in verifiable patterns. He can make science.

Some readers may wonder why I speak so insistently of "making science." It is not often appreciated to what degree Goffman was a serious empiricist, even perhaps what might be called (in some meaning of the term) a positivist. (In this he resembled, I might say in passing, Margaret Mead.) He believed that there was an empirical reality and was wary of anything that smacked of the supernormal, could not be verified empirically, or was overly speculative.

(Perhaps I will be permitted a personal reminiscence here. Many years ago, when he was teaching at Berkeley, Goffman asked me to come to his seminar to hear a student, Marvin Scott, present his research on horse racing. This excellent research dealt with the way the social organization of what Scott called "The Racing Game" (Scott, 1968) made it reasonable for some trainers, owners, and jockeys to want their horse to lose, rather than win. However, in the course of his presentation, Scott suggested in passing that gamblers, including horse players, sometimes had "winning streaks" or "losing streaks." Goffman, who had been listening appreciatively until that point, interrupted to say that of course Scott meant that they *thought* they had such streaks of good or bad luck. But Scott said no, these were observable "facts." Goffman, unwilling to accept such supernatural talk, persisted, appealing to the laws of probability to assure Scott that such "streaks" were natural occurrences in any long run of tries in such a game as blackjack or craps. And finally exploded in anger at Scott's "unscientific" insistence on luck as a natural phenomenon).

Goffman used his linguistic inventiveness to name things in ways that evaded conventional moral judgments and thereby to make scientific work possible. Instead of pointing with scorn at the "inhuman practices" of mental hospitals, or defending their workers as honest professionals doing the best they could with a difficult job, he situated their activities in a context of organizational necessity they shared with other organizations with widely varying degrees of moral repute. The resulting generalizations made possible a deeper understanding of these phenomena than either denunciation or defense ever had.

His generalizations about total institutions simultaneously made possible a far more serious moral evaluation of those practices, since the judgment was now based on a more than superficial understanding of the moral choices actors actually had to make. This leads, inevitably, to blaming organizations rather than individuals, and not even to blaming the organizations for doing what they have to do under the circumstances in which they exist. It is never easy to assign blame for what a whole society, in all its parts, is responsible for. As Goffman explains:

> I have defined total institutions denotatively by listing them and then have tried to suggest some of their common characteristics. . . . the similarities obtrude so glaringly and persistently that we have a right to suspect that there are good functional reasons for these features being present and that it will be possible to fit these features together and grasp them by means of a functional explanation. When we have done this, I feel we will give less praise and blame to particular superintendents, commandants, wardens, and abbots, and tend more to understand the social problems and issues in total institutions by appealing to the underlying structural design common to them all (123-4).

NOTES

1. This paper was given at a conference on Erving Goffman and the concept of "total institutions," held in Grenoble in November, 1999, prior to the planning of this volume. Since then, it has been published as "*La politique de la presentation: Goffman et les institutions totales,*" pp. 59-77 in Charles Amourous and Alain Blanc, editors, *Erving Goffman et les institutions totales,* Paris: L'Harmattan, 2001.

REFERENCES

Goffman, Erving. 1961. "On the Characteristics of Total Institutions." In Goffman, *Asylums: Essays on the Social Situation of Mental Patients and Other Inmates.* New York: Anchor Books, pp. 3-124.

Scott. Marvin B. 1968. *The Racing Game.* Chicago: Aldine Publishing Co.